Jesse Bowman Young

What a Boy saw in the Army

A Story of Sight-Seeing and Adventure in the War for the Union

Jesse Bowman Young

What a Boy saw in the Army
A Story of Sight-Seeing and Adventure in the War for the Union

ISBN/EAN: 9783337176075

Printed in Europe, USA, Canada, Australia, Japan

Cover: Foto ©ninafisch / pixelio.de

More available books at **www.hansebooks.com**

WHAT A BOY SAW IN THE ARMY

A Story of Sight-Seeing
and Adventure in the
War for the Union

By JESSE BOWMAN YOUNG

100 Original Drawings by Frank Beard

NEW YORK: HUNT & EATON

Composition, electrotyping, printing, and binding by
HUNT & EATON,
150 Fifth Avenue, New York.

PREFATORY NOTE.

A STRIPLING, in the stormy days of '61, heard the blast of a bugle and the beat of a drum—signals that the great war had opened. The sounds made his blood tingle and stirred his soul as they lured him to the front. He was then in the plastic period of boyhood, and the things which he saw and heard and felt took hold of him, biting into the quick—like the acid used in etching—and impressing upon his memory indelible pictures, in which terror and fun, privation and frolic, sorrow and joy, heroism and pathos, vie with each other for mastery. These pictures have haunted him for years, until at last he has transferred them to paper, in so far as he has been able, in the effort to portray some of the scenes, experiences, and surroundings amid which the boys who wore the blue and followed the starry flag lived, moved, and had their being, "for three years, or during the war." The lad was barely out of his teens when the struggle ended, in 1865, but his experience in camp, on the march, and in battle, is ineffaceably stamped into his life and character. He was trained in war times to love the Union and the flag; to appreciate the meaning of the word "freedom;" to revere the principles which, after a life-and-death struggle, became triumphant; to glorify the heroic spirits who were then in the forefront of the battle—in the cabinet, in Congress, in the field, and in the White House; and to admire and emulate the martial virtues of obedience, courage, patience, alertness, and dashing enterprise. He has many blessings to be grateful for, but chief among them he reckons the privilege of having been a soldier boy in the armies of the Union.

Frank Beard, the artist whose remarkable pictures so aptly illustrate the story, was himself also a soldier in those days. He has said, in regard to the drawings, that "he just reached back into the knapsack which he used to carry and brought out of it these sketches of men and things as he saw them then!" In the work of explicating and illuminating the graphic phases of this story Mr. Beard has been a most sympathetic and discerning artist. JESSE BOWMAN YOUNG.

OFFICE OF THE CENTRAL CHRISTIAN ADVOCATE,
ST. LOUIS, MO., *February* 1, 1894.

CONTENTS.

CHAPTER I.
SOME SKIRMISHING TO BEGIN WITH. . . . . PAGE 9

CHAPTER II.
GLITTERING TINSEL 28

CHAPTER III.
A BRIEF CAMPAIGN TAKES SOME OF THE SHINE OFF. 44

CHAPTER IV.
SIGHT-SEEING AT FORT DONELSON ON PRIVATE ACCOUNT. 66

CHAPTER V.
UP THE TENNESSEE RIVER. 84

CHAPTER VI.
THE BOY LEARNS AT SHILOH WHAT HIS LEGS WERE MADE FOR. 97

CHAPTER VII.
A CHANGE OF FRONT. 121

CHAPTER VIII.
THE HEIGHTS OF FREDERICKSBURG. 133

CHAPTER IX.
THE ARMY OF THE POTOMAC IN WINTER QUARTERS. 158

CHAPTER X.
OUT ON THE PICKET LINE. 174

CHAPTER XI.
A CONTRABAND'S WONDERFUL DREAM. 185

CONTENTS.

CHAPTER XII.
Once More on the Eve of Battle. 203

CHAPTER XIII.
The Thickets of Chancellorsville. 218

CHAPTER XIV.
A Battle Sunday in the Wilderness. 233

CHAPTER XV.
"About, Face! Northward, March!" 252

CHAPTER XVI.
"Maryland, My Maryland!" 267

CHAPTER XVII.
Smelling the Battle Afar Off. 282

CHAPTER XVIII.
The Struggle for Round Top. 300

CHAPTER XIX.
Gettysburg—The Charge on Cemetery Hill. 316

CHAPTER XX.
Gettysburg—The Great Victory. 331

CHAPTER XXI.
After the Battle. 348

CHAPTER XXII.
Back to Old Virginia. 362

CHAPTER XXIII.
Staff Duty in Washington. 380

CHAPTER XXIV.
The Pageant Fades. 389

ILLUSTRATIONS.

	PAGE
An Old-fashioned Training Day.	11
The Trains that Ran Southward were All Laden with Soldiers.	18
"How Would You Like to Go Along with Me?"	22
The Boy has His Picture Taken.	29
Ned, the Cook.	37
Saber-Practice by the Raw Recruit.	39
"Halt! Who Goes There?"	45
"Here, Old Fellow, is Your Revolver!"	60
Gunboat Assault on Fort Donelson.	75
A Pen and Ink Recollection of General Grant as He Appeared on the Field.	79
"Ole Aunt Betty."	87
Bringing the Mail.	92
He had Known for Some Years that He Had Legs.	101
Pen and Ink Sketch of General Sherman, 1864.	103
The Boy Recognized General Grant.	110
"O, Where's Reuben?"	127
"You are Absent from Your Regiment Without Leave."	129
Fredericksburg Lay at Their Feet.	138
Bullets Whistled and Hissed and Rattled All About Them.	142
As He Spoke He Doubled Himself up Convulsively and Groaned with Agony.	149
"Thank God, the Christian Commission has Come."	152
He Lay on the Earth Hugging the Ground.	154
"Wake Up! We are Going to Retreat!"	155

	PAGE
An Undercurrent of Comment and Criticism.	160
"Rock of Ages."	167
A Picket from Each Side Met in Midstream.	179
A Figure Stealthily Creeping Along through the Garden.	183
The Center of an Interested Group.	186
"Dat was de Day Trubble Come to Our Cabin."	190
Pen and Ink Sketch of President Lincoln.	197
"Father Abe."	201
They Tossed Him in a Blanket.	208
They Set Out to Make Calls of Ceremony on Their Generals	214
"Halloo, Major, Have You Not Lost Your Alignment?"	225
"Forward, Charge!"	229
"Do Not Skulk Here."	237
"How Can We Get Back to the Boys?".	243
They Proceeded to Prepare a Meager Meal.	246
The Roads were Dusty, and the Day was Hot.	257
Sergeant McBride.	265
A Newsboy Came Galloping by Laden with the Dailies	272
"Colonel, Don't You Know You're Inside the Rebel Lines?"	289
She Asked for One of the Pennsylvania Reserve Regiments.	295
Hancock the Magnificent.	311
"I Picked Up a Stone and Knocked Him to the Earth."	325
"Boys, Never Give Up Your Battery!"	337
"I'll Give Them One More Shot.".	343
The Glorious Flag.	353
Jack Took a Good Look at the Prisoner.	375
"Richmond has Surrendered!"	392
Pen and Ink Sketch of General Phil. Sheridan, 1863.	395
Peace and Liberty Born From the Mouth of the Cannon	399

WHAT A BOY SAW IN THE ARMY.

CHAPTER I.

SOME SKIRMISHING, TO BEGIN WITH.

IN the closing month of 1861—that far-away time of tumult and danger which has already receded into myths and shadows—a certain boy, still in his teens, responded to the invitations of the drumbeat and the bugle note which then were inviting volunteers to the front. His name, for the purposes of this record, shall be Jack Sanderson; but it must be understood that he was a real boy, and not merely a character in a story manufactured out of somebody's head and made up for the occasion. This boy was actually a live boy in the days of '61 and the aftertime; he went into the Union army and saw what was to be seen there; he took part in some of its campaigns, and shared in the dangers and excitements and terrors of some important battles, and came through it all without serious harm, and is now a man with children of his own, who love to hear stories about the war, and often beg him to tell them of life in the army. For their sake, and also to give pleasure to a host of young people who are interested in accounts of hardship, exposure, and romantic adventure, such as the volunteers realized in the late struggle, this boy has permitted me to write down some of the experiences through which he passed while he was a soldier for the Union.

In 1860, and the first half of 1861, when the storm of war was brewing, Jack was away from home at a boarding school. He had some notion of going to college after he had finished the preparatory course of study at the academy, for he was fonder of books and school than of anything else. He was a thin, pale, delicate-looking fellow, who liked to read an interesting tale better than play townball; who always felt afraid of getting hit when he helped to storm a snow fort, and who did not care for violent romps, outdoor sports, and active games. Indeed, he was so disposed to mope over his book and become absorbed in a story that very often he had to be chased from the house into the fresh air before he could be forced to take any outdoor exercise. Of course nobody supposed that such a boy ever would make a soldier.

There were but few martial influences or heroic surroundings, indeed, in this lad's neighborhood to develop soldierly inclinations. Once in a long while the people came from the back townships to the place where the militia, with their plumes and old-fashioned accouterments, went through the movements of training day—a great occasion in the young lad's life. His earliest impressions of "a trainer" left stamped upon his childish vision a vivid picture of a prancing steed and a dashing, be-feathered, full-armed creature, of an order higher than the human race, in some strange way permanently united to the animal which he proudly bestrode, the horse and rider making but one magnificent being, which appeared on earth once in a great while to

AN OLD-FASHIONED TRAINING DAY.

delight the assembled people! The sham battles of that time were frightful to the little lad, and it is within his distinct recollection that on the first occasion when he heard the cannon fired off on the Fourth of July he ran home as fast as his shivering legs would carry him and hid under a bed, ashamed to let anybody know how terrified he was, stifling his sobs as best he could, and striving to stop his ears at the same time and shut out the horrible sound of the big black gun. A standing memorial of one of these national salutes was known through the country in the shape of a ghastly artificial arm, ending in a steel hook, worn by a poor fellow who had been maimed by a premature discharge of the cannon. Once, it is true, the boy saw some real soldiers, a forlorn, sunburnt, weather-beaten body of volunteers, returning from the war in Mexico. The sight of these brave men, who had actually been in battle, some of them wounded and a few of them very ill, crowded upon a canal boat and greeted with cheers and enthusiasm and tears by the people on the banks, a tough little drummer waking the echoes with his drum, and a torn flag waving proudly overhead—this is one of the boy's very earliest memories of childhood. There was not much in these things, it is clear, to prompt him ever to become a soldier. But there dawned an hour when the boy became a man, when, although still in his teens, fragile and unmuscular, there was roused within him a love for his country, a spirit of devotion to the Stars and Stripes, an appreciation of the meaning of the words liberty and union, such as belong to full-fledged manhood. How all this came about we shall see in due course of this story.

One day at the school there was a serious commotion. Among the students were some boys and young men from Maryland and Virginia. Carter Burton, the recognized leader of these Southern students, was a handsome, graceful, hot-headed youth, who had been brought up on a plantation, with slaves to wait on him and plenty of money at command. He used to sneer at the "Abolitionists" and berate the Northern people because some of them opposed slavery.

On the day in question news had come that Fort Sumter was in danger; the very air resounded with the threats which had been made by South Carolina troops that they would destroy and take the fortress. The school was in a buzz of confusion all day long; the teachers themselves could hardly give attention to their tasks, much less keep the boys at their studies, and everybody seemed to be impressed that something dreadful was going to happen. It appeared as though a volcano was on the eve of an eruption or as if a mine was just ready to blow up.

In the late afternoon, as the boys were coming in to chapel exercises, Burton was noticed in the center of an excited and noisy group of students who were arguing, threatening, quarreling, almost fighting. Just as they reached the chapel door some one called out,

"Burton, what is that rosette which you have pinned on your coat?"

The speaker was a tall, ungainly youth from the mountain region of Pennsylvania, to whom the nickname of Lanky Jones had been given by his fellows in the school—a sturdy, quiet, hard-working lad, who was earning his way through the academy by ringing the bell and sweeping the halls of the institution.

"None of your business, Lanky," was the sharp retort. "If you mind your bell rope you will have enough to do without meddling with my affairs."

"Carter, that's a secession badge, isn't it?" persisted Lanky, approaching the Southerner, who, eyeing the questioner coolly, replied,

"Why do you ask me? You seem to know all about it beforehand."

Lanky came up gradually through the crowd nearer to Burton, his face pale and his voice trembling with excitement. He took a closer look and saw that the Southern colors were woven together in a knot of red and white ribbon on which was mounted a Confederate seal of some kind. As soon as he made the discovery he put forth a sudden and impulsive plunge with his hand, and, snatching the offensive badge from its place on the coat, he threw it to the floor and angrily stamped upon it. Instantly Burton dealt him a heavy blow, which was partly parried, and amid increased excitement and rage the two antagonists clinched and attempted to settle their dispute with the fist. The confusion brought one of the teachers out of the chapel, and before either of the young combatants had received any very serious hurt they were separated, and the boys were directed to come into the service that was just commencing.

This incident is a sample of scenes that were constantly taking place in various sections of the land. Many of the boys and girls of that time were just as patriotic as the grown-up people. They did not know much about the causes that led to the war; they could not see all the dangers that threatened the nation— they were but boys and girls—but they loved their flag, and they adored the Union, and they trusted Mr Lincoln, and they were ready to do their share toward saving the government from destruction.

Since the people everywhere were agitated over the situation of things in the South, it is no wonder that there was during that winter of '60 and '61 a state of continual disturbance among the boys on account of politics. In the literary societies week after week they had very exciting debates over the two questions of slavery and secession, which were then alarming and troubling the whole country. Once or twice, when the character of John Brown, who had just been executed for treason, was under discussion, and, after that, when the labors and principles of Abraham Lincoln were debated, the youths proceeded from bitter and hasty words to sturdy blows, and sometimes the meetings broke up in a row.

Those who are old enough to remember those months of uncertainty and tumult, of wrath and alarm, will ever pray that the country may be kept in all the future from such disturbances. Nobody knew what was before the nation. The very air was full of strife and hate and signs of danger. The wisest and the soberest men trembled for the safety of the government. Society was like the troubled sea, tossing and heaving in a terrible tempest. The angry and threatening proceedings of Congress that winter were repeated in the same spirit of violence in the homes and schools and business places of the people in all parts of the country.

One day the whole community was moved by the discovery that a Confederate flag was flying over the academy. Of course the offensive banner was removed and torn to pieces in a fervor of loyalty as soon as it was discovered, but the incident made a deep impression on the students, who gathered in noisy and contentious knots about the grounds in the intervals between recitations and discussed the situation. No one could be found to defend the act, as most of the boys were from loyal Pennsylvania, and in the present temper of the town and of the school secession sentiments were not popular.

"I believe it was Burton," said Lanky Jones. "He has the daring and audacity for just such a trick. You know what he wore yesterday. He believes the South is going to establish a great empire, and that all the North must succumb to it. I've heard him say he did not want to live under the Stars and Stripes."

"There he comes now, Lanky. Stick it at him. Say like a man before his face what you've just said behind his back."

"Certainly I will," said Lanky; and as the young Southerner came up he accosted him: "Burton, I remarked something about you just now that the boys want you to hear. I said that I believed it was you who put that flag on the belfry."

Burton stopped, and his cheeks glowed like fire. "Well," said he, after a short pause, "what if I did? What have you to say or do about it?"

"I have just this to say, Carter Burton. You'd better go and live under that thing you call the Stars and Bars. You're nothing but a rebel at heart, and you come North to flaunt your secession doctrines in our faces. If you do not clear out it will not be well for you. I give you fair warning."

"Curses on you and your flag!" said the hasty and imperious Burton. "It was I who unfurled that Confederate flag up yonder. It is the banner of my people and the sign of the rights and doctrines I believe in. I am ready to back up my opinions with my life, too. I'm sick of the whole Yankee tribe. I wish the *Mayflower* had sunk with her entire cargo before—"

A savage shout of indignation came from the crowd. They had heard enough to madden them. Half a dozen Southerners with like sentiments and sympathies ranged themselves about Burton, who was reckless and angry enough to defy the whole throng alone. In the midst of the brawl and before violence could strike a blow the principal appeared. He had overheard the conversation, and his presence quelled the turmoil for the time.

He simply said, "Mr. Burton, walk up to my room." The young man obeyed, and the two were closeted together for more than an hour. What passed between them no one ever found out. At the end of the interview Burton came out, went to his apartment, packed his trunk, and took the first train for his Southern home.

Soon after this event a dispatch was received that the Confederates had fired on Fort Sumter. The news set the boys clean crazy with patriotic excitement. A military company was organized, called "The Seminary Cadets," and drilling began. Jack Sanderson enrolled himself as a member of it, and wrote home to his mother for permission to go right into active service. He wanted to abandon school and enlist im-

THE TRAINS THAT RAN SOUTHWARD WERE ALL LADEN WITH SOLDIERS.

mediately, in a fever of loyalty. The thought that the flag had been insulted and one of the national forts bombarded stirred his deepest soul. He could not study; he was not able to think about anything else than the troubles that had overwhelmed the country; for a while, indeed—but this was not a long while —he even lost his appetite! When that event overtakes a boy it is a sure sign that something has occurred which really and deeply moves him!

Meanwhile the town was in commotion. The President had called for seventy-five thousand volunteers, and enlistment was going on everywhere. The sound of the merry fife and the rattling drum was heard by night and day. The trains that ran southward, passing the academy, were all laden with soldiers. Bluecoats appeared by hundreds on the streets. The glitter of bayonets and the flash of brass buttons shone out at every turn. Mass meetings were held, and impassioned speeches were made to great audiences of people, who were profoundly agitated at the incidents that were daily occurring at Washington and farther south. Thousands, amid tearful partings and patriotic admonitions, and, alas! sometimes dismal forebodings, hurried off to the front.

In a few days Jack had a letter from his mother. It ran thus:

"My Dear Boy: I am not surprised at your request. I have been looking for it during these troubled weeks. The war which some wise men have been for a long time foretelling is upon us. I am glad that my son has his heart full of love for his country. I am proud of his patriotism. But, my dear Jack, you are too young to think of enlisting. You would only risk, and maybe lose, your life without doing any service worth while.

"And have you forgotten that you are my only boy, and that I am left in widowhood to make my own way in the world, and that you will have to help care for and support your little sisters? If you should go off to the war and be wounded or killed, O, what would we all do? I dare not think of it. It almost breaks my heart, the very thought of such a fate for my son.

"There are plenty of men for the service. Let them do the fighting. The boys are not called to go.

"No, Jack, I cannot, my dear boy—I cannot let you go.

"In much love, Your Mother."

Jack read the letter hurriedly. He knit his brows and wiped his eyes and read it again. Then he folded it up and began to pace the room, compressing his lips and twitching his face and making random gestures with his hands and arms. Then he sat down and went over the epistle once more. At last he said:

"Well, I suppose I'll have to give up going with the boys just now. I can't get over this letter. She has been too good a mother for me to flatly disobey her—that is, just at this time! But there's no use trying to keep me out of the army. I *must* go. I feel it in my bones. I cannot stand it to have this thing continue—the country in danger, men needed, our glorious flag fired on, the capital threatened, and everything going to sticks —while I stay at home and do nothing to help save the land from ruin. I can't do it! One of these days I *must* go into service!"

And thus the question was settled for the time being, and thus the reason appears why Jack did not start out with those who went in the spring of '61 into the army.

But, nevertheless, he kept thinking over the question, and wondering how the way would be opened for him to enlist without wounding and squarely disobeying his mother. Sometimes he was about ready to go against her will, and then he would halt, and reconsider his plans. So matters continued for several months.

When the disaster at Bull Run occurred he was on the point of rushing off at once, but the recruiting officer would not accept him on account of his youth. What the outcome might be was a problem which gave him constant perplexity. At last an event occurred which changed the situation and secured for him a provisional consent from his mother.

The incident itself was in brief and abruptly announced to Jack one day early in December, 1861, by one of the boys of the town in which they both lived, as they met on the street, in these words: "Halloo, Jack, your Uncle Sam has arrived in a new uniform, and he looks like a general." Jack, as he hurried home, found that the whole community —an interior town in Pennsylvania—had within an hour been thrown into a tremulous condition of excitement and pleasure by the arrival of a tall and distinguished-looking gentleman in uniform. The whole family to which Jack belonged was thereby put in commotion, and throughout a wide circle of relatives the news was quickly carried that "Uncle Samuel" had come home to say good-bye before finally joining his regiment in the Western army. The person thus familiarly addressed and alluded to by his nephews and nieces on the Susquehanna was known now as Major Bowman. In the early settlement of California he had gone to that State, practicing his profession as a lawyer with high success in the city of San Francisco for ten or twelve years. He had come East the year before the war broke out to tone up his overtaxed brain and broken-down nerves; and for twelve months or so he had been hunting and fishing and running about over the mountains of the Alleghenies regaining his lost health. He had been for some time assisting to recruit an Illinois regiment of cavalry, and was now on his way to rejoin it at Cairo in that State.

This incident stirred up Jack's war spirit afresh. The autumn had gone by without seeing him enlist; but now that this military relative had arrived the whole question came up for reconsideration. The boy's mind was in a whirl of hope and wonder and perplexity. He had an idea that in some way the road would be opened now for the fulfillment of his cherished wishes.

Major Bowman had but a few hours to tarry, and these were busily occupied. Soon after he arrived he met Jack and said to him in a casual way, "How would you like to go along with me out into the Western army?"

The boy's eyes flashed with eagerness and his lips trembled with feeling as he replied:

"O, uncle, you do not mean that you have any thought of taking me with you, do you? I have been dreaming and hoping and longing to go into service ever since last spring, but mother is not willing for me to enlist. I cannot stand it to stay at home while all the rest of the fellows go to the front. Besides, I should not like to think, after the war is over, that I did not help to save the Union."

Major Bowman smiled at the boy's impulsiveness, and said:

"HOW WOULD YOU LIKE TO GO ALONG WITH ME?"

"I have been thinking over the matter very seriously. I need some one to go with me for the present, at least, to act as my secretary. In the organization of the regiment there is a good deal of writing to do, and I will have to get some one to do it. I think you are entirely too young to enlist as a soldier now. You are not rugged, and the exposures and hardships of a single campaign would soon kill you, I fear, even if you should escape the bullets of the enemy. What I have to suggest is this: I will take you along as an experiment, and maybe some position may open up that will be just the thing for you. For example, you might make a good quartermaster's clerk—"

"Quartermaster? who is he? What does he do in the army?" said Jack, in his ignorance.

"The quartermaster," said the major, "is the officer whose duty it is to procure and issue supplies of various sorts to the troops, such as clothing, tents, forage for the horses, and matters of that kind. He supplies wagons for transporting baggage, and has a certain number of sergeants and clerks to aid him."

"Does he go out and do any fighting?" said the ambitious youth.

"No, quartermasters usually have no actual fighting to do; but they often pass through all the danger and excitement they care about in an active campaign. Or you might get a place with the sutler of the regiment. He needs several assistants, and I do not know but that you—"

"You will have to explain your words again. I do not know what a sutler is. What are his duties in service?" was the further inquiry of the unsophisticated boy.

"The sutler is a man authorized by the government to sell certain kinds of goods to the soldiers. He keeps the camp store and makes money by the sale of various articles that are wanted by the men."

"Does the sutler ever go into a battle?"

The major laughed out at the boy's greenness, and then proceeded, "O, no; you would not find a sutler within gunshot of a battlefield. That is not his place of business. He and his clerks are very careful not to come within reach of the rebel bullets; and, indeed, they would be big fools to venture into danger for nothing."

"But, uncle, I do not fancy the idea of going into the army, or rather pretending to go, in such a position as that of sutler's clerk. Why, there's no glory in that. I would sooner stay at home altogether. I want to see some actual fighting and be a real soldier if I go at all." And the boy's cheek flushed with ardor and enthusiasm.

"Well, my boy, when you have seen some actual service I think you will have your enthusiasm dampened a little. The life of a soldier is a very serious business, especially in a war which will last as long and be as great an undertaking as this rebellion. It is no child's play, I can tell you beforehand. The glitter of a new uniform and the music of a clattering band and the appearance of a brigade on drill or the passing of an army in review may all seem very romantic and attractive to you at first. It may appear to the spectator like a beautiful and enticing vision. You imagine it a fine thing to camp out and live in tents and go on picket and be promoted for gallantry, and all that. But, at the start, I want to tell you that all this is merely the outside of the soldier's life—the shining shell—that's all. The romance soon gets rubbed off. To march or ride for hours or days with only half rations through the blistering heat or the freezing cold, in mud or dust or snow, hungry and worn out, and ready to drop at every step; to expose your life in the battle; to run the risk of capture or of wounds that may cripple you for life, or face and meet death in some shocking and ghastly form on the field; to get sick and lie in the hospital for weeks without a single relative near—that's what the soldier's actual career is like. Youngster, you will have another idea of 'glory' when you've been through a year of service at the front. If you go I want you to go with your eyes wide open. You must not expect to be sprinkled with cologne water and go to sleep on pillows of down. There's a deal of rough and dangerous and nasty work to be done. War is a dreadful thing, even at its best, when it is undertaken as a last resort in order to serve the cause of freedom; and it is very foolish to go into it with the notion that it is merely a romantic panorama."

"Well, uncle," said the boy, his cheek not so red now, and his eye not flashing so eagerly as a little while ago, "I've thought of some of these things before. I never had the idea that I would have a holiday in the army."

And then Jack's lips closed with an effort to hold in check the emotions that were at work in his heart. His face took on an aspect of new resolution and firmness. A look of purpose and decision came into his eyes. He realized more thoroughly than ever what was before him if he went to the war, and, as he took in the aspects of the case which had been presented by the major, his heart failed him a little. He questioned whether in some such situation as had been pictured he might not quail and prove unworthy of the name of soldier; whether he could stand the exposures and hardships of a campaign; whether, if he went, he would ever come back again. This train of thought sobered him, but in a few moments he said quietly, "Uncle, if you think I can be of service to you, and by and by get into the army in reality, I am ready to go along."

"But what will your mother say?"

"O, I think she has about made up her mind that I am bound to go, anyhow, and this will strike her as a good opening for me."

Just then the mother entered the room. Jack turned to her and said, with a sort of gasp, "Mother, the major offers to take me along to Cairo with him. I can come back whenever I want to. I can be of service to him for the present, and perhaps in time get into the army. What do you say?"

"My son, I have kept you at home already a good part of a year, and all that time you have been wild to go into service. I am not willing for you to enlist now. But if your uncle is willing to take you along with him I will not stand in the way. You ought to deliberate very carefully before deciding."

"Why, mother," said the boy, "I have been deliberating for months. I cannot endure it any longer to stay at home. I must have at least a taste of army life."

"How long will it take you to get ready, Jack?" said the major; "I have no time to wait. I leave on the early train to-morrow."

"I will be ready, sir, whenever you are. Depend on that." And with the words the boy hurried away to pack his valise and announce the project to his associates.

That night the household was in very serious mood. The boy himself felt deeply the importance of the step he was taking. What might lie before him he did not know. His imagination, quickened with the excitements of the day, was full of all sorts of flitting visions. He pictured the anxiety which his mother and sisters would feel during the long months of his absence. He saw himself now in camp, now on the field, now in the hands of the foe, now in an enemy's prison. Anon he beheld himself *an officer* (and at the word his heart throbbed the quicker), with sword and epaulets and elegant accouterments. And then, the scenes shifting, he said to himself, with a spasm of dread, "What if I should never get back again? What if this were to be the last evening I should ever spend at home? O, dear, what will it all lead to—where will it all end?"

Thus in the intervals of conversation his mind was in a whirl of exciting and changing pictures. The folks all spoke with cheerfulness and hope of Jack's plans; but once in a while a word half spoken, a fear half uttered, a sly tear hastily wiped away, would indicate the cloud that hovered over the group. Whenever Jack looked into the face of any one of that circle— mother, sister, or aged grandparents—he found loving eyes

SOME SKIRMISHING, TO BEGIN WITH. 27

regarding him with wistful affection. Then a big lump would creep into his throat, and he would choke it down with a violent effort and pretend to have a sudden fit of coughing and say to himself, "I do hope we will not have a 'scene' when I go."

The good-night kisses were not forgotten when bedtime came; and before that hour his sisters all clustered about him with gentle caresses, each with a little keepsake—a needlecase, a Testament, a necktie, and some warm woolen socks. They bravely kept back the tears while in the room, but Jack could hear their sobs after they went out. Once or twice his mother stopped as she passed Jack and stood for a while running her fingers gently over the boy's hair. The touch of her hand, strangely tremulous and tender, sent a thrill down deep into his heart. Striving to choke back the feelings that almost overcame him, at last he arose, and, putting his arms about her, said, "Never mind, mother, maybe I'll be back sooner than you will want to see me. You will not be ashamed of me, anyway; I will warrant you that."

And thus, with warm and loving kisses from his little sisters fresh upon his lips, and with the prayer of his mother, "God bless and keep my boy!" ringing in his ears, and with heart and brain dizzy with conflicting emotions, Jack started out to be a soldier.

CHAPTER II.

GLITTERING TINSEL.

JACK, until this journey, had never seen a prairie. Day and night ever since he was born he had been within sight of the mountains. Wherever he had cast his eyes all around the landscape he had been accustomed to see them—blue and misty afar off, dressed in greener tints close by, covered with forests or gray with granite bowlders, changing their hues with every passing hour, and seeming sometimes like living creatures with a voice and language all their own. Crossing the Alleghenies in the dim twilight, he bade them good-bye and woke up next morning to find himself in scenes that were strange and new. The prairies of the West were just beginning to appear. Looking back, he could barely distinguish the hills of Ohio fading away in the distance, while on either side of the track along which they were whirling the rolling sea of prairie grass stretched in yellow, snow-tinged billows.

Here and there was a settler's cabin, succeeded by a colony of yelping prairie dogs, with thriving towns and a few dawning cities intervening between great expanses of wheat and corn stubble, and then—Chicago, at that time a place of about one hundred and fifty thousand inhabitants. Here the boy was furnished with his uniform, made up of a roundabout and a singular sort of padded breeches, called "cavalry trousers," all trimmed with yellow braid, and seeming to have been made up expressly for some other fellow. Jack felt stiff and awkward in the suit, and

THE BOY HAS HIS PICTURE TAKEN.

yet there was mingled with his conscious awkwardness a sense of pride and elation, especially when he saw himself reflected in the hotel mirror, where he hardly recognized himself; and when he started out to see the city he was certain that all the people were looking at him and noting with admiration his new military garb.

Of course the boy had his picture taken at once, and sent

the treasure, showing him in his army dress, back to his friends in Pennsylvania. He could scarcely keep his face straight during the operation of securing a likeness, as he wondered what the home folks would think and say when the picture should reach them. It is a family tradition, on the other hand, that these same home folks could not retain their composure of countenance, either, when that remarkable portrait challenged their admiration, presenting their soldier-boy as a curious mixture of valorous discomfort, military ambition, uneasy vanity, and conscious awkwardness in his novel costume—sleeves two inches below the wrist, coat collar pressing rigidly up against the chin, tight against the throat; brass buttons by the dozen glittering down the front and scattered promiscuously on other parts of the roundabout; yellow tape of a cheap and showy variety wriggling and crawling here and there over the surface of the garment, and the trousers looking as though they had been cut out to fit some ungainly, bow-legged biped from another planet.

Moreover, there was an expression about the entire picture—an "atmosphere," so to speak—that seemed to say: "This trouble will very shortly be at an end. The country has been waiting for me, and here I am, ready for duty, accoutered for action, prepared to crush the rebellion at short notice, and thus save the land and the flag. The great object of my appearance on the scene is to quell the disturbance and summarily put an end to the hostilities of the war. This revolt will not last long after I commence active operations against the enemy. All I ask is a fair chance to get at him. I have any amount of latent courage, loyalty, strategic ability, and general military capacity hidden away under this new uniform, and the country will be startled when these powers begin to appear. If you want to see signs and wonders wrought, only wait until this raw recruit takes the field!"

A long ride on the cars brought the major and Jack from Chicago down through central Illinois, panoramic glimpses of fertile farms and pioneer settlements flitting before their eyes at every step of the way, until the morning showed them their destination, the muddy, water-locked city of Cairo, at the junction of the Ohio and Mississippi Rivers, where, after a tasteless breakfast at the St. Charles Hotel—tasteless, did I say? I was wrong; it was full of soda taste; everything was seasoned with it: hot biscuit, coffee, eggs, bacon, all revealed a thorough sprinkling of the caustic stuff—well, after this characteristic meal the major said to Jack, "The horses are here, and we must hurry out to camp."

They went to the door, and there stood a handsome black horse, fiery and wicked-looking, madly champing his bit and impatiently pawing the mud, and bearing an elegant military saddle, decorated with blue trappings and gold lace. A rough-and-ready-seeming soldier, tall, stout, with burly, overgrown shoulders, who was holding the animal, lifted his hat and made a salute, saying: "We're glad to have you with us again, major. Here is Prince all ready for you. Nobody can't do nuthin' with him when you're away, that's sartin. I've had my hands full this morning bringin' 'im here. He knows who is his master."

In a moment the major was in the saddle, and Jack was directed to mount the little bay, Charley by name, the man following as they galloped away.

"That's Jim Van Meter," said Major Bowman, as they rode along. "He takes care of my horses and acts as orderly to carry messages for me, and does all sorts of work about my headquarters. It will not take you long to get acquainted with him. He is a great character in the camp."

Jack had not had a chance to look about him upon the new region until this moment, and now he commenced to use his eyes and make a hasty exploration of the town and surrounding country.

"Why, major, this place is under water," was his first comment as he looked down from the levee upon the town and observed it swimming in a sea of mud.

"Yes," was the reply, "it is in that condition nearly all the time. You notice that the river is many feet above the level of the lowest streets. This great bank or levee is all that saves the town from making a part of the bottom of the Mississippi."

"And is this the Mississippi? I have been wondering what sort of an impression it would make on me when I should look on it for the first time. How muddy and wide and big it is! But see out there in the middle of the stream; what makes that part of the current so much clearer than the rest?"

"That is the Ohio River, a cleaner stream than the 'Father of Waters,' and its current can be traced many miles below here."

A few brick business houses stood on the bank, and here and there appeared a handsome house, but the most of the dwellings were low, squatty, and untidy. Everything appeared to be under the weather. The shores on the other side of the river were low and covered with scrub oaks or some other stunted species of tree down to the water's edge. It was a dismal, swampy, fever-one-day-and-chill-the-other-ish sort of region to look on. It required some resolution in Jack to keep down a feeling of disappointment. His enthusiasm certainly was not at the boiling point that dull and dreary winter day as he rode through the streets of Cairo.

"I must look at a map and find out the situation of this place. I forget just how the States come together down here," he said to himself, and then, speaking aloud, he asked, "Have you a map at camp?"

"Certainly, that's one of the things every intelligent cavalry officer needs. The generals and their staff officers have to study geography all the time while they are planning and carrying out their campaigns. We must note the roads and rivers, and trace the railroad connections, and examine the situation of the towns and mountains and passes, and take into careful consideration the whole lay of the land. Here, by the way, you will see something entirely new." And as the major reined in his horse he pointed down the river. "Yonder do you discover a line of earthworks? That is the Confederate fort over in Kentucky. Until lately the rebels had also fortifications on the Missouri side, but I think since the skirmish at Belmont they have withdrawn from that vicinity. I believe the general who commanded our troops in that fight is to be our commander here." And then, turning and accosting the orderly, he said, "Van, is General Grant here?"

"Yes, sir, our regiment is to serve under him. I heard this morning that he had been made commander of this military district, and the boys say that means they sha'n't have any winter quarters."

"Who is General Grant?" said Jack.

"He was once in the regular army, and a few months ago was made colonel of an Illinois regiment, and he is now the brigadier general commanding at this point. He is a very quiet-looking officer, but he made the rebels fly at Belmont, and those who know him say he can make noise enough when the time comes. He is to review all the troops in this vicinity soon, and then you can see him for yourself. But here we are at camp. How are you, Colonel Dickey? Good morning, adjutant. Why, Captain Dodge, I am glad to see you."

And as they stopped in front of regimental headquarters a group of officers gathered about the major, who dismounted and shook hands all around. Then Jack was introduced and welcomed, Colonel Dickey saying as he greeted the boy:

"Well, Jack, we'll try to take good care of you for a while. Hard tack and bacon will bring you out in a jiffy. My son is here with us, and is the bugler for regimental headquarters. Charley! ho! Charley! Where in blazes is the boy? He can get out of sight quicker than a squirrel. If he wants to be bugler for me he will have to learn to be on hand when wanted. O, here you are. Charley, this is Major Bowman's nephew, Jack Sanderson. He has come out here from Pennsylvania to try soldiering with us for a while. You two will be company for each other if you behave yourselves."

And thus Jack was made at once to feel at home in the camp. The major's tent was very comfortable and cheerful, furnished with a small stove, a desk, a folding cot, a trunk, a chest, and some other odds and ends which Jack hardly expected to find in camp. That was in the early part of the war, be it remembered, and a good deal more baggage was allowed and taken with the army than afterward, when everybody had to go in light marching order, and when the chief commander of the largest army in the field was said to require as his portion of luggage for a campaign nothing more than a toothbrush and a paper collar.

"Your tent is just back of this, Jack," said the major. "It is what we call an 'A' tent, on account of its shape. You can get some straw at the quartermaster's and fix your bed and get yourself settled in your new home, for I will have work for you to do this afternoon."

Jack went out, carrying his satchel and shawl-strap, and inspected his quarters. The ground was wet, and snow mixed with mud surrounded the new habitation. As he took in the situation he seriously questioned whether he could make himself at all comfortable even with plenty of straw.

"Van," he asked, as that dignitary approached, "where is the quartermaster's tent? I want to get some straw."

"I'll show you after a while. Just now I'm going to water the hosses down at the river, and if you want to go along you may ride Charley."

Jack was glad to have another chance for horseback exercise. He felt already as though Charley were bone of his bone and flesh of his flesh when he was in the saddle on the prancing and beautiful animal. Leaving camp, they loped down a road that abounded with deep mudholes, old buttonwood stumps, underbrush, and rotting logs, with here and there a cast-off boiler, the remnant of some old steamboat disaster. Soon they entered a miniature forest of singular-looking plants, slim, straight, smooth, and topped with feathery leaves. They were from six to fifteen feet in height, and some of them not much thicker than stalks of Indian corn. Many stems had fallen and become entangled together, so that it was impossible to see very far through the thicket. It was a strange and singular sight to the boy, who inquired at once, "What do you call this wilderness? I never saw such a growth as this."

"Why, boy, whar did you have yer broughtin' up? Did you never see a canebrake before?"

"No, I never did. We do not have them in our region at all. I have seen the canes that are sold for fishing-rods, but I never saw any of this size, and I never knew how they grew." And as he examined the strange and singular scenery an old stanza came into his mind:

"Down by the canebrake, close by the sea."

In the midst of his musings a shrill whistle suddenly roused him, and glancing ahead he saw the river, booming with its muddy waters, on which was a great steamer bearing right down upon him, as it seemed at first sight. Jack started and made a motion impulsively as if to check his horse.

"Ha, boy, that's a good one!" laughed Van Meter. "Don't be afeard; that old mudscraper isn't goin' to cut across lots this trip. She knows better 'n that. She has to bear in almost to the shore to make the bend in the river and git her head up in the right course on the other side." And as he spoke the prow of the vessel, which all but touched the bank, wheeled around and was soon lost to view around the curve in the river.

Dinner was ready when they returned, and the boy, like all of his species at mealtime, was ready for it. He found that he was to eat with the battalion headquarters mess, along with the major and half a dozen other officers. He saw on the table some hard bread or army crackers, some hot biscuit, an appetizing roast of beef, with two or three sorts of vegetables. He said to himself, "If this is army fare I shall not suffer."

Something of the same thought appeared in his face also, for the major said: "Jack, do not expect to get such rations as these every day. While we are here at Cairo we can get what we please. It will be different when we start out into the enemy's country. Ned, our cook, however, will go along with us, and he will see that we do not absolutely starve."

Ned, the important personage alluded to, was just pouring out the coffee into the tin cups that stood at each plate, and he grinned with delight and pride at the remark.

"Yes, sah, majah, you can allus depen' on Ned. As long as you done fuhnish me wid de perwisions I can cook 'em to de satisfaction of any gen'l'men. Trus' ole Ned fur dat work. Dat's w'at he's heah foh."

"I'm very much afraid that Ned will beat a retreat after we start down into the South. He will say that he has no 'call' in that direction. How is it, Ned? If we are ordered to advance into Dixie will you go along? Honestly, now, will you promise not to desert us?" was the inquiry of one of the officers.

"Cap'n, dat's a mighty delicate question to ax me. I'se gwine wid ye for a while anyhow; an' when it gits too hot fur me to stan' it any longer, den mebbe I'll done gone cl'ar out. I'se mos' powerful keerful o' my life, I is. It's de only one I'se got. Dis chile's not gwine to let the rebels get hol' ob him if his legs kin kerry him out ob deir reach. I'd soonah die dan fall into de han's ob de Confed'rits."

NED, THE COOK.

"Well, Ned, we'll try to take care of you. But why do you make the coffee so hot? Whew! it will never get cool enough in these tins to drink. If there is any region here or hereafter hotter than coffee in a tin cup, why, I hope I'll never get there, that's all."

Ned went out into the kitchen part of the quarters muttering to himself, "How do you s'pose Ned kin boil de coffee widout makin' it hot?"

When night came Jack was tired enough. He had fairly entered upon his duties, fixed up his tent, copied the papers assigned him, delivered the messages intrusted to him on several occasions by the major, and was ready to sleep when the buglers sounded tattoo. The wild, plaintive notes of their instruments sounding out into the air and reëchoed from sky and river and canebrake; the crackling log fires surrounded by groups of soldiers; the long lines of snow-white tents stretching through the encampment; the occasional song or hymn that came to his ears from different quarters of the grounds; the regular step of the sentinel pacing his beat close by, sword in hand and scabbard dangling and clattering after him on the earth at every turn; the racket and hubbub that came at brief intervals from the corral where the horses and mules were pawing, kicking, neighing, braying, squealing—these were the confused sights and sounds that mingled in his mind with thoughts of home and mother and loved ones far away, and with speculation and wonderment as to the future, while the boy laid himself down on his bed of straw, pulled the blankets about him, and fell asleep.

"Jack! Jack! Wake up! The bugles have sounded half a dozen calls; breakfast is ready; everybody and everything is astir, and you are not out of bed yet. Hurry and dress yourself!"

This was the first sound that penetrated the boy's ears next morning. He half opened his eyes, and in a stupid, bewildered sort of way gazed about, trying to realize where he was. As he slowly regained his senses and began to shake off the deep slumber that had held him in dreamless unconsciousness all night long, he saw the face of the major peering in through the parted curtains of his tent.

"This is a slow way to commence soldiering! Why, when the angel Gabriel sounds the last trump he will have to toot his horn the second time for your special benefit. Any boy who can sleep right on through all the noise that has been made ever since five o'clock can't be stirred up at the resurrection day with only one horn blowing. Shake yourself out in a hurry, my boy, or you will miss breakfast."

By this time Jack was roused effectually; he felt as though he was ready to sign a pledge never to adventure himself asleep again. After a hasty breakfast he was ordered to go out and spend an hour in saber exercise. He managed to learn at least the names of several of the movements of that weapon, and although his wrist was almost twisted out of joint by the time he was through with the task, yet he was glad that the words "moulinet," "guard," "thrust," "right cut," and other like terms had now a real meaning for him. In the afternoon, when his writing work was done, he spent some time with the drill sergeant, who had been for some years in the regular army, and was on that account regarded with peculiar respect. By him the boy was taught how to mount a horse, sit in the saddle, use the stirrups, wheel about, and dismount. He had plumed himself

SABER-PRACTICE BY THE RAW RECRUIT.

on knowing something about such matters before, but a feeling gradually crept over him during the instructions he was receiving that he had a good deal to learn in order to become expert and skillful as a horseman.

He noticed that almost every hour was taken up in the camp with some kind of work. At one bugle call early in the day the parade ground was filled with squads of two or three men apiece practicing in the use of the saber or carbine. A while later each company by itself would go through with various exercises. In the afternoon the battalions would perform separate evolutions, and later the entire regiment was drilled together. Thus it seemed to him that it was nothing but drill from morning till night—drill, drill, everlasting drill! He heard some of the men complaining of this, and listened to an officer giving a reply to their murmurs: "This is tiresome work, I know, boys; but you must not expect to have a play-spell in the army. The only way to keep men, as well as boys, out of mischief is to give them something to do. Besides, we will soon be ordered over into Kentucky after the Johnnies, and if we venture into active service without knowing our duties we shall be used up the first brush we get into. You can't learn the manual of arms out on the skirmish line. If you do not find out how to handle the saber and carbine skillfully, and how to go through with these different movements with ease and readiness before you go into a battle, you will be badly beaten one of these days when of a sudden you are shoved into a hot nest of 'rebs.' The soldier who shows himself most ready and skilled and prompt will be the most likely man to be promoted into the first vacancy that occurs."

In the evening Jack, by special favor of the major, was permitted to be present at a school of the officers of the battalion held to study cavalry tactics and the rules and regulations of the army. He had sense enough to keep his mouth shut and listen attentively to the conversations and instructions of the evening. The major's Military Dictionary and some works on "the art of war" were also at his disposal, and in these he read at odd hours. And as he read he found out that war is not such a plain and easy and simple matter as some people at that time imagined. In common with perhaps a considerable number of his countrymen, old and young, he had in his unsophisticated innocence supposed this to be about all there was of it:

Two rows of men in handsome uniforms, abundantly striped with gold lace, decorated with any number of epaulets, feathers, and brass buttons, and furnished with lots of guns, swords, cannon, and flags, in some way happen to arrive at precisely the same moment in a big open field, conveniently located for the purpose, one set on one side and the enemy on the other. At once, after arranging their lines, they fire at each other, and proceed to cut off each other's heads miscellaneously for a while, and make a terrible noise, and by and by the whipped party runs away, and the others hurrah, and everybody says, "It's a great victory!"

The boy, for his part, received some light on the subject, soon making the discovery that an army has to be created and drilled and disciplined; that it needs to be furnished with clothing and food and arms and tools; that it has to be taught how to build bridges and make roads—even railroads—and erect forts and use its various weapons with skill and self-possession and promptness. All this requires months of time.

The review was a notable event in the boy's experience. The afternoon was clear and bracing, and in spite of the mud the occasion was full of interest and excitement. The whole morning had been occupied in getting ready for the display. Boots were blackened, gloves were washed up white and clean, belt-plates were scoured, sabers and carbines were polished until they glittered like silver, and each company did its best to outshine its neighbor. At last the bugles sounded the "assembly," and the regiment formed into line, and then at the command, breaking into column, four men abreast, marched to the parade ground, a couple of miles away.

Arriving at the ground, they saw the infantry regiments stationed in line, their gleaming muskets resting with the butt of the weapon on the earth in the position called "order arms." Half a dozen batteries of artillery, some with bright fieldpieces of brass, and others with iron cannon, were at their posts, making a very threatening appearance.

When at last Jack's regiment reached its place in the long line and had been properly formed, the boy eagerly took in the brilliant scene, and was captivated with the waving banners, the sounding bugles, the exciting music of the bands, the handsome appearance of a multitude of richly dressed officers, the prancing steeds that seemed as proud as their riders, the flashing arms, all reflecting the bright rays of the sun.

At the appointed hour the general commanding appeared with his staff. Jack was near enough to Major Bowman to ask, "Which is General Grant?"

"That quiet-looking man yonder, with closely trimmed brownish beard," was the answer. "The officer next him, with black beard, is Captain Rawlins, the assistant adjutant general."

"But who is that dashing general off to the left with so many staff officers about him, and rigged out with epaulets and feathers and an elegant sword? I thought surely that must be Grant. Why, he has the most splendid uniform of the whole party."

"No," said the major, "that is General Blank. He is an old political trickster who has managed to get himself commissioned brigadier general. He knows no more about war than my horse Prince—not as much, indeed. But he is full of airs, and he puts on more style and affects more importance and military dignity than all the rest of the generals put together. He is only—"

What the major was about to call General Blank can never be found out, for in the midst of the sentence the command was shouted forth and repeated all along the line, "Present arms."

At the word the banners all drooped low in the air, the bugles sounded a wild, shrill blast, the drummers beat a loud roll, the infantry presented arms, the cavalrymen brought their sabers to the front, making the proper salute; artillerists who had no sabers lifted their hands to the visor of their caps.

In a few moments the whole cavalcade of general and staff

officers galloped down the line, making quite a flutter as they rode, and splashing the mud in all directions. When the retinue had returned to its place again the order was given, "Pass in review."

At once the whole command of twenty thousand men or more wheeled into column and marched in front of General Grant and party. As the regiment was filing back to camp after it was all over, amid the music of bands and the booming of cannon, the boy said to himself, the beautiful vision still casting a magic spell over his soul: "What a grand thing it is to have a military command and exercise control over men! How handsome these officers look in uniform! The generals especially, how happy they must be, with their rank and big pay, with their honors and their sense of power! What an honor it must be to be associated with them on staff duty, to be trusted by them and be on friendly and intimate terms with them! O, how many things there are in the life of a soldier that are splendid and stirring and magnificent! Somehow it takes right hold of a fellow and lifts him up until he feels as though he were flying through the air. My brain tingles all through with that display. Shakespeare must have been a soldier at some time in his life or he could not have pictured it all as he does. I never knew till now what he meant when he wrote of the 'pride, pomp, and circumstance of glorious war.'"

CHAPTER III.

A BRIEF CAMPAIGN TAKES SOME OF THE SHINE OFF.

THE night was dark and blustering. All day long it had rained; and now sleet, snow, and drizzle mingled in the air and were driven hither and thither by the wild winds. The camp had settled down to rest, and the boy, listening to the whirl and confusion of the storm, was about to blow out his candle and go to sleep, when suddenly he heard in the distance the splashing feet of a horse galloping through the mud. Into the gloom he heard the sentinel ring out his challenge, "Halt! who goes there?"

The rider stopped and replied, "A messenger from General Grant's headquarters, with dispatches for Major Bowman. Where can I find him?"

The sentry shouted, "Sergeant of the guard—post number three—dispatches from headquarters!" From one to another of the line of guards this was repeated until it reached the sergeant at his post, who came at once to the spot. By this time Jack had hastily thrown some clothes on him and bounced from the tent, and called out, "Sergeant, I will take the message to the major."

"HALT! WHO GOES THERE?"

In a moment he was rapping with haste and excitement on the tent-pole and rousing Major Bowman with the announcement that important news had come. That officer arose quickly, untied the folds of the tent curtains, and took the papers. Removing the envelopes, he signed his name upon each of them and handed them back, to be given to the orderly as the proper receipt for the inclosures. Jack watched his uncle's face and saw it assume a serious look.

"What is it, major?" the boy asked, anxiously.

"We are ordered to move at four o'clock to-morrow morning," was the response; and with the words he handed Jack to read the following order:

"HEADQUARTERS MILITARY DISTRICT OF CAIRO,
"January 8, 1862.

"*Special Orders, No. 5.*

"The Third Battalion, Fourth Illinois Cavalry, Major Bowman commanding, will report for duty to Brigadier General Blank, and will continue with his brigade during the contemplated movement of the army.

"Major Bowman will see that his command is at the wharf and on board the steam transport *Clio* by five o'clock to-morrow morning. He will have his men supplied with five days' rations and forty rounds of ammunition apiece on their persons. He will take a sufficient number of wagons along to supply forage for the animals and additional ammunition enough to supply sixty rounds per man. The troops are to be but lightly equipped with camp equipage, as the movement must not be encumbered with a large wagon train.

"By order of BRIGADIER GENERAL U. S. GRANT,
"Commanding District.

"JOHN A. RAWLINS,
"Assistant Adjutant General."

"Jack," said the major, "call Adjutant Pike at once. Take this order to him, and tell him for me to issue the necessary directions to each of the company commanders. The men must be in line and ready to move at four o'clock in the morning to the very minute. This means business."

The boy hurried off with the message and came back to find the major at his desk writing a hasty note to his wife. "Jack," he said, looking up as the boy entered the tent, "we cannot expect to get much sleep to-night. We have a good deal to do in order to make ready for this movement. I want you to pack up enough blankets to make us tolerably comfortable, lock up these books, put away my clothes, and see that everything about my headquarters is ready at the right time."

Jack did all that could be done, scrawled a hurried letter to the friends at home, telling them what was going on, and then threw himself down on his bed and was soon asleep. It seemed to him that he had barely done so when the loud reveille sounded at three in the morning. The whole command was soon astir, the horses were fed and saddled, the men drank their coffee and swallowed their morning meal, packed their blankets, put on their overcoats, filled their haversacks with hard-tack and bacon, secured their portions of sugar and coffee, and at the hour assigned were mounted and in line. Everybody was cross, chilly, restive, and disagreeable. The sleet was still falling, and it was hardly possible to keep in any measure dry even with the help and shelter of the rubber "poncho." The bugle sounded the order "Forward," and on into and through the darkness and mud and slush the horses went bearing their riders forth to rebeldom.

The wharf in the vicinity of the transport presented a busy scene of bustle and confusion with army wagons rumbling to and fro, batteries of artillery struggling to get into position and

A BRIEF CAMPAIGN TAKES SOME OF THE SHINE OFF.

station themselves on the levee in a "park" until an opportunity to get on board should be furnished, teamsters swearing and whipping their mules, orderlies rushing with dispatches in every direction, infantry marching and then countermarching, horses eagerly and hungrily stamping and neighing, rain falling, steam puffing from the engines of the boats, bells ringing, whistles blowing, details of soldiers loading boxes of ammunition and provisions, and, withal, everybody shouting, yelling, pushing, pulling, all at once. "Where are we going?" was his inquiry of the major.

The answer was in the form of a quotation:

> "Theirs not to make reply,
> Theirs not to reason why."

The boy saw that if his uncle knew what direction the troops were to take he was not going to tell. He tried another tack: "How do you like the idea of being under the command of General Blank?"

"Not at all," was the gruff response; "but I have to obey orders as long as I am in the service. For the time he is my superior, and my duty is to respect and obey him. I can do the one part of this task in some sort, I guess, but the other is out of the question. We shall see some rare work if we go into battle under his command. However, it is not worth while to indulge in gloomy forebodings before we are fairly started on our campaign. I will do the best that I can for my own command, at any rate. Meanwhile we shall see what we shall see."

It was noon before the troops were all on board the transports and ready for the forward movement. Then came a tedious wait for orders, which lasted the rest of the day. Everybody wondered why the boats did not start and what was the matter, and nobody could, or at least nobody did, throw light on the question. The night came again, thick, murky, and wet, and as soon as the darkness had fairly settled down the steamers received orders to push out from the levee and drop down the river.

"Why did we not start by daylight instead of waiting for the night to come?" was Jack's inquiry as he stood on the deck with the major, watching the lights of the city of Cairo receding and vanishing in the distance behind them.

"I cannot positively answer your question," was the reply, "but I think that one reason of the delay is that Cairo is full of rebel spies on the watch for news of our movements. If we had gone in the daytime they would have watched our course and their generals would have known our destination almost before we had reached it. On the other hand, I have learned that to-night the picket guard is doubled all around our line, and it will be impossible for anyone to get over into Dixie with news concerning our advance. Our movement may be a part of a general push along the whole western line. But it is idle to speculate about the matter now. We shall be wiser in the course of a week than we are to-night."

"Do you think we shall get into a battle before we get back?" pursued the curious youth in quest of information.

"I do not know any more about the matter than you do," replied the major. "It all depends. If we should find any rebels in our path, and they do not run away, and there is any fight in our boys, and the weather does not interfere, and all the other conditions are favorable, it seems to me within the limits of likelihood that we may have what Van calls a scrimmage before we return. And that we may be ready for that possible event it behooves us to go to bed."

The boy awoke before day next morning, and on going on deck found the boat tied up with the other transports of the fleet at a landing on the Kentucky side of the Mississippi River, about midway between Cairo and Columbus, near the mouth of the Mayfield Creek. The troops were already getting ashore, and very soon orders came for the cavalry to disembark and take the head of the column.

"Well," said Jack to himself, "if we go ahead we shall at least have the first sight of the rebels if there are any to be seen."

An aid of General Blank at that moment came galloping up with orders to start at once, and march toward the interior from the river for about ten miles and then take the main road to Mayfield. The men and horses were both glad to put their feet on land once more, in spite of the rain and mud, and the column moved forward with spirit and life. Jack had an opportunity to see the precautions that must be taken in an enemy's country on the march to avoid surprise. The most vigilant and cautious lieutenant in the battalion was ordered to take with him a sergeant and half a dozen men and assume the advance. His instructions were to keep about a quarter of a mile ahead of the rest, and if any rebels were discovered he was to fire off his pistol as a signal shot and send a man back at full speed with the news. A full company of cavalry came next, followed by a pioneer corps with axes, picks, and shovels. Then marched a couple of regiments of infantry, a battery of artillery, and the rest of the troops guarding the wagon train, with two companies of cavalry in the rear to close up the column and keep an eye on the crossroads. In addition, along the whole length of the column, on both sides of the road, at the distance of two or three hundred yards, a line of skirmishers marched to prevent a sudden attack from either flank. Jack watched with interest all these arrangements and precautions, and felt his pulse quicken with a vague sense of uncertainty and an apprehension that there was danger ahead, when the command was repeated by voice and bugle all along the line, "Fall in! Forward—march!"

The country was level and finely wooded with oaks, elms, and walnut trees of goodly size. Here and there appeared tracts which had been cleared and were now occupied as farms, and the soil seemed rich and fertile, but the buildings were—most of them, at least—old and tumble-down in appearance. One large and comfortable dwelling was the only one of its kind they saw that day; all the other human habitations were log cabins of the rudest and most primitive style. As they were riding along through the mud Jack inquired, "Major, what ails this region? If we had such a tract of land in Pennsylvania it would be thickly settled. Saw-mills would be at work in these splendid forests, and the houses would be fit to live in, and the fields would be covered with crops. What is the reason everything looks so dilapidated and forsaken?"

The officer glanced sharply into the face of the boy, and with a look of surprise replied, "There is but one secret of this state of affairs, and an intelligent youth ought to know what that is without telling."

"Slavery?" said Jack, inquiringly.

"Nothing else," was the comment of the major. "This State is the equal, in fertility and in many natural advantages, of any commonwealth in the Union. It has coal and iron and timber in abundance, and many sections of the State are unrivaled for grazing purposes, while you can hardly find anywhere in the country a better soil for the growth of wheat and Indian corn. The climate is delightful. A man seeking comfort and health will find all the conditions filled right here. And then its commercial advantages are wonderful. Its rivers alone bring the heart of the State into easy and rapid communication with all the rest of the world. Its northern front is traversed by the Ohio; along its western border runs that immense artery of trade, the Mississippi; while throughout the interior for hundreds of miles flow two splendid rivers, navigable for a good portion of the year, the Kentucky and the Tennessee. With these advantages this region ought to be in the forefront of trade and overflowing with prosperity and business life. Yet you see a fair sample of the situation and condition of things in this section through which we are passing. Other sections, it is true, are more prosperous than this region immediately about us; but nevertheless a blight rests on the whole State. A curse has paralyzed enterprise, checked commercial activity, deadened everything. Nature and Providence have done all that it is possible to do for any land in affording it such ample resources and opportunities. But all these advantages are wasted, clean thrown away, just so long as Negro slavery is revered and worshiped as the 'sacred institution.'"

By this time the command had arrived at a point where the road forked, and the major detached a company of cavalry and ordered it out toward Paducah to reconnoiter. A couple of hours after they had passed this place the major called Jack to him and said: "I want you to ride back and follow after Captain Shepardson's company until you overtake it, and deliver him this message: If he has found no traces of any Confederate forces in the vicinity he may return and join us at our camp, wherever that may be, this evening. If there is any sign of the presence of the enemy you are to let me know as quick as possible, while he guards the road and keeps them in check. Do you understand?"

"Yes, sir, I will see that he gets the word," was the eager reply of the boy as he wheeled about and galloped down the road. He found at one point a battery stuck in the mud and the drivers doubling their teams on each cannon to pull it through the slough. A little farther back he came to the infantry regiments scattered along in the slushy roads trampling through the mire wearily enough under their loads of ammunition, knapsacks, and rations. In the middle of the column he saw the general in command of the brigade riding cheerfully and contentedly in apparent leisure and comfort. Nearer the rear was the wagon train, delayed by a broken bridge which the pioneer corps was trying to repair. Then came the rear guard, and at last Jack found himself alone. The troops had all marched toward the front. The whole command had passed by, and he had still several miles of country to traverse with which he was totally unfamiliar, and which might contain some Confederate troops. He quickened his speed and urged Charley on at a rapid gallop. Soon he arrived at the turning-off place and struck away in the direction pursued by the company he was in search of. He kept his eyes and ears open, and the sense of danger and the novelty and romance of the situation lent a strange fascination to it.

After riding a couple of miles from the main road he happened to look back, and as he did so he made a discovery: he was pursued. A cavalryman, who had just entered the road from a bypath that led through the woods in the distance, had caught sight of him and had struck in pursuit. Jack did not know exactly what to make of this, and, looking at his revolver, to make sure it was in shooting trim, and putting spurs to the horse, he rode more rapidly on. Glancing back, he found that the stranger was gaining on him. He saw, too, that the man was making signs to arrest attention, and, taking a closer look, he discovered that the pursuer was no other than Jim Van Meter.

The boy felt a little foolish as he halted and allowed Van to catch up.

"You thought I was a 'Johnny reb,' and was going to eat you up, now, didn't you?" was Van's salutation. "I had a good laugh while you were running away. You see I've been out foraging. I've laid in a couple of chickens and a roll of butter and a pie and some corn bread and lots of good things. See here "—pointing to his overweighted haversack of provisions and to the fowls strung over the neck of his horse—" I believe in livin' on the fat of the land as long as you can git the fat from the rebs."

"Where did you get all that stuff? What did you have to pay for it?" said Jack.

"Pay! That's a good one! Who's goin' to pay for vittles in Dixie? I believe in the doctrine that the country owes us a livin', and as long as I'm soldierin' I'm goin' to have it, one way or another."

"Why, Van, you didn't steal that provender, did you?" inquired the boy, with some anxiety.

"Steal? What d'ye take me for, boy? I'd scorn to do such a act. I cramped it; confiscated it; tuk possession of it as the property of the enemy; condemned it as contraband of war; held an inquest over it and ordered it to be seized and used by the forces of the United States; and then tuk it under my protection as one of the duly app'inted agents of the guv'ment. And look 'ere, my canteen's full likewise. I found some of our boys guttin' a corner grocery store down at the crossroads. They'd rolled out a bar'l o' Bourbon into the road and knocked in the head and was a dippin' into it pretty free and eager; and I was a helpin' myself too, when, lo and behold, along comes one of the officers of the staff, and he sees what was goin' on, and he clears 'em all out mighty quick. And now give an account of yourself. Why aren't you with the battalion? What in Hail Columbia are you doin' 'way out here?"

"I'm taking a message to Captain Shepardson. Will you go too?"

"Yes, come along. Let's hurry up; for I do not want to be caught at night on this road so far from the rest of the troops."

By this time they had arrived at the top of a hill from which the country for miles around could be seen. Away ahead they caught a glimpse, apparently, of the men they were in pursuit of. No signs of the enemy were to be discovered anywhere. But few natives were visible, and these did not have anything to say unless they were accosted. Suddenly, while they were pacing along at a rapid gait, Van stopped and said, " Hold my horse. I've found somethin' wuth looking after." And dismounting he picked up a handsome new revolver, and, examining it carefully, put it in his pocket. They had scarcely resumed their ride before a picket guard caught up with them, anxiously scanning the ground and eagerly looking for something. He saluted the two with the words: " Say, comrades, ye didn't see a new revolver along here, did ye? Mine dropped out of my holster somewhere on this road this afternoon, and I'll be hanged if I can find it. I've been searchin' for it high and low for more than an hour. I wouldn't 'a' lost it for a twenty-dollar gold piece."

And while he spoke he looked all about the ground near by in search of the missing weapon.

"Whar was you when you dropped it? Mebbe you didn't have it with you this trip. What sort of a lookin' pistol was it? It's a pity to lose a good revolver. It's a thing wuth havin' in this country of rebs." This series of mingled comments and questions Van uttered coolly, but with some show of sympathy, as he pretended to aid the man in looking for the pistol. In a moment or two the latter went on, greatly troubled on account of his loss.

The boy was shocked. He had been brought up to believe in some old-fashioned notions, among which was the doctrine that it is wrong to steal. He was so inexperienced and unsophisticated that he did not know that a man may be strictly honest, and highly respectable, and a very proper sort of a gentleman, and have a good name in society, and yet steal, if he only call the act by some less offensive name. It is the word "steal" or "thief" that hurts, oftentimes, more than the deed or the character thus described. If these bad names can be put out of sight people may take the property of somebody else and escape all blame. The act may be styled going into bankruptcy, or getting up a corner in stocks, or organizing an oil company, or discovering a gold mine, or getting somebody to become one's bail, or confiscating the goods of an enemy, or finding things—any one of these terms will serve the purpose. The boy, I say, was not educated in these new ideas, and hence he was shocked.

We will agree that it is mighty uncomfortable for a boy to have such old-fashioned notions. They often come up in his thoughts just at the nick of time when but for them he might make some money, or enjoy some sort of pleasure, or keep possession of property that has by some unlooked-for chance fallen into his hands. Then, without warning and in a way that cannot easily be overlooked, these old-fashioned instructions begin to clamor and threaten and rankle and make all manner of inward disturbance; and of course one's peace of mind is destroyed. It is a troublesome thing, in short, to have what is called a conscience coming in every little while to interfere with one's plans and pleasures. If this clamorous organ could by some means be thoroughly abolished and effectually put out of the way boys and men could act out all sorts of mischief and enter into all manner of adventures and, in fact, do whatever they wished, without experiencing any of the inconveniences that happen to a fellow now if he does not mind what his conscience tells him to do. Some very unpleasant—indeed, one would be justified in saying *painful*—consequences often follow when this everlasting busybody, the conscience, sets up to act as a general committee of investigation upon our deeds and then proceeds to execute her peculiar penalties. I believe that the effort has been made at times to kill the conscience, but the experiment is attended with some risk, and is understood not to have been a perfect success.

Another characteristic prank of the conscience is that it is perpetually interfering with its neighbor conscience. It will not stay quietly on its own premises, but is ever trying to invade some one's domain next door. It is not satisfied to go on and command and forbid and advise and scold and punish the fellow that it belongs to, but it insists on having its say often to somebody else. And on this particular occasion this was the whim that came over the boy's conscience. If he had just reflected a moment he might have said to himself: " This is not any of my business, and I will have nothing to do with it. I did not take the man's revolver. I do not really know that Van has it. The one he picked up may belong to another man altogether. Besides, I cannot make myself the guardian angel of careless soldiers who go through an enemy's country losing their weapons. If he did lose this particular pistol, then very likely the most valuable lesson that can be taught him is to suffer him to bear the loss. Why should I interfere in the matter? Let providential events follow their due course."

And then, afterward, he and Van could have sold the pistol for fifteen or twenty dollars, dividing the proceeds, and they would have been just that much richer in worldly goods. That would have been the thrifty way of doing the business.

But, as I started out to say, this boy's conscience was fussy, officious, and of a meddlesome disposition. In this particular case it was not satisfied to assume authority over the boy and his conduct alone, but it was impudent enough to try to interfere with Van's plans and speculations. So, acting out the impulses of his crotchety faculty within, Jack looked into the face of his companion and, in a tone which showed how horrified

he was, said, "Why, Van, you are not going to keep the fellow's pistol, are you?"

Van looked sheepish and crestfallen. He was a big, strapping, muscular chap, who could have whipped Jack and six others like him all in a pile. Yet at this question he colored and then grew pale; he shrugged his shoulders and wriggled uneasily in his saddle, and at last stopped his horse and yelled to the fast-receding trooper: "Here, old fellow, is your revolver! It'll be a lesson to you, I hope, not to be so careless with it in the future. You'd 'a' had to pay for it next payday, and that would 'a' been a nice hole in your pile. Better take care of these 'ere weapons that Uncle Sam gives you, my crony. The next comrade as finds it won't be as kind to you as I've been. Now take it and skedaddle as fast as you can, or you'll not get to your regiment again afore night."

The rejoicing man overflowed with thanks, made an offer of money as a reward for finding the pistol—which, to Van's credit be it recorded, was refused—and then galloped away.

The subject was not again referred to by either of them, except that Van remarked, in a tone of injured innocence, "I wanted to teach him a lesson as he'd remember."

He afterward said that it was the tone and look of the boy that "fetched" him. He remarked, in alluding to the incident, "I never felt so mean in my life. I couldn't stand them innocent eyes o' his'n starin' at me in a wonderin' and accusin' kind o' way. So I handed over the six-shooter, and I'm that much poorer by the operation."

Delivering the message to Captain Shepardson, the two hastened back to the road which they had left, and followed hard after the advancing column. With all their haste it was night before they could overtake it, coming about dark to an open space on a gentle slope, where they found the artillery parked, the wagon trains arranged in order, and the men going into camp.

"Where's the cavalry to camp, captain?" Van asked of one of the staff.

"Somewhere about here, I guess. I'll ask the general," was the reply; and soon the word was brought that they had been sent for to come back from the head of the column and would be in by and by. After waiting an hour Jack and his companion ventured ahead to meet them. They found them, long after night had set in, still in the dark and mud, a couple of miles from camp, and showed them to their bivouac.

The major was effervescent with indignation and wrath at the way in which things had been conducted as to the camping arrangements of the troops, and he let out his feelings to Jack when the latter appeared: "This is just what I expected when we began this movement. Here was a column of troops stretched out over six or eight miles of territory. The lofty military genius who presides over its destinies rides with his staff safely and comfortably in the center of the column. When nightfall comes he looks about him for a convenient camping ground, and when he comes to one that strikes his fancy he selects it, orders the tents to be put up, and sends ahead five or six miles for the troops that have been in the advance all day to come back and settle down for the night. Confound such stupidity and mismanagement! If the man had an ounce of common gumption, let alone any military knowledge, he would have sent one of his staff to ride with me at the front all day. We could have selected the proper place, and then as each part of the command arrived it could have gone into camp by daylight. As it is our horses are tired and hungry, the infantry have had to march and countermarch five miles more than there was any reason for, we have come into camp in the darkness, and before we do anything toward getting a bite to eat for ourselves or animals we must send out a party to picket the roads in the neighborhood. I pity the men. They are not to blame, and yet they are the ones who suffer."

The battalion was ordered to take position on the higher part of the hill just in the edge of the woods that crowned the slope. It was amazing to find how, in spite of the discomforts and inconveniences of the situation, the men soon made themselves tolerably comfortable. The ground was soaked with water and covered with a light scum of snow, and yet, when the fires were kindled and the indispensable and blessed coffee was made, and the pork began to sizzle in the pans, and the beef was broiled on the coals, it was remarkable how cheerful everybody grew.

Jack ran into a Negro cabin near headquarters to find out what the inmates had to eat. He learned that the old "auntie" in charge could make hoecake at short notice. He ordered enough for half a dozen, and watched her making preparations to bake it. Seeing it in a few moments spread out on the hot hearth, he went back to camp and found supper almost ready. Telling them of the treasure he had discovered, he ran and brought the cake. It was made of the meal from the white Kentucky flint corn, now common all over the country, but at that time rare in the Eastern States. As Jack spread the cake with some of Van's confiscated butter, and ate his fried bacon, and enjoyed his beefsteak he thought he had never in all his life before tasted such a delicious meal. Then, spreading his rubber blanket on the wet and snow-covered ground, he made his bed. The rain had ceased and the stars shone out clear and bright, and from where the boy had unrolled his blankets he could look down over the whole encampment. The smoldering camp-fires, gleaming all over the hillside, the dark woods in the rear, from which even now there might be peering the vigilant eyes of a rebel host ready to pounce down on the Union forces at dead of night and take them by surprise, the cordon of sentries round the camp, the bugles sounding tattoo—all this gradually and indistinctly mingled with the visions of dreamland as the boy, tired out and drowsy, took a speedy departure for the dominions of Nod.

The next day, and the next, and the next, through the mud and snow and slush, the march was continued. No rebels were to be found except some pickets in the distance. The whole campaign seemed aimless and vague. Everybody asked the conundrum, "What is General Blank driving at?" and, after pondering it carefully, everybody "gave it up." Finally, after running around loose in Dixie for a week or more, they all returned to Cairo.

"What does all this mean?" was the question of the perplexed boy to the major on their return.

"The King of France with twice ten thousand men,
Marched up the hill—and then marched down again!"

was the reply of that officer; and then he continued his comments: "You see, my boy, that we have a precedent almost classical in its character for this campaign. General Blank is not the first distinguished genius to accomplish such an undertaking. But, seriously, you will find in a few days that this campaign was not for nothing. I take it to have been a feint. The line of battle out here is very long. Halleck is at work somewhere. For some reason or other he wants to draw the rebels to defend Columbus. Hence this feint. You know an expert boxer will make a seemingly desperate lunge at the chest of his antagonist, who, while parrying the expected blow, receives instead a stunner on the nose. This is the game of experts in war also. Halleck, who has command of all this western territory, has, I

A BRIEF CAMPAIGN TAKES SOME OF THE SHINE OFF. 65

think, been simply pretending to attack Columbus, but all the time his real aim has been to deliver a tremendous blow at some point along the Tennessee or Cumberland. If the rebels have been induced to reinforce their threatened strongholds on the Mississippi, and withdraw troops for that purpose from the regions east of those places, they have been playing directly into our hands."

In a few days the news reached the troops at Cairo that General Thomas had won a notable victory over the Confederates at Mill Springs, Ky.,—an announcement which threw light upon the seemingly aimless and fruitless march against Columbus, which we have just had a glimpse and a taste of in this story. This latter campaign was clearly intended to keep the Confederates from reinforcing the troops which Thomas was about to attack in eastern Kentucky.

CHAPTER IV.

SIGHT-SEEING AT FORT DONELSON ON PRIVATE ACCOUNT.

"HURRAH, boys, Grant has captured Fort Henry, and we are ordered to advance up the Cumberland River at once against Fort Donelson!" was the salutation that electrified the Fourth Illinois Cavalry one morning soon after its return from the expedition into Kentucky, recorded in the last chapter. These twin forts, built by the Confederates to command the Cumberland and Tennessee Rivers, and to protect the railroads which lay south of the fortified points, had been coveted for months by Halleck and Grant; one of them had already fallen, and the other was doomed. The boys received the news with gladness, and rejoiced at the prospect of seeing active service in the field and the opportunity of pushing into the South.

Instead of leaving Cairo for an expedition of only a few days, the troops were ordered to break up camp there altogether and proceed to the front. There would be no longer any opportunity to go into town and purchase delicacies and luxuries not issued by the commissary department. All chances for the boys to slip off from duty for a day or a night and spend the time in seeing the sights and tasting the amusements and sharing the dissipations of the so-called city of Cairo were at an end. Active service in the field, an advance through the land occupied, guarded, and fortified by the Confederates, a forward movement into the South, not now as a feint but in earnest—all this was clearly seen to await the troops. In a short time they tore down their tents, stored all the equipage that could not be taken along, and then reported for transportation to the officer in charge of that branch of the service. A fleet of gunboats and mortar boats accompanied the expedition. These iron-plated monsters were novel sights to Jack. Most of them had been hastily built by altering small river steamers, cutting down their decks, and plating them over with iron. A few new vessels had been constructed as an experiment, and they looked like old-fashioned arks or barges roofed over and armored throughout with metal plates. The huge mortars were studied with a good deal of curiosity, each one occupying an open boat by itself, while around it were piled the great shells by and by to be thrown into the enemy's ranks. The unsophisticated boy examined them all with interest, wondering what sort of a dreadful noise the explosion of both would make, and even eagerly anxious for the hour of battle to come, so that he might see and hear the awful-looking weapons in actual use.

At last the expedition was ready to start. The array of steamers of all sorts and sizes, the fleet of gunboats, the parade of the troops as they marched to the levee and embarked on the transports, already laden with ammunition and provisions, the final good-bye to Cairo, and the start on the journey are still vivid pictures in the memory of the survivors of that command.

Up the Ohio to Smithland the boats directed their course, while the soldiers crowded the decks, scanning the low shores of the river, now lined with farms and now guarded by bluffs. Then the Cumberland River was entered, and from that time the interest and even the pleasure of the trip were enhanced by the additional spice of danger which the possible presence of the foe imparted. The expedition was on the edge of an enemy's country; the banks at any point might conceal hostile pickets, while at any stage of their course a volley of musketry or a cannon shot might be expected from the bluffs. No one knew exactly what to look for, and hence all were on the *qui vive*, in suspense, vigilant night and day.

It was a cold, snowy morning—the 13th of February, 1862—when the cavalry landed near Fort Donelson. At once they were sent out to picket the roads. The region about the fort was thickly wooded and quite rough. In such a country only infantry and artillery could be used in a battle, so that the cavalry had simply to await orders and keep a sharp lookout on the surrounding district and guard the roads in every direction. Rugged hills, dense forests, and high bluffs were the marked features of the landscape. Through these thickets and up the wooded heights only foot soldiers could make their way.

When the regiment arrived the skirmishing had already commenced, and all around the line an occasional rattling fire was going on. Fresh troops, however, were on the way, and no general attack was desired until these should arrive.

As the cavalry had no actual work except picket duty assigned them, and Jack was curious to see what was going on and investigate matters for himself, he started out with Charley, the bugler, on a little private exploring expedition, in the effort to get a glimpse of the line of battle as it ran through the woods and over the hills around the fort for several miles. Starting out from the boat on which the headquarters were established and near which the regiment was encamped, they climbed a hill covered with undergrowth and dense with scrub oaks. Here they found some infantrymen throwing up earthworks and digging intrenchments. Stopping to talk a while and take observations, Jack asked a burly soldier from Iowa, "What's the latest news you have this afternoon from the front?"

The man ceased his work and said dryly, "The Johnnies are looking around to find a hole big enough to crawl out of, and they cannot discover any."

"How do you know?" said Charley.

"We just captured one of their pickets. Do you see the poor grayback yonder at the foot of the tree? He's tired out with poor rations, long and hard marching, and constant activity. He was at Fort Henry last week, and escaped from there when Admiral Foote bombarded the place, and came over here with several thousand others, under Colonel Heiman, and this morning he ventured out a little too far and our boys nabbed him."

The youthful explorers went up to the prisoner and said:

"Good morning. How are your folks coming on over yonder?"—pointing in the direction of the fort.

The captured man was a wretched-looking object, to be sure, and clearly not a typical Confederate soldier. He was evidently a representative of the lower class of whites in the South, the crackers, or "poor white trash." Tired, hungry, scrawny, and thin, he was wrapped in a ragged blanket, and chewing, with as much vigor as his constitution permitted, a big quid of tobacco. While he shivered with the cold at the foot of the tree an Illinois trooper stood guard over him, this part of the performance seeming, however, to be needless, for the man did not appear to have strength enough in his frame to allow of his running very far or fast. He looked up at the salutation and drawled out in answer to the question, "O, right smart, I reckon. We uns haven't got much to eat, and its hard to fight without suthin' besides hard bread and rye coffee. I dunno what we'd 'a' done if it hadn't been fur our terbacker. That's been more'n meat and drink sometimes."

"How many soldiers have you over there?"

"O, right smart chance of 'em altogether. I heerd some on 'em say that the Yanks was sure to be licked this time, we had so many in our army. But then, agin, I heerd some say this mornin' as there was talk of our gittin' out of this afore long."

The boys shared the contents of their haversacks with the prisoner and went on, wondering if he were a fair specimen of the Southern soldier. They had a good view of the rebel works at the next opening. The Confederate sharpshooters were trying to keep the Union men from planting a battery. Once in a while a bullet had come into the midst of the detail of men who were assigned to the task of putting the guns in position. Some of them had already been wounded, but there appeared no enemy in sight. The battery was on the brow of a gentle knoll in the edge of the woods. In front of it was a deep ravine, on the other side of which were the rebel works. Their side of the hill was covered with little pits dug out as a shelter for riflemen. In a zigzag course were to be seen several lines of fortifications, some made of logs, others of bags of sand, others of sheaves of brush and sharp sticks, the pickets standing out and pointing toward the besiegers. At the top of the hill was a line of cannon, their gaping throats, black and threatening, all ready to send out fire and death.

The boys stood quite a while in the woods and looked about over the scene. Their thought was on this wise: "How can General Grant expect men to charge such strong works as these? It is not possible for any force to take them. Even if our men should be brave enough to come out of the woods and advance down this hill into the ravine and try to climb the slope on the other side they could not climb over those fortifications. They would be stopped by the trees that are cut down yonder. They would only run into the sharp branches and get entangled in them. There seems to be no place where they can get through; and all the while the rebels would be pouring into them a dreadful fire of shot and shell. It will be a fearful scene here if Grant orders an attack."

While the boys thus watched the strong works they ventured forth from the woods to get a better view, not noticing that they were exposing themselves to the observation of the enemy. The first intimation they had of that fact consisted in a peculiar sound which can never be forgotten by any one who has ever heard it. It is like no other sound in the world. It makes an impression on the ear and on the nerves which hardly anything else does. It is a whistle and a whine, a hiss and a rattle, altogether, and it ends with a "thud" that is striking and peculiar too. This sound, coming close to their ears, startled them so that they jumped, and both exclaimed at once, "What's that?"

At this instant the officer in charge of the building of the fortifications noted them and angrily cried out, "Get out of that, you young rascals. You'll get a bullet through your head before you know where you are. Don't you know any better than to venture out in front of the embankment? What are you doing here?"

The youths by this time were safely hidden from the view of the sharpshooters, just beginning to realize the danger of being at the very front. One of them replied, "Captain, we are just looking around to find out what is going on. We were curious to see the two lines of battle. We did not see any rebels over there, and did not know that it was a risky thing to stand out yonder."

"You young fools," said the officer, "do you expect that the rebels are going to come outside their breastworks and lift their hats and say,' Good morning, gentlemen, we give you fair notice that we are about to open fire on you, and if you want to keep your hides free from bullet-holes you'd better remain under shelter?' Didn't see any rebels, indeed! Clear out and join your regiment, or I'll arrest you for straggling."

This rebuff threw a damper on their taste for exploration, but they were not satisfied yet, and when they had passed out of sight of the officer they tried to penetrate further along the line, but found pickets and guards stationed to prevent men from passing from one command to another, and they had to content themselves by turning back to the river.

That evening Jack saw for the first time men who had been wounded in battle. The boat on which the regiment had come up the river was now turned into a hospital. Just after supper the boy noticed a commotion in the cabin, and, pressing through the crowd of soldiers, he found out what was the cause of it. A couple of wounded men had just been brought in from the picket line to be examined and attended to by the surgeon. The latter appeared a little nervous, as he had never before dressed a gunshot wound, but in a moment he showed no signs of hesitation or shakiness. He summoned the first one to his side at the operating table. The man had been shot in the hand, his middle finger being torn away and the bones connected with it badly crushed. His clothing was covered with blood and his face was pale from the long walk he had taken since he had received his wound. Jack felt a cold chill run up and down his backbone as he saw the ugly sight and looked at the case of instruments lying in view on the table ready for use.

"Do you want me to give you anything before the operation?" said the surgeon to the patient.

"What do you mean?" asked the latter.

"Shall I give you ether or chloroform while I dress your wound?" explained the doctor.

"How long will it take you to put me through?"

"About ten minutes," was the reply.

"Well, then, fire away; I guess I can stand it," said the man, coolly, as he gritted his teeth and compressed his lips and braced himself up to endure the operation.

The surgeon, noticing that he was chilled and worn out from exposure and pain and by the long walk he had taken from the picket line to the hospital, made the man drink a glass of liquor to nerve him up for the task. Then he took his knife and began to cut into the torn and bleeding flesh, which he trimmed away neatly, exposing the crushed bone. Jack watched him till he saw the nippers at work cutting off the bones of the broken finger and the saw doing its harsh work among the larger ones of the hand; and just then he felt a strange sensation of numbness creeping over him. The blood seemed to leave his heart and then rush violently into it again. An attack of dizziness made his head swim, and a nauseating feeling disturbed his stomach. The wounded man, the surgeon, the furniture of the saloon of the steamer where they were gathered, the spectators, all seemed to mingle in mad confusion. It appeared as if they were all having a crazy dance together. Conquering the faintness by a convulsive effort, he turned quickly away from the scene and rushed out on deck and into the fresh air, which soon revived him. But to this day—although the boy afterward saw thousands of wounded men, many of them mangled and torn far worse than this one—that first soldier, brought in from the front at Fort Donelson with his torn and bleeding hand and operated on by the surgeon, is vividly stamped on his memory.

That night the gunboats all arrived, anchoring a couple of miles below the fort. Next day, February 14, early in the afternoon, they slowly steamed up toward the line of fortifications called the water batteries, situated on the river bank. Jack had no task on hand, and his curiosity was not yet fully satisfied.

He therefore concluded to walk up the stream, keeping abreast of the boats so as to watch their movements. By and by he came to a turn in the river, and, looking ahead, he saw about a mile distant in his front the lower batteries of the Confederates, and higher up on the bluffs the frowning guns of the upper works.

While he stopped and gazed on the scene the gunboats carefully steamed around the bend and maneuvered into position. Before they were ready to commence operations Jack noticed a puff of smoke appear at a certain point in one of the embankments. In a moment afterward he heard a boom and a terrible screech which filled the air, sounding like the wail of a human being in awful agony, or like the yell of a fiend in torment. In the midst of the impression made upon him by the sound he saw the air filled with pieces of shell just over one of the gunboats, and then he knew what had happened. The rebels had opened fire on the fleet, and this was their first bomb!

The boy had hardly time to draw his breath before the leading boat returned the fire, that boat being the *St. Louis*, under Flag Officer Foote, who had charge of all the naval forces in the Western waters, and who had captured Fort Henry without waiting for the army to cooperate in the attack, on board. This heroic spirit was leading off in the present attack, and now it was under his personal direction that the first shot was fired from his flagship against the water batteries. In a moment the *Louisville* also was in action, and then the other ironclads of the fleet, the *Carondelet* and the *Pittsburgh*, followed at some distance down stream by the wooden gunboats, the *Tyler* and the *Conestoga*.

The stream was not very wide, and the boy, from his perch on the bank, as he walked along, keeping abreast of the leading boats, could look right into the faces of the gunners as they handled the great black cannon. He saw the air filled with smoke, he heard the scream of the shell as it flew through the half mile of distance between the boat and the batteries, and then he could see it explode right over the rebel guns. He could not tell what effect had been wrought by it, of course, but he saw that at once the whole line of cannon on the side of the enemy

GUNBOAT ASSAULT ON FORT DONELSON.

opened fire. The fleet—a half dozen boats, large and small—were during this time coming into position, one by one wheeling about so as to get into range with the fort, all the while advancing. When each arrived at the proper post it delivered its fire and then circled around to reload and give the other boats opportunity to deliver their broadsides. Once in a while a solid shot from the fort would strike an iron-plated ship, make a deep dent in its armor, and then glance off with a terrific splashing into the water. Then a shell would burst just over the deck, sending a perfect storm of iron hailstones down on the metal plates. Many times the boy watched a ball ricochet in the water, touching the surface ten or twenty times before finally sinking in the waves, bringing to mind the occasions when he had often made pebbles skip in a similar way across a milldam.

The whole scene was full of fascination. Once in a while the shells would come dangerously near to where the boy was standing, but none of them happened to hit him, and he grew accustomed to it all, forgetting the peril in the excitement of the battle. He had the rare opportunity of watching a gunboat fight without taking any part in it. His frame quivered with a thrill of excitement as he watched the preparations made at the fort for hoisting new guns into the place of those which had been disabled, as he noted a shell burst in the midst of a crowd of the combatants there, or as a shot would come skipping across the water perilously near to him on the bank, or as a bomb would burst in the very air over his head and send its pieces flying in all directions.

In the very height of the engagement he saw a well-aimed bombshell of the foe enter the porthole of the *Carondelet*, exploding just within the opening, dismantling a cannon and wounding a dozen or more men. Through the din and confusion of the conflict there could be distinguished the officers' voices giving command to the gunners, the cries of the wounded, and the battering and hammering of the detail of men who at once were set to work to clear away the wreck which had been made by the shells, so as to get the decks ready for action again. Thick and fast came the shot and bombs from the batteries, crashing on the iron plate, skipping across the waves, going clean through the smokepipes, tearing down the rigging; but still the plucky Commodore Foote kept his flagship, the *St. Louis*, in the forefront of the fight, and kept signaling to the others what to do. He had been severely wounded in the ankle, but he would not leave the field without doing all that he, with his fleet, might achieve toward capturing the fort.

After an hour and a half of this sort of work a couple of the boats, the flagship *St. Louis* and the *Louisville*, were noticed to be in trouble. They could not come up to the scratch at the proper time. They moved wildly and falteringly hither and thither, and it was seen that the officers could not manage them. The signals soon told the fleet what was wrong; the steering apparatus of both boats was out of gear, the pilot house of the *St. Louis* had been almost destroyed by round shot, and the machinery injured so that the ships could not be maneuvered; they would not obey the helm, and soon began to drift helplessly down the stream. The loss of these two disabled ships so weakened the fleet that it was soon found necessary to suspend the gunboat attack. That battle, however, between the guns of Fort Donelson and the agile, gallant, armored vessels of Flag Officer Foote, never to be forgotten by the nation, made a picture that will hardly fade from the memory of the boy, who stood on the bank that wintry day, heard the awful cannonade, listened to the shouting, and watched the varying stages of the fight.

One issue was decided by this engagement: Fort Donelson could not be taken, as Fort Henry had been, by an attack on the waterfront by the fleet. It would need more than a mere bombardment by cannon and mortar to conquer and capture it. The land forces would have to try their powers at it. The works would have to be stormed by the infantry.

That night was a busy time for everybody. It was generally understood that an attack was to be made upon the fortifications from the landward side, and all knew that it would be an affair of severity and blood. The lines were all arranged, the troops stationed, the roads picketed, and all the preparations completed.

Next morning the army was startled by heavy firing in the woods at a certain point where a road led off in the direction of Nashville. Word came to General Grant, "The rebels are trying to cut their way out and get away from us." In military language this sort of a movement is called a sally, or sortie. The Confederates knew that their communications were cut off with the rest of the world, that there was no hope of resisting a siege, that Grant would be sure in the end either to capture them or starve them out, and they determined to make an effort to get away by breaking a hole in the Union line of battle and running through it toward Nashville.

That Friday night, February 14, was bitter cold, and there was much suffering in the trenches and along the picket line. Before daybreak next morning the Confederates had opened the battle, concentrating their troops against the Union right, and, for a time, breaking in that flank, amid much havoc and with desperate fighting on both sides. What noble names pass before the eye as one studies anew that terrible day: McClernand, at the head of the First Division, winning his commission as major general of volunteers by his gallantry, with W. H. L. Wallace, one of the noblest spirits on the field, soon afterward to yield up his life at Shiloh, McArthur, full of daring, and Oglesby, still living to be honored again and again by the franchises of his splendid State of Illinois, as brigade commanders, and John A. Logan, his eye like that of an eagle, his voice sounding above the storm of battle, with magnificent courage leading his Thirty-first Illinois; General C. F. Smith in command of the Second Division, a gifted veteran soldier, who nearly forty years before had graduated at West Point, and ever since had been in military service, having indeed been Grant's instructor in tactics

A PEN AND INK RECOLLECTION OF GENERAL GRANT AS HE APPEARED IN THE FIELD at the academy twenty years before the battle in which they were both now engaged, and under him Colonels Lauman, Morgan L. Smith, and J. Cook, commanding brigades; and the famous Lew Wallace in charge of the Third Division, with the gallant Crufts and Thayer as his acting brigadiers—these were some of the heroic leaders who under Grant during those perilous days at Donelson helped to win the fight.

We may not tarry to depict the varying fortunes or describe the details of the engagement; suffice it to say that there were charges and countercharges; that the fight between the "ins" and the "outs" was desperate and lasted nearly all day, and that finally the Confederates were driven back into their intrenchments, while there were heavy losses on both sides.

Next day was Sunday, February 16. Grant had his troops in line of battle at an early hour, and was about to give orders to open the engagement, when the skirmishers, advancing through the woods, heard the sound of a bugle, and soon afterward met an officer bearing a white flag.

"What do you want?" was the question of the skirmishers.

"We have a message for General Grant; where will we find him?"

"Halt here and we will send the dispatch to him," was their reply; and at once a courier was sent with the letter to the general. It was found to contain a request for the battle to cease till noon, and a proposition for commissioners to be appointed to arrange terms of capitulation.

The good news flew quickly along the ranks that a flag of truce had come in, and all sorts of rumors spread out through the army as to the contents of the dispatch which had been received.

The reply of General Grant is now one of the famous sayings of history. He said to the rebel commander, "No terms except an unconditional and immediate surrender can be accepted. I propose to move immediately upon your works."

Soon there came another flag of truce, and this time it bore a letter announcing that General Buckner, the chief officer of the Confederates in the fort, had accepted the terms and that the place was ours.

That was a stirring Sunday. The word passed along the ranks like a flash of lightning, "Fort Donelson has surrendered." The men went wild with joy. They screamed and yelled and shouted and cheered in the wood and all along the line of earthworks, from one end of the army to the other. The boys on the gunboat fleet and on the transports took up the cheers and made the sky resound with their glad hurrahs. The Confederate flag was hauled down and the Union banner was unfurled on the staff, and at the sight the band played Yankee Doodle, and Hail, Columbia, and other national airs, and then everybody cheered again. Soon the two armies were mingling together as freely as if they had been all members of the same family. The bluecoats traded off greenbacks for tobacco, and supplied bacon and hardtack to those who were in need. Groups of Yankees and Confederates were to be seen all around the works conversing and laughing and jesting with each other on the most friendly terms. For days they had been trying in the most desperate and determined fashion to kill one another; now they were brothers again, all sectionalism, feuds, hatreds, and strifes forgotten or ignored. The men of Illinois and Iowa, and the soldiers of Tennessee, Alabama, and Georgia, conversed and commingled with delightful sense of comradeship—each side recognizing the valor, the skill, and the military capacity of the other, and each army feeling that it had met in the other's forces foemen worthy of its steel.

Very soon the prisoners were embarked on steamers and sent

SIGHT-SEEING AT FORT DONELSON.   83

to places of safe-keeping in the North. The sight of the transports laden with this strange freight was unique. From one end of the boats to the other the decks were covered with motley crowds of Southerners, some arrayed in butternut-colored garments, some clad in neat gray uniforms, and others scantily dressed only in dirty blankets. For the first time in many months they were under the Stars and Stripes, but now, alas! they were prisoners of war, on their way to places of captivity, while, as the steamers on which they sailed off down the river bore them away, they saw the works which they had so gallantly defended manned by Union soldiers.

CHAPTER V.

UP THE TENNESSEE RIVER.

THE cavalry battalion to which Jack belonged was ordered to go into camp and perform picket duty as soon as the surrender took place. It was encamped for a while at Randolph Forges, on the estate of John Bell, called the Cumberland Iron Works, near the village of Dover, a few miles from the fort. This large property belonged to the gentleman who had been the candidate for President on the "Bell and Everett" ticket in the preceding election in 1860.

Many slaves were still on the place, and the question of the bearing of the war on their destiny had not yet been settled. Nobody knew what would become of them or what the Union army ought to do with them or for them.

One day while in this camp a middle-aged Negro came to Jack's tent, where he was reading, and, after elaborately taking off his torn hat and politely bobbing his head up and down and courteously scraping the earth with his right foot at the same time, he asked permission to talk a while. He had looked about him very carefully first, in order to be sure that his words would not be overheard. Then he began: "Massa, I hopes dat you won't reckon it imp'dent if I axes you a pertick'ler question."

"O, no," was the encouraging reply of Jack. "Go ahead. What do you want to know?"

"Well, massa," said the black man, bowing and scraping as he spoke, and so nervous and anxious that his lip quivered and his voice trembled with excitement, "massa, de fact is dat I'se curyus to find out what dis yer wah means. I'se hearn tell a good deal about it, an' I'se been a-wonderin' if it's gwine to help my people any afore it's over. Duz you think, now, massa, dat dis yer wah's gwine to—" and here he stopped and held his breath and glanced about him, afraid to speak, lest even his whispers might be reported to the overseer, who was still on the place.

"You needn't be afraid," said Jack; "there is no one around here who would harm you. I will not tell on you. We are all your friends, and you may be certain that no Union soldier would betray you. Speak right out what you have in your mind."

"Well, massa, tell me, now, duz ye think dat dis wah's agwine to do anything for us poh cullud folks? Sometimes I spec' dat it is, and den again I spec' dat it isn't, an' I has no one to talk to dat knows about dese yer mattahs. I'se laid awake nights a heap since de trouble done gone commenced, a-thinkin' it all ober, an' now I'se in a snarl wuss nur I was afore. Now dar's ole Aunt Betty, she's shore dat we's all gwine to get our freedom by an' by. Dat's wot I'd like to fin' out. Is de wah gwine to set us free?"

"Why, Tom, who put that into your head?"

"Well, massa, it's a good while ago sence dat notion come inter my min'. Ye see, dar was a lot ob Yankee folks out yar in de woods gittin' out timber fur de big ships, and I was sent out dar wid de oxen to tote de long sticks down to de ribber. I felt like askin' 'em about dat strange country, de Norf, whar all de folks is free, but I was afeard to say a word to 'em about it. But one day one ob de men sez to me, sez he, 'Duz you know dat you black folks will all have yer liberty arter a while?' an', someways, dat question struck clean froo me. It seemed as if somebody 'd done gone and tole de man just what I'd been a-thinkin' about. I was knocked all through-other. I could har'ly answer him, but I makes out to say, 'How you know dat?' An' he says, 'Nebber you min' how I knows it; jis' 'member what I says to you. De time 'll come bimeby when you kin have your chillens in de school, and you kin larn to read yerse'f, and you'll have de chance to make yer own libbin' and be a man wid de rest ob men.'

"Dat's what the Yankee gen'l'man said, and his words hab nebber lef' me. I 'membered 'em all dese years; an' when de sojers commenced for to go from dis yer place to de wah, and when dey all said dat dey was agwine to cut loose from de Norf and not let any of de Yankees rule any longer, den I 'membered it all de mo'. I didn't see how it was gwine to come aroun', but I wondered what dat man meant and how he come to know so much about it; an' sence you gen'l'men done gone come and took de fort an' has matters all yer own way I'se been a-wonderin' an' conjurin' an' 'quirin' 'bout de matter till I'se almos' los' my wits. Nobody 'mong us 'pears to know anything 'bout it 'cept ole Aunt Betty."

"And who is this old Aunt Betty? Tell me what she says about it," said Jack.

"Ole Aunt Betty is a great woman 'mongst us, massa. She 'pears ter know moh dan any one else when we's in trubble. She's ole and blin' and all cripple up wid de roomatiz, and de little pickaninnies follers arter her when she goes along roun' de plantation, makin' all sorts ob sport wid her; but she nebber minds 'em, an' when dey gets sick she comes an' says words ober 'em, an' dat makes 'em well again and dey nebber forgets ole Aunt Betty arter dat. She's no good no moh for to work in the fiel', but she does little chores 'roun' de house for de missis. Ebery once in a while, when she's down in de cabin wid de cullud folks roun' about, den she does talk to 'em like one ob dem kronikles de Bible tell about."

"Ole Aunt Betty."

"Well, but what does she say about the war and the time when you will be free?" inquired the interested boy.

"O, massa, I can't begin to tell you all dat ole auntie says. She 'pears ter know all about dese yer mattahs. She smokes her pipe and mumbles to herse'f, an' says, sort a-whisperin' like, 'Min', now, what yer ole auntie tells yer. She ain't got long to tarry wid you no moh. Pretty soon de Massa will call her to go on de long journey. Her eyes is not to see what your eyes will see arter a while. An' when I'm dead an' gone, den ye will 'member dat ole auntie saw what was a-comin' to pass. De fire mus' burn, an' de dross be burnt up, an' de lan' mus go froo de fiery furnace, an' den bimeby all de people will go free. O, chillens, dat's what the hymns mean dat we sing:

"Keep a-inchin' along, Keep a-inchin' along,
Jesus will come bimeby."

What does dat mean, chillens? He's comin' to make you all free. We's all got to stay a long time down in Egypt's lan', an' den de Lord 'll lead us out froo de Red Sea. It's de Red Sea, shore enough—red like de fire, red like de blood. But min' what I tell you, all de people will be free.'"

And here the man stopped for a moment. The vision which the old colored woman had seen now seemed to flash before his eye also. He spoke after a little while of silence:

"Now, massa, what duz you say about all dis? Is you gwine to do anythin' fur de black folks afore you finish de wah?"

At first Jack could not reply. His feelings were solemn and peculiar. He had never before talked with a slave. He had been brought up in free Pennsylvania, and had not even up to the time of the war seen a bondman. This interview gave him some new feelings and thoughts. The glistening eyes of the slave, his trembling and agitated voice, his homely and expressive language, and the anxious and plaintive inquiries which he offered—all these taken in connection with the hurried and fearful glances about him in the midst of his conversation, showing his dread of detection, deeply touched the boy's soul. He felt a sense of brotherhood to the black man who crouched before him trying to unravel a problem that was just then puzzling wiser heads than his—a feeling of relationship such as he had once thought it would be impossible for him to feel toward any one of the colored race. For the first time the boy really took into his mind the possible issues of the war in regard to slavery. He saw what might result from the success of the Union army in this respect, freedom and equal rights to all men of every race. He did not see clearly, however, the end of the matter. It was not plain to his mind, the work of setting free the bondman. He did not see how it was to be done, and yet he hoped that this would be one fruit of the struggle. So, more to brighten the hopes of his questioner than to satisfy himself or solve the puzzle, he replied:

"Tom, I guess Aunt Betty is right. Some of these old aunties can look very far ahead and see what none of the rest can see. If she has seen a vision of liberty for you all, the good Lord may have sent it. I can't tell yet what the upshot of the war will be, and it is hard for any one to see through it to the end. But a good many believe that when at last it ends every black man in the land will be free."

The man's face was lighted up with a new expression of hope and patience combined as he shook the proffered hand of the boy and, uttering his hearty thanks, went out of the tent and back to the colored quarters of the estate. Jack watched him, and noticed him stopping to talk with a little group of his own people in the distance. They conversed with eagerness and interest, and meanwhile pointed toward the tent where Jack still remained. The boy saw that the talk he had just engaged in with the slave was the subject of discussion. Those few words of comfort and cheer, how they were whispered around that estate from one to another of the lowly blacks! what pictures of freedom did they paint before those benighted minds! what patience did they inspire! what sorrows did they assuage! Ah, who can tell now?

Not long were the troops allowed to enjoy a season of rest at Randolph Forges. Soon orders came to cross over the country to the Tennessee River; tents were struck, supplies were packed, and once more the command ventured forward still farther into the Confederacy.

The region between the two rivers, which here run for some distance almost parallel to each other, is a rough, hilly, and nearly barren wilderness. The ride over the rocky roads and through the woods in the bleak winter wind and through the snow that fell, mixed with sleet, was cheerless and uncomfortable enough. The sight of a deer, once or twice, bounding through the forest in the distance, the occurrence of singular-looking mountain bushes and winter berries here and there along the route, the blocking up of the roads by breakdowns and deep ruts, were the only matters of interest that took place to vary the tedious day's march over the hills. The boy was chilled to the very marrow long before he arrived at the camp on the banks of the Tennessee. Reaching there, he bustled around with all his might to help put the tents up before night should close in. Then a bright, snapping fire was built, and Ned mixed him a tin of something hot and stimulating to check the chill, and before he fell asleep he had forgotten the toils and exposure of the mountainous ride.

The transports were all ready, and in the morning the command was ordered aboard. This time the battalion was assigned to the division of General Hurlbut, with General Crufts as the commander of the brigade.

Just about the time of starting the question of Jack's relation to the army was partially settled. He had made up his mind to enlist if the officer who had charge of the muster-in of the troops would pass him. Accordingly, his name was entered on the rolls of one of the companies of the battalion, and he waited anxiously for the visit and decision of the mustering official. The major said to him one day, "Jack, you will have to serve for the present without pay or allowances, and it is possible that you cannot, under the rules of the service, be sworn in. If you are satisfied to serve under these conditions you can be set down as one of our recruits."

The boy assented to the conditions, and in a few days he was announced by order of General Crufts as the postmaster of the brigade which was made up of the Thirty-first and Forty-fourth Indiana and the Seventeenth and Twenty-fifth Kentucky regiments of infantry, with Major Bowman's Third Battalion of the Fourth Illinois Cavalry.* He had entered on his duties just before the start was made up the river. After the troops were on board and the transports were laden with baggage and the gunboats were all ready for the expedition a delay of some hours took place. The night came, and no orders to move had arrived. News came to the boat on which the cavalry were awaiting the movement that at division headquarters, a mile or two down the river, on the transport *Neptune*, a large package of mail matter was ready for distribution. The night was dark and the river rough and the rain coming down fiercely; but all this was accounted as no hindrance at all when letters from home were so near. A boat was launched from the steamer, two men were assigned to it from the crew, and Jack was put in charge of it and ordered to bring the mail with the utmost possible dispatch. Out into the darkness they swiftly sped, and in a short time they saw ahead of them the lights of the *Neptune*. The sentinel on deck challenged the boat, and Jack made known his errand and was allowed to come on deck, where he found about five bushels of letters and papers that had been accumulating at Cairo and had just been forwarded to the army from that point. While Jack was attending to the duty of receiving and stowing away the mail General Hurlbut came up and asked, "Is Major Bowman on your boat?"

The boy replied, saluting the general promptly, "Yes, sir; I am on duty at his headquarters. Have you any word for him?"

"Yes; I want to send him a message. If you will remember it I need not write it down. Tell him to assume command of

---

*Among the afterward famous men connected with this brigade was Benjamin H. Bristow, Lieutenant Colonel of the Twenty-fifth Kentucky, and afterward Secretary of the Treasury under President Grant.

his steamer, and at daybreak in the morning to lead the way up the river. We will follow."

"All right, general; I will deliver the message."

Back to the steamer from which he had come Jack and his precious freight were quickly rowed by the stout arms of the boatmen. Arriving there, he found that Major Bowman had gone

BRINGING THE MAIL.

to bed in his stateroom, fatigued with the constant exposures and toils of the past week, during which he had been in the saddle night and day. For the first time in many days he had a chance to get into a bed, and he had embraced the opportunity at an early hour. Jack was nonplused. He said to himself, "I do not like to wake him out of his first sleep. I can give the message to him in the morning just as well. He is tired and half sick, and it would not be right to rouse him now." And so the boy went on with his duty as postmaster, working until late to get the mail for the different regiments assorted, and not willing to go to bed until he had found out whether his night journey had brought him any news from his own dear ones far away. It was after midnight when the boy went to sleep, and long after daylight when he awoke. He thought of his message, and in alarm dressed himself and hurried to the major's stateroom. No one was in it. He ran up on deck, and found the major pacing to and fro in perplexity and fretting on account of the delay. "I do not see what this means," he was saying to an officer near him. "They are making some sort of signals to us from the *Neptune* down yonder, and the other transports have steam up and are all ready to go, and yet here we stay. They must be waiting for something, but what it is I cannot tell."

"O, major," Jack faltered, "General Hurlbut told me last night, when I was down at his boat to get the mail, that you were to take command of the troops on this steamer and lead the way this morning at daybreak. You were asleep when I got back, and I was afraid to disturb you and break your first rest, and so I put it off till this morning, and I overslept myself, and—"

"Thunder and lightning! Didn't you know any better than that? Afraid to disturb me!" And in high dudgeon the officer strode away to give orders to the captain of the transport to move up the river at once, and in a few moments they were under way. After seeing that the orders, thus delayed, were carried out, the major came back to the affrighted boy, from whom even the appetite for breakfast had been scared away.

"Jack, once for all, let this be a lesson for you! I thought you knew more about military matters than to make such a blunder. You have delayed the whole expedition, and I do not know how much damage you have done. Here for an hour or more General Hurlbut has been waiting for me to lead off and wondering why I did not start, and meanwhile you have been asleep, with his orders locked up in your slumbering brain. If you ever do an act like this again it will lead to your being tried by a drumhead court martial."

All this was a very galling and bitter experience to the boy. It is worth while to put on record the fact that after that incident he did, to the letter, just what was told him, and never stopped to ask whether the major was asleep or awake when he had an order to give him.

The views that were afforded along the route of the expedition, which included more than eighty steamboats and a dozen ironclads, were many of them charming and romantic. Sometimes a dozen transports would be in sight at once, decked with flags, crowded with bluecoats, and heavily laden with artillery and military stores of different sorts. In places the banks were high and steep and the current narrow and swift. The steamers made a gay and inspiring appearance as they sailed along through such gorges, the rocky bluffs and wood-crested heights forming a charming background to the picture. Then the scenery would change and the banks would recede and a dense canebrake would appear, followed by a rural steamboat landing. Here and there on a lofty crag would be seen a group of people, natives of the region, summoned to the river by the news that the Northern army was advancing up the stream. Once in a while these little knots of spectators would greet the troops with cheers and the flapping to and fro of tiny Union flags, and again a few sullen, silent, frowning men and women would be noticed in the woods on the brink of the river or at a wood wharf or at some little hamlet, showing by their demeanor that they wished the waves would swallow the whole expedition.

Every little while the wild echoes of the woods were awakened by the music of the bands, and they would often resound with the cheers given by the soldiers when they discerned signs of Union sentiments among the few inhabitants visible. Thus the time passed on until the transports one morning were found tied up at an obscure little point on the river called Pittsburgh Landing. Orders were given to land and go out into the woods and encamp.

For many weeks afterward this before unheard-of place became the depot and rendezvous for the Army of the Tennessee, and in a short time it was christened with an event that will never be forgotten, one of the fiercest and bloodiest battles of our time. The bluffs here are high and steep, and it was with much difficulty that the cannon and wagons and stores were unloaded and taken up the hill. After a good deal of work and an immense amount of profanity the army was on its feet again and distributed through the woods and over the little patches of farms that were to be found here and there in the region near the Landing. The division of General Hurlbut was ordered to go into camp a couple of miles from the place of debarking in the woods near the bank of the river. Here for a couple of weeks the usual duties of camp life went on without disturbance. The regiment went out on picket, ran into a lot of Confederates, got a good deal excited, captured some rebel cavalry, and soon began to wonder again what was before them in the shape of a battle.

Near the camp, right on the brink of the high bluff, were a couple of Indian mounds, singular in form, quite high, and an object of curiosity to all who noticed them. The woods abounded with wild turkeys and other game. At one place were to be seen some remarkable springs of water. From a high wall of rock were discovered, gushing out of the fissures in the limestone, a score or more streams of fresh, clear, cold water, some of them as large as a man's arm.

The night they went into camp Jack deemed himself fortunate in being able to get a good place for his bed. He found a nice lot of dry leaves, and, gathering them in a heap, he spread his blankets down, thinking of the comfortable couch he would have to sleep in. Just before he went to bed he had occasion to hunt for something he had lost among the blankets, and, turning them back, he made a startling discovery. He had made his bed in a big nest of wood ticks! That was his introduction to a species of tormentor of man and beast which abounds in that latitude.

On the morning of the 5th of April the Third Battalion of the Fourth Illinois Cavalry was ordered to report to General Sherman for duty. Down came the tents, the wagons were packed up, and by sundown the command was in its new quarters. It was Saturday evening, and orders were given to be ready at sunrise next morning to go out on a scouting expedition. Some signs of the enemy had been noticed for a day or two, and it was desirable to know whether any Confederates were near.

General Sherman's division was encamped at Shiloh Chapel, a little, old, rough log church about three miles from the Landing, at the very front of the army. Here the battalion bivouacked in the woods that night, little thinking of the events that would happen on the morrow, and nobody dreaming that within two miles of the spot where they were lying an army of forty thousand Confederates had already formed line of battle for the morrow's dreadful struggle!

CHAPTER VI.

THE BOY LEARNS AT SHILOH WHAT HIS LEGS WERE MADE FOR.

EARLY in the morning of Sunday, April 6, the cavalry battalion to which Jack belonged had risen and prepared for work. Orders had been issued the night before to start out on the Corinth road as soon as possible the next day to reconnoiter the country round about and see whether any rebel force might be near. Before sunrise the men had breakfasted, fed their horses, and were ready to saddle up and get into line at short notice. The morning was a bright one. The robins had been chirping in the woods since dawn, and the trees were full of music, when suddenly a sound not so melodious broke in on the ears of the soldiers, an occasional shot from the picket line a mile beyond the camp. At first nothing was thought of this, as the guards had been permitted at times to fire off their guns to clean them in the morning on being relieved of duty and returning to camp. The horses, which had already been saddled, began, as well as the men, to show signs of nervous excitement, which was not lessened any as the firing continued, and as wild birds, in great numbers, rabbits in commotion, and numerous squirrels came flocking toward the Union lines as though they were being driven from the woods in front. It was now almost six o'clock, and the neighboring infantry regiments showed tokens of alarm, and some of them began to form line of battle. By the time that hour actually came the firing had become quite heavy, a cannon shot now and then being heard in the midst of the musketry. An officer said, "That means trouble. There is something wrong out there. The rebels must be attacking our outposts." The words were scarcely spoken when a straggling squad of men came running by in great excitement, their officers in vain trying to keep them in order. They shouted the news that the Confederates were making an attack on the picket line with a heavy force. Still, no one thought of anything more than a little skirmish. It was strange that nobody in that army, from the commander down to the smallest drummer-boy, had thought of the possibility of an attack upon it. No fortifications had been thrown up, no rifle-pits had been dug, no extra precautions had been used in order to guard against surprise and disaster. It is difficult to believe what is the simple truth in the case, that Albert Sidney Johnston, with his army of Confederates, was engaged nearly all day Saturday arranging his lines of battle, about two miles in front of the Union picket line, without let or hindrance, no Federal soldier being near enough to molest or make him afraid! If there had been a single line of earthworks, a few rifle-pits along the Union front, the advanced position could have been held against any force that might have been thrown against it. It is scarcely comprehensible now that Grant and Sherman were both overconfident in their belief that their enemy would not dare venture from Corinth, twenty miles away, to make any attack on their forces at Pittsburgh Landing.

By this time the bugles had sounded, "Fall in—mount!" and the cavalry was soon in line. The long roll was beaten among the infantry regiments in every direction. The men were just at breakfast, and many of them had to spring into the ranks in a hurry without waiting to drink their coffee or eat their hardtack.

Following pellmell after the first squad of retreating men came the whole regiment of infantry to which they belonged, and one or two wounded soldiers, all very much frightened, and running in dismay. At once it was seen that something serious was the matter.

Major Bowman had drawn the battalion up in line, and was about to report with them to General Sherman, whose headquarters were not far away. He called Jack to his side and said: "The first thing you are to do is to see after this baggage and have it hauled back to the rear. It looks as if we were going to have a battle. The teamsters are here, and I will leave everything in your care. As soon as you have had the camp equipage taken away you may report to me for duty with the battalion, wherever it may be. This will be a desperate day for us, I fear. We will not make any expedition on the road to Corinth this morning. Gracious, that firing is heavy! It is drawing nearer to us very fast. You have only a few moments to get out of this. Take care of yourself and get this stuff removed as speedily as possible. I hope to see you safe and sound after a while. Good-bye!" And the major, with the words on his lips, rode off rapidly on Prince, who was excited and wild with the sounds of the battle which he heard.

Jack turned in haste to the teamster, who was all ready with his wagon. The man was badly scared, and his horses were frightened too by the musketry, which was now sounding in rapid volleys in the woods not far away. "Come," said the boy, his own heart beating with a good deal of anxiety, "let's get these boxes and trunks on the wagon as soon as we can. The rebels are coming, and we do not want them to get this baggage. Hurry!"

The man needed no urging. His own fears were hurrying him up fast enough. He seized a roll of blankets and the boy another, and between them they carried a trunk, and without ceremony ran to the wagon and dumped the things into it. The teamster was all the while muttering and cursing under his breath and telling what he would have done to his head and eyes before he would let himself be taken by the rebels. They returned to the tent for another load, and as they did so a shell burst above their heads, the horses began to jump, the teamster himself was overcome with fright, and, leaping into the wagon, he grasped the lines and whipped the team into a run, shouting back, "I'm not going to let the Johnnies take me! G'long! Get up! Whoa, there! Every man for himself now!" In a moment he was out of hearing, and Jack was left standing in the midst of the baggage, with trunks and boxes and bedding lying in confusion all about him, the picture of bewilderment and despair.

At first an insane notion seized the boy that he might carry the goods away to a place of safety, and with that aim he took hold of a trunk weighing over a hundred pounds and tried to shoulder it and lug it away. He found that to be impossible. He looked around in fear and flustration. The bullets were beginning to whistle among the leaves. In the midst of his perplexity another shell burst near him among the branches of the tree to which his horse was tied. The frightened animal made a furious leap, tore loose, and ran away, leaving a part of the bridle fastened to the limb. Jack looked out through the woods in the direction of the attack, and a hundred yards away, coming into the other end of the camp on a full run, he saw a long line of men clad in uniforms of gray. Beyond them, half hid by the smoke and hardly to be seen through the trees, was a battery of artillery getting ready to fire. The boy almost fainted at the sight of his danger. He thought, in his fright, "There comes the whole rebel army! I don't believe I can get away from them. My horse is gone and I am left alone in the camp, and here are these things that I was ordered to remove, and the wagon's gone, and I'm between the two lines! I'll have to leave the goods all here for the rebels to capture. What will the major say? The Lord have mercy on me now! I'm a gone customer, I guess!"

HE HAD KNOWN FOR SOME YEARS THAT HE HAD LEGS.

While he was thinking this in the twinkling of an eye he seized the broken bridle from the tree, saying, "Maybe I can pick up a horse somewhere."

And then he ran! He had known for some years that he had legs, but he had never before tested their strength and endurance and speed in a race for life. He looked back over his shoulder, and a glance told him that the dreadful-looking line of

Confederates was gaining on him. They were now ransacking the camp he had left, and he saw that he must run nearly half a mile to get really within the Union lines. A stake-and-rider fence was in his way. Just as he neared it and was wondering whether he had strength enough to get over it a cannon ball swept away a section of rails, and through the gap he leaped, hardly knowing whether he was dead or alive. His lungs heaved and panted, and he gasped for breath in the spasmodic effort he was making to escape the hands of the foe. He heard their yells behind him, and their shout of onset seemed to be just in his rear. All along in front he saw the hastily forming lines of battle getting ready to receive the attack. Boom! Whiz! Bang! Rattle! went the sounds of the opening engagement all around. Just ahead of him as he neared the Union ranks he saw a battery wheel into position on a little hill in front of Shiloh Chapel. In an agony of alarm he saw the men loading their guns. The cannon seemed to be aimed right in his face. He called out—forgetting that in the confusion nobody could hear him—" Don't shoot me! O, do wait till I get inside our lines before you fire!" And even while he spoke he saw the flames belch from the guns, and the air all about him was filled with smoke and his ears were torn with the awful noise.

"It's no use! I cannot hold out any longer! I can hardly breathe now! My lungs will burst, my legs are giving way, I'll be captured surely and die in a rebel prison," he thought, still struggling to breathe and to run. He did not know whether he was going in the right direction or not, the air was so smoky and his wits were so confused. At last—his tongue parched, his lungs almost collapsed, his heart nearly bursting, and his limbs ready to sink under him—he found himself within the lines of General Sherman's division. He saw that great soldier riding all along the ranks, stationing the infantry, putting the batteries

PEN AND INK SKETCH OF GENERAL SHERMAN, 1864.

into position, aiming the very guns with his own hands, seeming to be everywhere at once. Toward the rear scenes of confusion and alarm were prevailing, but among the ranks about him the boy saw many who were cool and self-possessed, and he began to recover his wits again.

But he could not report for duty until he should find a horse. He thought within himself, "I reckon this is going to be a great battle, such as I have been anxious to see for a long time. I think I have seen enough of it. I wish I was safely out of it and at home. I wonder where that teamster went with what baggage we did save. What if that should be lost too? O, here is the battalion! Major! Major Bowman!" the boy shouted as he ran to the head of the line where that officer was in command; "O, major! The teamster ran away before we could get the baggage into the wagon, and the watch you gave me to keep for you I had put into the big chest and locked it up safely, and that is one of the boxes we had to leave behind, and I could only save about half the bedding! All your best clothes and the camp furniture and the mess dishes and other things are gone, and my horse broke loose, and he is gone too, and I don't know where the driver went who took the things we did get into the wagon, and I'm almost dead running so fast, and—"

Just then General Sherman rode up, and in his rapid, nervous way said, "Major, give me some extra men for orderlies. One of mine has been shot already. Take the rest of your battalion down toward the Landing and drive back all the stragglers you can find. The devil's to pay, sure enough. Hundreds of men all around here have run without firing a gun. I see no chance to use the cavalry in these woods at present, and you must keep them employed as best you can drumming and whipping up the stragglers." And off the general galloped, his clothes torn and soiled, and his hand bleeding from a wound he had just received.

The major sent the men with him and ordered the battalion back toward the rear to perform the service requested by General Sherman, and as Jack walked by his side for a moment he said: "Take the best care of yourself you can until you find a horse, and then join us. Never mind about the lost property. That is the fortune of war. I'm sorry about the watch. Why did you not do just as I told you, and keep it on your person? It was natural, however, for you to think it was safer in the box. Good-bye." And off they rode.

The noise and confusion of the battle had increased in every direction. Jack turned for a moment to look toward the enemy. Lines of blue-coated infantry could be seen stretching through the woods and across an open field and over a little knoll, and thence the smoke hid the view. Just in front a battery of artillery was playing on the enemy. As he watched the scene he noticed with concern a mass of men in gray and brown clothing pressing into line in the woods beyond the cannon. In a moment they came charging out of the forest and against the battery. The infantry that had been supporting the battery gave way, and almost before anybody knew what had been done the guns were in possession of the Confederates. The woods resounded with the victorious huzzas of the enemy, and in the confusion and excitement that followed Jack found himself in the midst of a terrible stampede.

A panic is a singular and a dreadful thing. When it strikes into the heart of a man or a mob or an army it can hardly be conquered. It bewilders and unnerves and maddens. It is the one thing that scares people out of their wits. Whether the ancient god Pan, who used to frighten armies in the woods by his terrific yells, according to the old Greeks, was at work that day, or whether the alarm came from surprise and lack of discipline and going into the fight without breakfast we will not say now, but at any rate there was a good deal of a panic at the beginning of the battle. The roads were filled with all manner of fugitives running for their lives. Army wagons, some empty and others full of rations and camp stores and baggage, were being driven down toward the Landing, and other wagons with ammunition were trying to get to the front. In the midst of the crowded roads at one point was a battery of artillery minus their guns, running away without firing a single shot. They had been frightened by the death of their captain, who was shot dead while he was giving command to them to come into line and open on the foe. Sutlers' wagons were jammed into the midst of the throng of pale and frightened men, some of whom were only half dressed, some carrying their muskets and others without any weapons or accouterments, having lost or thrown them away in their alarm. Colored servants, bleached almost white now with terror, were scampering out of the reach of the rebel bullets. Here and there a soldier had seized a mule or a horse and, with only a rope or a strap to manage him with, had mounted the animal and was trying to force his way to the river. Officers were in vain attempting to quiet the alarm and organize the wild, surging, frantic mob that was pressing toward the place where the transports were tied up. Word was sent quickly down to the Landing to have the steamers anchor in the middle of the stream and to let no one come on board.

The replies of the stragglers to the appeals made to them to go back to the front and help those who were fighting there were piteous enough. "Come, men, do not act the coward," urged the officers. "There is no reason for your fears. We can whip the cursed rebels if you will only turn back and aid your comrades. Stop, boys, stop, and listen! I'm ashamed of you! Have you no reason or souls at all? O, do not leave your flag! Don't give way to this panic. Back, men! you must not crowd this way! Back, I say, or I'll shoot the first coward that dares to pass this line!"

The poor fellows who were thus brought to a halt cried out, in one voice, "It's no use, captain! Our regiment's all cut to pieces; there's nothing left of it at all. Most of 'em was captured by the rebs before they got their breakfasts. We're all whipped to blazes!" Another clamor from a dozen voices was heard, "Captain, I'm sick—'deed I am. I can hardly walk now. I'm too weak to load a musket, let alone carry one." And still another excuse formed itself in this wise: "O, lieutenant, I have to go to the Landing after ammunition. The colonel said I should. I must get through."

And so, with one excuse after another, and with the same cry of danger and disaster, they infected each other with their fears and spread the panic far and wide, until thousands were the victims of it.

Before Jack had gone very far he caught a loose horse, and, putting his bridle on him, he was soon mounted; but where to find the battalion by this time was more than he could tell, and so he went on down with the throng—the restless, panic-stricken, anxious throng—to the Landing, where he saw an appalling scene. Fully five thousand soldiers were slinking out of sight wherever they could hide. As it happened, they could not retreat any farther than the wharf, for a creek on one side and a swampy bayou on the other hemmed them in; but here, within the space of half a mile, lining the bluffs, hid behind stumps crouching under the bushes, concealed in the trees, digging holes in the banks of the river, and finding shelter in the dark ravines that everywhere abounded, a vast multitude of cowering wretches huddled together.

Between nine and ten o'clock Jack saw an officer with several attendants pushing toward the front. Ahead of him were

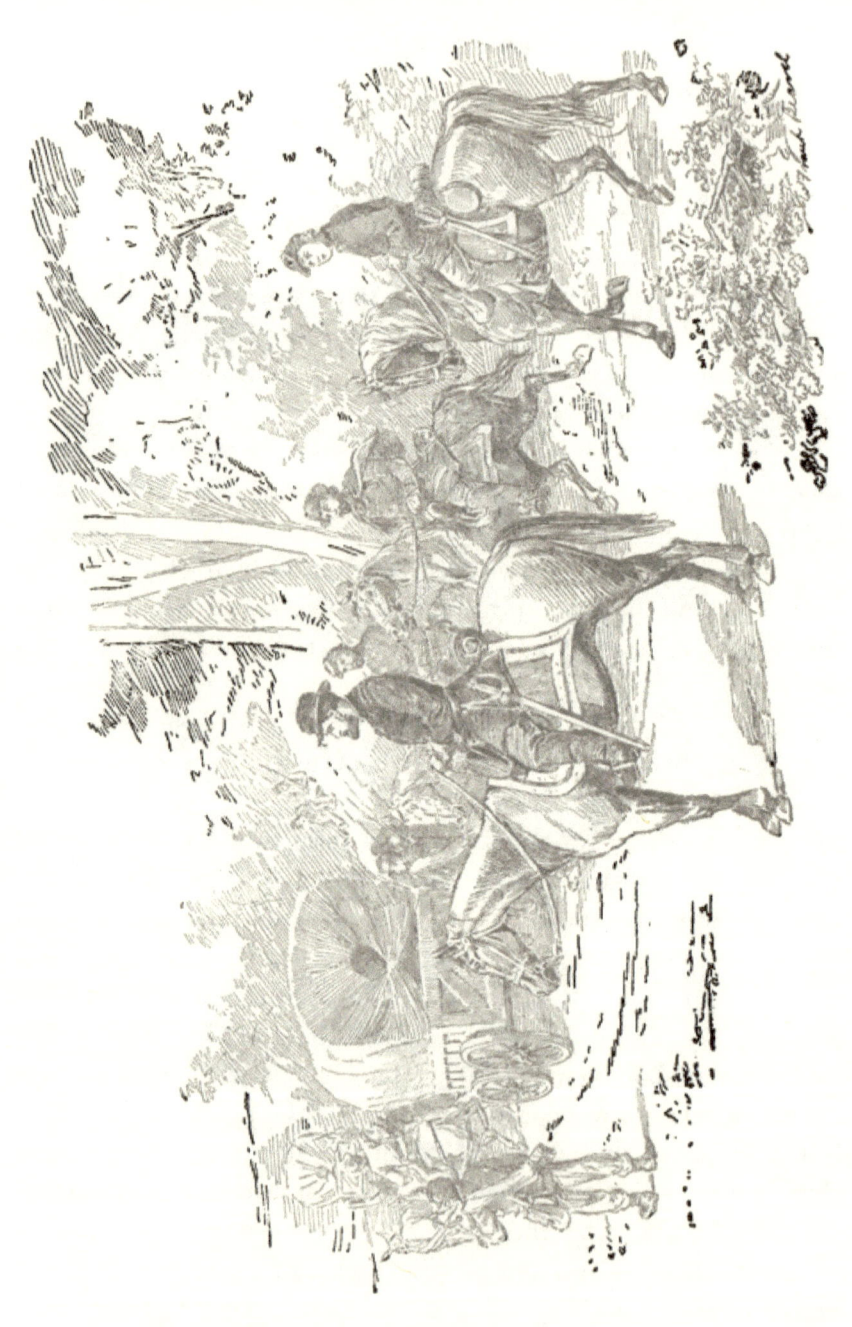

THE BOY LEARNS WHAT HIS LEGS WERE MADE FOR.

several ammunition teams which he had just hurried on. The officer tried, as he passed by, to cheer and encourage and rebuke those within reach. The boy recognized General Grant. That officer had been overnight at Savannah, six or eight miles down the river, anxiously awaiting the arrival of General Buell's troops, who were marching overland from Nashville. As soon as he heard the firing he came to the spot as fast as a steamer could bring him. He was cool and self-possessed in the midst of all the excitement, and seemed to mind the confusion no more than the scenes of a review. Some one said to him, "General, ought we not to have the other steamers that are down the river sent for? We may need them if we have to retreat." The general quietly replied, as he puffed his cigar and turned on toward the front, where the firing was becoming more and more terrific, "We have enough transports for such a purpose, if it comes to that;" and as he said the words there was an ugly look in his eye and a slight compression of his lips that signified more even than the spoken utterance.

Just then a German artillery officer belonging to General McClernand's division came riding up in great haste, covered with dirt and grimed with powder and smoke. Jack had often laughed at the broken English of Captain Schwartz as he drilled his men and screeched out the command, "Batter—ee! Right veel—martsh!"

Now the captain said, "Sheneral—Sheneral Grant, de repels, dey have took my cannon. Dey captured my batteree!"

"Why, captain, I'm sorry to hear that. Did you spike the guns before they captured them?" inquired the general.

"Vot, sheneral? Shpike dem new shteel guns? No, sir; it vould shpile 'em. Ve did better as dot."

"Well, what did you do? Tell me quick, captain; I must hurry on."

"Ve didn't shpike 'em, no, indeed; ve shoost took 'em back again. Hurrah!"—and away galloped the proud artillerist.

In a little while the boy found his command at work trying to form the stragglers into companies and regiments and send them to the front. It was an almost hopeless task, for many officers and men were used up so completely with fear that not even the saber and bayonet could force them into the field again.

Meanwhile the line of Union troops had been slowly forced back. Again and again they were made to retreat before the larger numbers of the enemy. The sound of the firing came nearer and nearer to the Landing, creating fresh panic among the cowards there.

A few days before the battle Jack had been much impressed by a remark of one of the men of a neighboring regiment, a stalwart, blustering fellow. The latter had been cursing all cowards and pronouncing his opinion of the man who would not stand fire. "Why," said he, in his indignation and bravery, "if I thought there was a drop of cowardly blood in my veins I would open 'em this blessed minute and let it out with my knife." The boy thought on hearing the word that surely here he had found a model of soldierly valor. Alas! among the crouching and demoralized masses at the Landing who should turn up but this hero? He was wallowing in a hole he had dug in the bluff, his head bandaged and the pretense of a bloody piece of muslin around his ankle, groaning and carrying on at a great rate.

"What's the matter?" said Jack.

"O, I got hit in the head with a piece of shell, and a bullet went through my leg. I know I'll die, I know I will."

"Get out of that, you wretch," said a voice close by; and just then the officer who had spoken the words came up in anger. "I've been watching you for the last few minutes. You haven't been near enough to the rebels all day to get hit with a shell. You cut your own flesh and bloodied that dirty piece of stuff and bound it on your ankle to make believe you had been wounded. Get out of that, or I'll saber you, you rascal!"

Toward night the major came back to where the boy was waiting for orders with the rest of the battalion and called him aside.

"Jack," said he, "the issue of this battle is doubtful. We have been forced back all day. We may be able to hold our present line till Buell comes. But I want to say to you that if we are surrounded here and hemmed in, and there is any danger of surrender, this battalion is going to cut its way out at the risk of everything. We will force our way through the rebel army."

The words burned into the boy's brain like fire, and started afresh the fever in his blood. He had been in a state of terrible excitement all day with the strange and awful events that had taken place. The words of the major stirred his already excited imagination to work afresh, and he saw in a moment a heated vision of a terrific night battle, with a regiment of cavalry heading a forlorn hope and trying to cut its way through the enemy's lines. He said to himself, "If it comes to that I will do all that I can to help it through."

They rode out toward the front again. The woods were so full of smoke that scarcely anything could be seen. Here and there a battery at work, a struggling line of infantry, making their last stand on the ridge that commanded the brow of the hill, at the foot of which was the wharf, an aid dashing across the bullet-swept space with messages, Grant and Sherman seemingly everywhere at the same moment, staying the retreat, and reforming the lines, and directing the artillery fire, and, beyond, the yelling, crowding troops of Beauregard, making a final struggle to drive the Union men into the Tennessee—this was the picture that was dimly discerned through the battle smoke and tumult.

All at once a booming sound came from the river. It was the report of a gun larger than any that had been used on the field.

"Hurrah, boys, the gunboats are driving into them! The rebels are flanked! We have 'em now," was the cry that passed along the ranks. The *Tyler* and the *Lexington*, two of the iron-clad fleet, had been watching all day for an opportunity to help in the battle. All at once their gunners caught sight of the Confederates pressing through the woods on the bank of the river, and they opened fire with the great cannon with which they were armed and which they had used at Fort Henry and Fort Donelson with such force; by this means the Confederates were checked in that direction.

Returning to the Landing again late in the afternoon, Major Bowman and Jack noticed a commotion on the other side of the river. Transports were there waiting for something or somebody. As the two watched the spot they saw a squad of men appear in sight on that side of the river. Then came a general and staff, and then on a run a regiment with its battle flags floating gayly in the air. They quickly embarked on transports, and in a short time were on the Pittsburgh Landing shore. Jack could hardly believe his eyes as he saw the advance guard and realized that Buell's troops had come to the rescue of the Army of the Tennessee. The arriving troops cheered and were cheered in return, and, nimbly marching up the steep bluff from the steamers as soon as they landed, and spurning the mass of cowards that lined the banks, they went on the double-quick out to the front and into position, just in time to aid in checking the last advance of the Confederate army for the day. At the top of the bluff the advance was cheered by a gallant fellow who, with

THE BOY LEARNS WHAT HIS LEGS WERE MADE FOR. 115

one arm shot off, heroically waved the other and shouted, "Hurrah, boys! We are glad you've come. We will whip 'em yet!"

A night of suspense and uncertainty followed the awful Sabbath day struggle on the plains and in the woods of Shiloh. Shortly after the arrival of General Buell's advance the fight closed for the day. Beauregard, who after the death of General Albert Sidney Johnston, killed early in the morning, took command of the army, is said to have sworn that before sundown he would water his horse in the Tennessee River, or in another place, where the fluid that horses drink is supposed to be very scarce. He was forced by the situation and circumstances of the evening to postpone his equestrian exploits, and at nightfall he ordered the attack to cease, and a sort of quiet reigned for a while over the field.

The Confederates made captures of a good deal of spoil that day. They said the Union army was as daintily and richly supplied as though it was out on a picnic. This was true, and this fact had something to do with the issues of the fight.

Early in the day some of the attacking force, tempted by the abundance of food and drink and camp furniture that was everywhere scattered through the tents of the Union forces, stopped to plunder. The opportunity to ransack and feast was too strong to be resisted. Sutlers' goods, commissary stores, quartermasters' supplies, private property of officers and men of various sorts, clothing, liquor of different kinds—all this was at their command. They would have showed themselves possessed of a good deal more than the average amount of self-control if they had resisted the temptation to help themselves to what was so plenty and so valuable and so greatly needed by their army and themselves.

On the one side thousands straggled from cowardice and in a panic; on the other, thousands left the ranks early in the battle and began to carry away their plunder, first filling their mouths and their bellies with the good things that were so tempting and delicious. Thus both armies were weakened.

In the woods to the right of the Union line the battalion whose movements we have been following in this story found a place for their bivouac. There in the darkness they tried to sleep. They durst not make any fire lest the light might draw the shots of the enemy, and hence had to go to bed without coffee. A bite of raw pork and some hard crackers afforded the only supper that could be got under the circumstances, and when that was munched in silence and sadness the men threw themselves down on the earth to rest as best they could in such a plight.

About nine o'clock a terrible noise was heard. It seemed like the explosion of a mine of powder. Everyone was startled and affrighted. A messenger was sent out toward the front to see what was the matter. He came back with the news that an immense siege gun had been mounted on the ridge not far from the Landing, at the keypoint of the position, and that it was going to be fired off at the Confederates all night long. It carried a ball or shell weighing over sixty pounds, and made a fearful concussion. About the same hour the gunboats began to fire their shells into the rebel camp from the river. At every little interval a terrific boom and shriek would wake the echoes of the wilderness, telling that another bomb had been dropped into the enemy's camp. At the same time the groans of wounded men could be heard all about through the forest. All this made up a dreadful situation.

About midnight Major Bowman came to Jack and roused him, saying, "Get up; we are going to have a drenching storm in a few minutes. Come with me, and we will find shelter."

Not far away were the abandoned tents of an Ohio regiment

that was now in another part of the field. The two had hardly entered one of these when a thundergust broke in fury over the woods and swept through the battlefield. Thunderbolts crashed among the trees, their awful peals mingling with the loud reports of the siege guns and the great cannon of the gunboats, deafening the ear and appalling the souls of those who listened to the "confusion worse confounded." As the boy peered out of the tent through the woods he saw them alternately lighted up with the glare of the lightning and then darkened with the gloom of the tempest. In a moment the darkness would be illuminated once more by the firing off of the cannon on the hill in front, and through the forest he could dimly discern the details of men who were searching with hurrying feet for the wounded and bearing them to hospitals in the rear. Mixed with other horrid sounds that smote his ears, he would catch every now and then an occasional cry of a maimed and mangled soldier crawling over the ground in quest of aid or lying helpless and bleeding on the wet earth, the sousing rain in mercy moistening his parched lips and cooling his fevered wounds. It all seemed more like a spectral vision, a ghastly dream, than an actual fact, as the boy gazed out into the midnight and was transfixed with the horrors of the scene.

By and by the morning broke again, giving the signal for the commencement of another death struggle. The whole army of Buell had arrived and was in position. General Grant did not wait for the foe to attack, but at an early hour ordered an advance against the rebel line. From that hour till late in the afternoon the battle continued. Cheers, now from one side and now from the other, booming of cannon, and fluctuations of defeat and victory marked the day. Gradually, however, after a stubborn fight, the Confederates were pushed back until they were forced to yield all the ground hitherto occupied by them.

By the middle of the afternoon the advanced line of Union camps abandoned on Sunday morning was in the hands of Grant's army again. The rebels had been driven slowly from one point to another, until finally there came a ringing cheer from our whole line. It was the token of victory. The Confederates were retreating. They had tried in vain to drive the Army of the Tennessee into that river, or make it surrender, or force it to give up its campaign against Corinth. They had failed. The Union host had been caught napping, had been driven four or five miles back from its position, had lost considerable of its goods and some artillery; but it still had strength and energy and pluck to rally again, and with Buell's help to drive back its antagonist to the region whence he came.

The troops were not in any condition to pursue very far the retreating army. They had as much as they could do to make him let go his hold and draw off from the attack. Probably both sides were glad enough to cry "Quits" and stop without fighting any more just then.

And now the boy's duties called him to traverse the great battlefield from one end to the other. The earth was muddied by the rains, and in places reddened with blood. Step by step the cavalry pursued the stragglers of the retreating army, picketed again the various roads, and passed over the whole scene of strife.

Here, kneeling behind a tree, was a tall, lithe, well-built Southerner, shot dead in the act of firing off his own gun, which had fallen to the earth beside him. He had just taken aim when the fatal bullet struck him in the forehead and instantly killed him. He had stiffened in the posture which he had taken; and there the dead man still knelt after the battle, his hand extended to hold the musket, his eyes glazed in the act of sighting the piece, his motionless body still leaning against a tree.

Near him was a fair-haired boy, clad in a fine uniform, with the signs of rank on his collar indicating him to have been a lieutenant. His face, his neat and cleanly and well-kept person, his slender and shapely hands, his thin lips, his rosy cheeks, ruddy even in death, his clear-cut and handsome features, all betokened a youth of a good family and breeding and wealth, while his regimental insignia showed that he was from South Carolina. He lay on the ground, his head resting on his arm, and seemed to be wrapped in a gentle sleep. The boy, in the hope that he was not dead, dismounted and felt the pulse of the youth. It was still and cold as ice. But there was not visible at first the sign of any wound, until Jack noticed a torn place in the clothing just over the left breast. Looking there the boy found a bullet mark in the flesh—the stripling had been shot through the heart. He seemed about Jack's age. His youth, his manly beauty, his apparent position and refinement, his early death, his appearance as if in slumber, all appealed deeply and touchingly to the heart of the spectator. Jack said to himself as he stood by the side of the dead and passed his hand for a moment tenderly over the soft and silken hair, and touched reverently and lovingly the cheek, which was as velvety and delicate as a woman's: "I pity the poor mother and sisters of this lad away over in the Palmetto State. He was—who knows?—their pet, their stay, their all. Here he lies among the unknown dead, and will be buried with a great multitude in the trenches. Poor fellow!" And a tear fell from the eye of the sympathizing boy as he lingered there. But he could not tarry. A wounded man close by made a signal for aid. Jack hurried to his side. A gaping wound in his chest showed that he was near death. The breath was slowly coming and going in convulsive and painful throbs.

"Can I do anything for you?" said Jack.

The man made a motion, pointing with a desperate effort to his wound, and gasped, "I wish you would tell my—" and then suddenly stopped in the midst of the sentence. His breath failed, his head fell back, the blood gurgled from his mouth, and he was dead! No name was to be found on his clothing, and the message which he was about to utter was stilled forever.

Farther on was the spot where one of the Union batteries had made an heroic stand, the guns battered and dismantled, and the horses lying dead in every direction. The scene now seems to the boy, as he reviews it, more like a sojourn in the abodes of the lost in hell; and it is recalled now only to remind us what our Union has cost.

Nurses by the score from the North were soon on hand. The Sanitary Commission and its twin, the Christian Commission, in a very few days after the battle came to the spot with delicacies, medicines, and needed articles of comfort for the wounded. It was wonderful the attraction and reverence and admiration that the sight of a woman created in that wilderness. For months the army had been out of sight of the gentler sex. The soldiers, hungry to see a woman's face and form, stood about the hospitals and transports, waiting by scores until one of the female nurses appeared. Then they would crowd up with grateful and respectful attentions and beg permission simply to shake hands. And as they exchanged a few words with her they thought, often with tears, of mother, children, and home.

CHAPTER VII.

A CHANGE OF FRONT.

THE army at once commenced a general advance upon the city of Corinth. After the battle of Shiloh General Halleck took command of the troops, with General Grant as his next in rank. Heavy siege cannon were brought to the spot and mounted on great gun carriages and directed against the fortifications of the Confederates. Slow approaches were made on the threatened city. Deep trenches were dug, and parapets were thrown up, and batteries were established commanding the rebel forts; and thus step by step the Confederates were crowded back, and mile after mile of the distance between Shiloh Chapel and the village of Corinth was slowly traversed. Once in a while a skirmish would take place, or the cavalry would have a brush with the rebel horsemen, or a day of cannonade would put the army on the alert and give the impression that an assault was about to be made, but with these exceptions the siege was a tedious piece of business.

The boys on picket used to call out to the rebels near them that the Union army was making a new edition of the Scriptures, since they were bringing and bearing to its destination "Abraham's Epistles to the Corinthians."

Meanwhile as the army ventured out farther into the region back of Pittsburgh Landing, and away from the river, the drinking water was found to be scarce and nasty. Springs were rare, "branches" were low and brackish, and very often the only thing in the shape of water was that which might be dipped up from stagnant pools and wallow-holes along by the roadside. Sickness, of course, followed the use of this slimy and putrid stuff. Among those who were stricken down were the major and Jack. First the appetite gave way; then the various ails that accompany the use of impure drinking water ensued, and finally the trouble became so bad as to threaten their lives unless it could be checked.

This was the time that tried Jack's soul. He was ill and homesick, weak and growing weaker every day. It was hard to get away on leave, or procure a furlough from the army in the midst of active operations, and at a time when an assault was looked for at any hour of the day or night; but it was still harder to stay there in the ditches and die of malarial disease and be buried in Mississippi mud.

The boy's spirit and fortitude left him. In addition to his ailments the mustering officer had refused to muster him into the service. He must be eighteen before he could be received. So he had no pay, no position, and no hope of either. He gave way to the accumulation of disappointments and ills, and grew pale, emaciated, depressed, and had barely strength enough to drag himself once in a while from his tent.

One day the major came in with good news.

"Jack," said the officer, "brighten up; I have word from headquarters that will be better than medicine for you. The division surgeon tells me I must leave this region for a little while or I will die. Get ready at once. General Sherman has strongly indorsed my application for leave of absence, and I think it will be here so that we can leave by the steamer to-morrow afternoon. Cheer up, my boy, we have another chance for life."

The news was a tonic for Jack. In a day or two the expected leave arrived, and the two rode down to the Landing. As they left the camp they said good-bye—gladly, for it was the hope of life that took them away; sorrowfully, for there was a probability that they might not return to their comrades in that part of the army. An offer of a higher commission in the eastern armies had been made to the major, and he was seriously considering it.

They embarked on the steamer at Pittsburgh Landing just before the evacuation of Corinth, barely missing that stirring incident, and with hope and cheer turned their faces away from the muddy and malarious trenches in which they had been living for weeks, toward rest and health and home in the North.

At Cairo the major left the boy and went east. Jack was to go on to St. Louis and await orders, and see that the horses were properly taken care of.

It was not long before he received directions to come on after the major, who had just been commissioned colonel of one of the best regiments of Pennsylvania infantry, the Eighty-fourth. The organization had been broken down and wasted to a skeleton by hard fighting and toilsome marching, and the new colonel was authorized to recruit it full again.

This was good news to the boy, who had been restored to health and had regained his strength, and was glad at the prospect of seeing his friends once more at home. He saw, too, in this new situation a hope of seeing service as a real soldier.

Down the Mississippi to Cairo, and up the beautiful Ohio, by vineclad hills and charming tracts of lowland and splendid cities and thriving villages, opening his eyes wide at the enterprise and commerce and business life that "boomed" everywhere in the journey—thus the boy traversed the rivers by steamer until at last the dim and distant mountains of Pennsylvania rose in the horizon. Then he was at home. He had been homesick as much to see the Alleghenies as to meet his relatives. The first glimpse that he had of them thrilled him to his finger ends with a wild, strange delirium of joy.

He found at Alexandria, Va., the regiment with which his fate was to be henceforth connected. It had been cut to pieces in the valley of the Shenandoah, had lost many of its officers by sickness and wounds and capture, and had seen its gallant Colonel Murray killed at Winchester. The new commander, Colonel Bowman, was ordered to fill it up by new recruits and then lead it into the field.

The first order that Jack received on arrival at the camp was to go home and commence recruiting operations. He had no time to look around, make the acquaintance of officers or men, or inquire how he would like his new military relatives, but hurried off to begin his labors.

Camp Curtin, at Harrisburg, was the rendezvous for recruits in the eastern part of the State. The soldiers who there saw their first experience in martial affairs will not easily forget it.

All sorts of officers and men, of different shapes and sizes, good, bad, neutral, indifferent, were massed here together on their way to the front. Patriotic youths, burning with zeal and ardor for their country and flag, here lay down in the same bunk with bounty jumpers, who had enlisted for the sake of the extra five or six hundred dollars offered in some quarters at that time for recruits, and who, a few hours after they had received the greenbacks, would doff their uniforms, put on citizens' clothes, and walk off to the depot and soon be over the hills and far away.

Here were a few regular army officers, prim and cultivated, trying to shape things into order and regularity ; and here were hundreds of fresh volunteer officers utterly ignorant in their inexperience of everything connected with the army or military life.

Shrewd rascals who saw in the war a good opportunity to make money were here by the hundred, on the watch for pickings and stealings, and likewise men, young and old, who were looking for positions of honor and good pay somewhere that would not require them to risk their lives in battle. Thousands of soldiers, raw recruits, or trained veterans from the Army of the Potomac, going, coming, drilling, shamming, stealing, working, receiving and distributing clothes, tents, arms, and accouterments, made up a scene of endless and perplexing confusion.

During that hot summer of '62 the long street leading out to the camp was half knee-deep with dust a good part of the time. Tramp, tramp, back and forth, night and day, with fife and drum and bands to diversify and enliven the occasions at times, were heard the feet of the volunteers of Pennsylvania along this highway, and through the terrible heat and the choking dust.

Jack found his friends in Columbia County interested in his plans. His schoolmates, and many older ones, seeing his uniform, hearing his experience, knowing the fame of the regiment that he now belonged to, and taking a just pride in the name of the new commander, joined heartily in the project. In a short time Jack had the pleasure of seeing parts of three companies on their way to the command, enlisted in part by his instrumentality.

Back and forth to and from Camp Curtin he traveled many times in this sometimes tedious and sometimes ludicrous business. He saw men at the camp who had no front teeth and who, therefore, could not possibly bite off the end of the cartridges in loading their muskets, and others who were blind in one eye, or lame, or half deaf, and hence were not fit for soldiers at all; and yet in some way they had passed muster and were on their way to their regiments.

"Jim," said the boy one day to one of these nondescript recruits, "how did you manage to pass the surgeon's examination? He has no right to accept men with a game leg and no upper teeth. Did you pay him to pass you, or straighten out your leg for the occasion and put in a new set of teeth and fool the doctor—or how?"

"Well, to tell the truth for once," said the fellow, "I did not see the surgeon at all. We were all in the barracks together, and when my name was called the lieutenant, who was very anxious to make up a certain number so that he would get his commission and was bound not to lose me, said he'd fix it all right. So he had Sam Champlin go in and answer to my name; and Sam, you know, is as big and strong as a bull, and the surgeon said, as soon as he looked at him, 'O, you'll do; pass out and send in the next man.' And so my name was checked off."

"Well, but how did Sam pass for himself?"

"O, easily enough. The lieutenant waited till the assistant surgeon was on duty, and then he had Sam's name called, and he went in and was examined and came out O. K."

Drinking was common everywhere. The city was full of concert saloons and drinking places of all grades in full blast.

Among the recruits were two brothers from the backwoods, both of them raw, green, awkward, and uncouth. They were made the butt of sport on all sides. The older one's name was Reuben, and the younger lad clung to him persistently and was not willing to be for a single moment without him.

One afternoon Reuben went down into the city while his brother was asleep. By and by the barracks were filled with a strange bellowing sound. Scores of soldiers were alarmed by it, and they came flocking in from all directions, crying, "What's wrong here? Is anybody being killed? What's the matter?"

The poor, lonely, homesick youth from the mountains sat blubbering on the edge of his bunk. He had waked from his nap and found himself deserted by his big brother, and alone among thousands of rough and strange men in the great camp; and at once he bawled out so that the barracks were at first alarmed and then convulsed with laughter, "O, where's Reuben? I don't want to be a soldier no more! I want my brother! Where's Reuben? I want to go home!"

"O, WHERE'S REUBEN?"

The summer sped away, and at its close Jack found that he had done about all the recruiting that was possible for that season, and accordingly he reported with his last squad of men at Harrisburg at the office of the Superintendent of Recruiting Service, Captain R. I. Dodge, proud of his success and anxious to be sent off to the regiment, then with the Army of the Potomac, on its way down into Virginia. While the recruits waited on the pavement outside the office—at that time in Market Square—the boy went in and reported. He found the adjutant, Lieutenant Liedtke, a young Prussian officer, in charge of the place, a stickler for etiquette and a rigid believer in red tape and in the most stringent military proprieties. The following conversation took place:

Jack.—" Lieutenant, I have brought a squad of recruits, from Columbia County, for the Eighty-fourth Pennsylvania Volunteers."

The Lieutenant.—" Recruits from Columbia County? Who enlisted them?"

Jack.—"I did a part of the work, sir. Mr. Forrester, who expects to be commissioned in the regiment, is with us, and he did the rest."

The Lieutenant.—" Do you belong to the regiment?"

Jack.—" Yes, sir; or at least I expect to when I join it."

The Lieutenant.—" What authority have you for being absent from the regiment and engaging in recruiting service?"

Jack.—" Here is my original order from Colonel Bowman, the commander of the Eighty-fourth."

The lieutenant took the paper, glanced at it, and in anger replied: "This is no authority whatever. You are absent from your regiment without leave. I will arrest you and send you to the guard house. No one has any right to enlist men in this State without authority from the governor or from these headquarters. We are going to stop these irregularities." And with the words the officer tapped the bell at his side and summoned a sentry, in order to put into execution his threat.

The boy was now thoroughly frightened and deeply humiliated. His men were at the door waiting for orders to proceed to the camp, and here he found himself in the predicament of having enlisted them without due authority and in danger of arrest. What would become of them? How would he get out of this difficulty? He began to protest and explain and appeal; but the officer was impatient and would hear nothing, breaking in on Jack's entreaties with the surly reply, "You are away from your regiment without authority. No colonel has a right to send a man off on recruiting service. You are under arrest, sir."

"YOU ARE ABSENT FROM YOUR REGIMENT WITHOUT LEAVE."

Just then Jack noticed a trim, soldierly-looking noncommissioned officer who had been occupied at a desk in the room come forward and speak with the lieutenant. While the two conversed the boy saw that they were talking about him, and he wondered what they were saying. Soon the sergeant came to Jack and said, "Are these men for the Eighty-fourth?"

"Of course they are," was Jack's reply. "You recall Lieutenant Jackson, who was on duty as recruiting officer in Columbia County early in the summer. I was of his party, and after helping him with his work I stayed, at Colonel Bowman's direction, to help Lieutenant Forrester recruit his squad. Here is the letter of the colonel."

The sergeant looked at the letter, and then said, "Let us go to the door and glance at the men." While he stood there, noting that the recruits were of a good class, and satisfying himself that the representations made by the boy were correct, he whispered, "My name is Sergeant Mather. I have been in this office, detailed as a clerk, for some weeks, but I belong to the Eighty-fourth, and expect to be sent back to the regiment soon. The adjutant is a rigid disciplinarian, and is impatient with anything like irregularity. I will see that you do not suffer. I think I can persuade him not to carry out his threats. Just keep yourself in check a little while and it will be all right." With these encouraging words Sergeant Mather returned to tackle his superior officer, the irascible lieutenant; and in a few moments he came out from the inner office bearing with a look of triumph a paper which he handed to Jack. The boy looked at it and was delighted to find it a pass for admittance to Camp Curtin with his recruits and an order for immediate transportation to Washington *en route* for the Army of the Potomac. With a glad and grateful heart the boy shook hands with Sergeant Mather, thanking him for the services rendered in this trying hour, and hurried out to take charge of his men and conduct them to the camp. This was the beginning of a lifelong comradeship with Sergeant Mather, who in a little while after that became the adjutant of the Eighty-fourth—comradeship welded in due season by common experiences at the bivouac fire, on the march, and in battle.

Finally, late in November, 1862, the whole party was sent out from Camp Curtin, and after shifting about from one camp to another, and making some bewildering journeys by rail, by steamer, and on foot, they found the Eighty-fourth Pennsylvania Volunteers encamped near Falmouth, Va., opposite Fredericksburg, in the Third Army Corps.

The new recruits were received with some curiosity, with some raillery for their evident greenness, with some familiar remarks about the "awkward squad," and yet with a right soldierly welcome, after all.

Soon after the arrival of the detachment, and while Jack was wondering what was to become of him, the colonel summoned him into his presence at headquarters and surprised and gladdened his heart by some amazing information:

"My boy, you have been wondering all through this work which you have done what your fate is to be in the new command. You have now served for an entire year without place or pay in the army. You have worked hard and received nothing for it but experience. I have been watching your conduct, and I now have the pleasure of telling you that you have fairly earned a commission by your services in recruiting the regiment. I did not promise you this, for I did not know that I could give it to you. But a vacancy has occurred which you can fill, and I am glad to be able to tell you that you are now Lieutenant Sanderson, of the Eighty-fourth Pennsylvania Volunteers. I wish you success and honor in your new position."

The boy was taken aback by this announcement. He had hoped all along that by and by he might get a commission, but he had not dared to expect it so soon. He could hardly contain himself, but, smothering his joy as best he could, and trying not to get top-heavy on account of his promotion, he reported to his new captain and was assigned to duty at once. He got a new uniform, took pride in seeing his shoulder straps attached for the first time to their place, girded his sword about his waist, went into the study of the infantry tactics, began to post himself in the duties of the new place, and was at once at home among the noble fellows who made up the command.

The camp was at Stoneman's Switch, on the railroad from Acquia Creek to Fredericksburg. No one knew what would be the plans of the new commander of the army, General Burnside, who had just relieved General McClellan. Fredericksburg was a mighty stronghold that lay directly across the path to Richmond. Whether it was to be flanked by going around on one side or the other, or whether it was to be stormed by assault in front, no one could tell.

For a little while the Army of the Potomac lay there on the plains of Falmouth, in the vicinity of Washington's early home, with the rebels gathering in force every day in their front. They performed picket duty, made some preparation for winter quarters, drilled daily on the hills and across the fields, and waited for orders. At last came the marching orders, and then everybody connected with the army knew that there was to be made a desperate struggle for the heights of the city of Fredericksburg and the road to Richmond.

CHAPTER VIII.

THE HEIGHTS OF FREDERICKSBURG.

ON Wednesday morning, December 10, there was a stir in the camp. Soon after breakfast, while some officers were together in the headquarters of the company to which Jack had been assigned, Captain Bryan came in with a look of seriousness on his face.

"Boys, I have news for you," was his first remark.

"What is it, captain? Are we going to move again 'on to Richmond?'" was the inquiry of one of the group.

"I think we are going to have another fight. General Stoneman has ordered the corps to be ready to move to-night, at an hour's notice, any time after sunset. We are to leave our tents and baggage and knapsacks behind, and are to take along four days' cooked rations and sixty rounds of cartridges per man."

"That means that we are to attack Fredericksburg," said the other. "It will be a desperate struggle if we have to storm the rebel position there. I was out at the river yesterday to get a glimpse of it. Be ready to score one more for Robert Lee if we try it."

"Do not lose heart so early, captain. We are bound to win at last."

"Yes, at last we shall win; but I am tired of this folly, —and it is simply folly to butt your head up against such hills and forts as the rebels have on the other side of the river. I will stand to my duty right through if I die for it, but I think it is nothing less than murder to try such a mad scheme as that which seems before us. Good-bye." And the officer went out to prepare for the forward move.

Captain Bryan turned to Lieutenant Sanderson and said, " I wish you would go to Quartermaster Kephart and get this requisition filled for shoes and blankets. We must see that the men are as comfortable as they can be made while on this march. Orderly Sergeant Simmons, I want you to inspect the guns this afternoon and have every piece in perfect trim. Draw the rations and have them distributed, and see to it that the men are ready to march at an hour's notice."

The boy went at once upon his errand, procured and issued the clothing, and helped to get the company ready for a forward move.

The feelings of soldiers under such circumstances can hardly be described. Thoughts of absent friends, of distant loved ones in their far-off homes, of the possibilities of the battle, of the dangers and hardships, the wounds and imprisonment and death, that must shortly overtake many of their number, along with a thousand other wild and excited fancies, rush through the mind.

The night came, but no orders were received to move. Tattoo was sounded at the usual hour, and the regiment went to sleep knowing that it might have to spring out of bed in the middle of the night and march toward the expected field of battle. Accordingly, at two the next morning a courier came from the headquarters of General Carroll, the brigade commander, summoning the forces to start out on the march at four o'clock. The camp was astir at once, the coffee was soon boiling, the pork was fried, a hasty snack was eaten, and in the dark, chilly, early morning the brigade set out for the river. On the way, before sunrise, the sound of the cannon was heard booming in front. The boys said all along the line, "The fun has begun; the Johnnies are up early too."

On the road Colonel Bowman met an aid of General Whipple, the division commander, and asked him, "Captain, what is the outlook? Have you any news about the situation? What is going on in front?"

The officer replied with a significant look and a shrug of the shoulders, and added, "There is trouble ahead. General Burnside is determined to charge the heights of Fredericksburg. No army can carry the works in front. It is madness to try it. His pioneer corps have just been trying to lay the pontoon bridges, and have been so annoyed and delayed by the rebel sharpshooters in the houses along the bank of the river on that side that the general has ordered the town to be shelled in order to drive the fellows out of their hiding places. I do not know what the upshot will be. I wish we were all well out of it."

"When do you think we shall be able to cross?" asked the colonel.

"Nobody knows. It all depends on getting down the bridges. If that attempt succeeds we may get to work in earnest this afternoon. For the present General Whipple desires the men to halt and make themselves comfortable."

The region was full of rolling hills and ravines, with here and there a clump of trees, and it had a cheerless, desolate look that winter morning. The country all around was stripped of fences, outbuildings, fruit trees, and indeed everything that was destructible. Each army in turn had overrun the territory, the inhabitants had nearly all abandoned their homes, which stood bleak, deserted, and comfortless, all except those that were occupied as headquarters by commanding officers.

The troops threw themselves down on the ground near the Phillips house, after stacking arms, and many of them, in spite of the cannonade not far away, were soon asleep.

About noon Colonel Bowman returned from the river bank, where he had been exploring the situation. At once a bevy of officers, Jack among them, gathered about him to hear the news. The colonel said: "Our guns are damaging the town somewhat, but we have not dislodged the sharpshooters yet. I watched the work of trying to lay the pontoons, and offered the services of my regiment to take the boats over if we were needed. What do you say to it, Major Opp? Would the men undertake such a task?"

The major, a modest, gentle, cultivated man, and withal as brave a soldier as ever lived, replied with a smile, "O yes, colonel, they would follow wherever you would lead them, but I do not think they are hankering after the perilous enterprise. Was your offer accepted?"

"No, it has not been yet, but maybe we shall hear from it by and by. I told General Whipple we would attempt it should he give the order, and that I was confident that we could do it, hard and dangerous as it appears. All that is wanted is a sudden dash across the stream that will surprise the rebels; but that, to be sure, is difficult enough while they have their sharp eyes at a thousand loopholes along the bank."

In the afternoon Jack and some of his friends started out to see for themselves what was going on along the river. After a

FREDERICKSBURG LAY AT THEIR FEET.

walk of half an hour they found themselves on the edge of a high bluff overlooking the Rappahannock. All about them were batteries shelling the town. Fredericksburg, pretty, old-fashioned, staid, and aristocratic, lay at their feet on the banks opposite, which were considerably lower than the point where they stood.

Away down the river, two or three miles off, could be plainly seen the bridge that had been thrown across by Franklin's men, while all around, behind the bluffs, and screened from observation, were the Union troops waiting for the completion of the bridge at the town so that the crossing might be made at both places at once.

Near by was a large balloon, which was occupied by a couple of signal officers. They had just ascended several hundred feet, and were steadied and held by ropes at that height so that they might, if possible, discover and report what the Confederates were doing.

Captain Dalton, of General Whipple's staff, was present, and he indicated the different places of interest. "Yonder," said he, pointing toward General Franklin's men, "is the left of our line. That is one of the places where an attack is to be made. The hills that lie back of the region in the vicinity of the pontoon bridge which they have made will be stormed by the men lying on the shore; if you look sharply you can see them now. Then in this other direction, off to our right, is another point to be attacked, the hill of St. Marye. That will have to be assaulted too. And in our front yonder, just back of the town, are ridges which must be taken in the same way. The rebels will surely not come down out of their strong forts to meet us in the open plain, and if we want to get at them we must climb the heights, if they will permit it. The struggle must be a terrific one. I do not see how anyone can escape. The place ought to be flanked."

No troops of the enemy could be discerned, but the fortifications could be plainly traced. A circle of hills, rising one above another like the seats of an amphitheater, almost surrounded the place. These heights, commencing near the river, some distance east of Fredericksburg, swept nearly around the town in an almost unbroken half-circle, jutting out toward the stream again on the lower side. The village was thus shut completely in on every side except in front, and here it was defended by the Rappahannock. The hills were crowned with forts, lined and furrowed with intrenchments, pitted and pock-marked with batteries. Nowhere could anyone discover a position that seemed assailable by direct assault.

"Yonder is the spot where we may lie to-morrow waiting for some one to come and bury us," was the half-serious, half-jesting remark of one of the officers.

"What do you think of the site, captain?" was the response in the same vein.

"Those hills have a good exposure for a vineyard, and they afford a good site for a cemetery, too; but, boys, I am not overanxious to rest my bones over yonder. I prefer the graveyard at home. I have a lot there, and if I am to have any choice in the matter I would prefer Pennsylvania to Dixie as a burial place."

"O, stop all this talk about funerals and graveyards!" was the exclamation of a jolly lieutenant, whose spirits were always in a ferment of gayety; "you'll take all the cheerfulness out of the command and throw a coldness over the meeting if you go on in this way. Halloo! see there! Now there is going to be a scene worth looking at. Hurrah, boys, look at that! That is the way to begin to put down the pontoons. It is worth while being buried in Dixie to do a gallant deed like that."

Every eye was at once directed to the river beneath, while

the effervescent lieutenant poured out his soul in his fervid way in emphatic exclamations of admiration and enthusiasm at the sight. A party of men was about crossing the river in pontoon boats right in the face of the fierce and rattling fire of the rebels!

It had been found impossible to drive out the Confederates by shells or minie balls from the houses where they had secreted themselves on the other side. There the riflemen stayed, picking off our men, and preventing work on the pontoons, and delaying the advance of the whole army. After cannonading the town General Burnside at last selected a trusty band of men and ordered them to make a dash across in boats, and, by a sudden attack and charge up the hill, to expel the sharpshooters from their refuges. This order was just being obeyed when Jack and his friends stood on the hill and watched the sight.

Several pontoon boats were lying at the bank. Suddenly, and without any word of command being heard, nearly a hundred men rushed out from a place of concealment, jumped into the boats, thrust out from the shore, and were one third of the way over the river before the rebels realized what was being done. The aim of the rifles from every loophole and casement and house along the stream was concentrated on the party at once. Bullets whistled and hissed and rattled all about them. But the gallant fellows threw up boards as shelter, hid themselves in the boats as best they could, except those who had to row, and thus in the face of the musketry fire they swiftly crossed the stream, a few of them being shot on the way.

Touching the shore, those who were unhurt rose from their places in the boats, leaped out into the water or upon the land, and ran up the hills and into the houses whence the fire had come. The rebels evacuated their strongholds and ran up into the town, and at once the way was clear for the engineer corps to go on and finish the bridge.

Strong boats, quite flat, about twenty feet long, were anchored in the stream a few feet apart, lengthwise with the current. Upon these were placed beams or girders to join them together, and across these girders planks were laid so as to make a roadway about ten feet wide and strong enough to bear horses, cannon, and the tread of a multitude of men. In order to hasten

BULLETS WHISTLED AND HISSED AND RATTLED ALL ABOUT THEM.

matters the engineers would build two or three boats in sections, with girders and planks complete, above the bridge and then float them down and out into position. Thus three or four gangs could work at once.

They were not allowed to do all this without annoyance and disturbance from the enemy. The rebels tried, by dropping their shells miscellaneously in different directions along the river from the forts behind the town, to put an end to the work. Some of the bombs struck close to the pontoons, others exploded just over the heads of those who were at work, but luckily none happened to hit the bridge itself. On the other hand, it was clearly to be seen that the Union artillerists were not idle, for the air was heavy with the smoke of their guns, which lined the bluff for two or three miles along the river. Immediately opposite the town the cannon were aimed at the houses which had sheltered the rebel sharpshooters, and some of these places of refuge had been pretty well battered, while here and there a dwelling was on fire; other batteries were shooting across the pretty little city at the fortified hills beyond. Once in a while a Confederate shell would come flying over town and river, to explode among the guns that lined the banks on which the Union batteries had been planted. Altogether it was a scene of confusion, excitement, and tumult that the boy looked upon, that hour when the battlefield of Fredericksburg first flashed in bird's-eye view before his tremulous vision.

That night the brigade to which the boy belonged bivouacked on the ground not far away from the upper pontoon bridge, anxiously wondering what the morning would have in store for them.

After breakfast on Friday the brigade of Carroll started down to the river. They marched along the brink, the fog concealing the other shore, and had just reached the pontoons when boom! whiz! came a Confederate shell. It was the signal for a general cannonade, which was answered by the Union guns. The rebel shots came so near the bridge as to endanger it, and the command was ordered back behind the hills again.

Early Saturday morning the boys were up and stirring about again in the fog. The firing had already begun. The attack had been made upon the rebel intrenchments **by the troops** already on the other side, and orders were received for the brigade to cross the river and join in the action.

On the way over Jack noticed here and there packs of cards and empty whisky bottles strewn by the roadside. Those who in camp and at rest liked to pass the time in seeking recreation by the use of cards and liquor did not relish the idea of being shot, or of dying, with packs of the one or flasks of the other on their persons. So they cast them aside as they marched to the battlefield.

Down to the bridge the command marched again, and this time they were led across the river. "Boys, we are in for it now," said the soldiers one to another. "There is no getting out of this. The die is cast. Once more we are to meet the rebels."

As they crossed an aid came galloping up with news from the left. General Franklin had advanced against the hill, had not been supported aright, and had been pressed back again to the river. The sounds of a fearful struggle were heard still in that direction.

Now the firing grew heavier and louder just back of the town. As the troops marched over the bridge and up into the town their faces looked serious enough. Here and there, however, was some irrepressible joker, who, even amid such circumstances, would keep all about him in a roar of laughter. One of these was the lieutenant who had called the attention of his comrades to the building of the bridge. He kept up a running comment all the while—"Who would not be a soldier? Terms, 'thirteen dollars a month, and found'—dead on the field! Come on, boys, we are going to make a friendly call on our old friend Bobby Lee, and renew the pleasure of his acquaintance. Do you hear the music?" (The rattle and crash of the battle had by this time become awful.) "Now, that is melody indeed!

They are getting up a ball for our special delectation. They have started a regular dancing tune—the Confederate waltz, the Fredericksburg polka, the Stonewall Jackson round dance, all in one. The ball has opened. Choose your partners." At the top of the hill, along one of the principal streets, the command was halted for a while. While awaiting orders the joker said to the colonel of the regiment, with a serious air, and in tones loud enough to be heard by all about him: "Colonel Bowman, I have a special favor to ask of you. I want you to excuse me from duty for the rest of the day. I have a sad errand to perform. I desire to pay my respects to the locality where the mother of the lamented Washington died. I believe the good old lady took her departure in 1789 from this ancient village; and I would like to embrace this opportunity to hunt up the spot, meditate on her virtues, and ponder the illustrious events that have taken place in our land since her decease. Besides, I think a change of location just now would be good for my health. This is a malarious region, and I have to be very careful."

The colonel replied to the joker in a like vein, in spite of the depressing surroundings, saying, "I am very glad to find you so patriotic and sentimental. If you are anxious to ponder the virtues of the mother of General Washington, then I can expedite your desires, if you will stay with the regiment, for it looks now as though, at the rate the battle is going, we would be in the neighborhood of her monument within the next fifteen minutes! That, I understand, is just between the two lines of battle, on the hill back of the town. If you can repress your ardor for a brief interval, and if your sentimentalism will stand the strain of the occasion, you will have the chance of meditating on her example and influence right in the thick of the fight on the front line within the next half hour!"

At this sally of drollness everybody laughed; but just then

the musketry firing became more frightful, shells began to drop in the streets, and wounded men came trooping by from the front, so that it required all the nerve and courage of the very bravest to keep cool and self-possessed under the circumstances.

The brigade was somewhat sheltered by the houses while in the town, but every man knew that in a few moments they might be ordered out into the open fields behind the village, where the works would have to be stormed, and the dreadful heights faced and assaulted, and the very thought was a trying one.

The mounted officers all sent their horses to the rear, as the fire was too deadly to be ventured into except afoot. The air in the streets of the deserted town resounded with the cannonade, making each explosion seem like the reverberations of half a dozen guns. Houses, windows, doors, and alleys repeated and reechoed the thunders of the cannon, making the effects still more unnerving and awful.

While they were halted in the upper streets Colonel Bowman sent for Jack and said: "Lieutenant, take this message down to headquarters at the river. Deliver it and bring back the answer as soon as you can. I do not know where we shall be; you will have to hunt us up. Tell the brigade surgeon that General Carroll directs him to send the ambulance corps to this point to await instructions."

The boy took the dispatch and hastened to deliver it. The streets by this time were confused and crowded with batteries, ammunition wagons, regiments moving to the front, wounded men hurrying to the rear. Into the midst of the mass once in a while a shell would drop from the Confederate batteries, creating havoc and a dreadful scatterment in the vicinity of the explosion. The firing meanwhile had become more terrible, the clouds of smoke from the guns gathered all about darkening the sky and filling the air with the odor of gunpowder. The whole scene resembled a dream of the lower regions.

Jack, after dispatching his errand, climbed the hill again and proceeded to the spot where he had left the regiment. It was nowhere to be seen. The streets in that part of the town were deserted. Now and then for a moment a soldier would appear and then suddenly vanish. Jack soon found out the reason— the Confederates were sweeping the streets with artillery, having secured the range of them from the hills beyond.

The boy ventured back to the edge of the town, and there he saw an appalling sight. The heights around the place were wreathed and fringed with fire and smoke. On every bluff and ridge about the whole amphitheater of hills cannon were ranged, which were all firing at once. Down in the hollow—in the pit of the theater, as it were—scattered here and there over the uneven ground, were detachments of Union troops, the focus of observation and aim from every standpoint on the heights. From all directions at once a rain of fire and death was sweeping in upon them.

As Jack surveyed the scene he saw a wounded man from his regiment hurry along with his hand bleeding and tied up in a bandage. "Tom," shouted the boy, "where is the command? How can I reach it?"

"You cannot get to them now," was the reply. "They are in a railway cut out yonder. We made a little dash across the open space from one cut to the other, and so escaped the front fire of the rebels. You cannot reach them now. The whole plain is swept by the guns from the hills out there. Nothing can be done this evening, anyway. Do not go; it is sure death to try it."

Jack stopped and looked about him. While making ready to venture forth, in spite of the warnings he had received, he saw an officer some distance off whose actions were queer and suspicious, hidden away behind an old outbuilding. With pallid face, and his body trembling and shaking as if with the palsy, with furtive glances the fellow looked hastily around to find out whether any-one was noticing him. Not seeing any observer, he took out his pistol, fixed it in position, took aim at his own arm, and fired! He had so aimed the piece as to make simply a trifling flesh wound. At once, with the blood streaming down to his hand, and dripping and smeared on his clothes, he started to the rear, holding his arm and making a great ado about the bullet that had gone through it! Jack watched him with disgust and curiosity, and then said to himself, "Well, I think I am about as much afraid as I well can be, but I do hope I will never so far forget myself as to fire a bullet into my own flesh in order to keep out of a battle! Phew! what a story of danger and disaster that fellow will have to tell!"

Just then he saw another officer, this time one whom he knew as belonging to a neighboring regiment, staggering loosely along in a limp, disjointed sort of way, looking as if his backbone had been taken out of its place and his flesh was trying to get along by itself without the aid of the spinal column.

"Halloo, Dick, what is the matter?" said the boy.

"O, my old complaint has come back on me. I am deathly sick; I can hardly stand; I have pains all over me; I feel faint; I'm afraid I'll die if I do not get relief. I wonder where I can find a surgeon. Have you a little whisky about you? I think if I had a good drink of 'commissary' it would help me along until I get to the hospital."

"No, I have no liquor," said the boy. "Where is your regiment? Why are you not with them? When did this attack come on?"

"O, just a while ago. I was with my command till we came

here, and then I was seized with this attack and overcome. I guess I must have fainted. O, dear, I am getting the cramp, too. I guess it is an attack of bilious colic; I used to get that terrible when I was a boy."

And as he spoke he doubled himself up convulsively and groaned with agony. Great beads of perspiration stood on his forehead, and the throbs of his heart could be distinctly heard.

Jack looked at the poor sufferer with pity. He saw the truth in the case; the man was deathly sick — with cowardice. He was not merely shamming; he was in mortal fear, almost dead with fright. He had succumbed to his terrors, and was now beside himself with anguish and dread.

AS HE SPOKE HE DOUBLED HIMSELF UP CONVULSIVELY AND GROANED WITH AGONY.

"If I were you," said Jack, "I would try to rejoin my regiment. It will not be a good thing for your record to be sick at such a time as this. Cheer up and go back. You will get over this by and by."

"O no, I won't. It is killing me. I cannot stand it. The pain is eating my very insides out. Oh-h-h-h!" he groaned.

"Well," said Jack, "good-bye. I am going to find my command if I can."

Just as the boy started he heard increased sounds of battle off on the right, and looking in that direction he saw the hills occupied by the enemy burst forth into flame, as though their very crests had become one vast volcanic crater. The Confederate troops were on the top of a steep and fortified hill around which skirted an old sunken road, like that which Victor Hugo imagines to have existed at Waterloo, dug out of the side of the ridge and walled up on its outer edge. Behind this wall the foe had lain, invisible and impregnable. Jack had seen Humphreys's division, made up in good part of men who had never before been in battle, march out in that direction earlier in the afternoon, and now they were in the act of charging the invincible hill crested with the stone wall. Their magnificent leader, losing one horse after another in the awful fight, leading his men on in a vainly heroic attempt to carry out the insane "demand" of Hooker and Burnside that "the hill be taken before night," had ordered all the officers to the front, had forbidden the troops to fire, and had commanded a bayonet charge. With a valor and steadiness never surpassed on any battlefield, his brave men obeyed orders, charging again and again, some of them getting within thirty steps of the wall and dying on the bloody slope. The division melted away as the boy looked upon it, dissolving into nothing under the dreadful fire of the enemy, which now at last covered the scene from view. The broken remnant of Humphreys's men rallied again and again, but their effort was vain. Half their number lay on the ground, dead or smitten with fearful wounds, and their comrades, repulsed but undismayed, coolly fell back, shouting and singing, to a point where the rolling hill would somewhat shelter them, to wait for orders.

One of Jack's friends, Charles Beaver, told the boy afterward this incident of that charge. He said: "I was shot down during our advance, and fell bleeding to the earth, unable to move. When our boys fell back I was, of course, left behind. I lay there tortured with my wound, bleeding to death, my mouth parched with thirst, and hearing the bullets and shells every second pass close to my face, as the hilltop was scathed with the fire from the rebel lines. I was sure I would die, and I tried to compose my thoughts and breathe a prayer for help. When the darkness approached the fire slackened and then came to an end. I began to sink into unconsciousness, and supposed my hour had come to die. As I opened my eyes once in a while I saw strange figures dimly in the darkness, and now and then a moving light, like a torch or lantern. As I watched these appearances I hardly knew where I was, on earth or in another world. The last thing I recall is the fact that I woke from a stupor and looked into a human face, felt a cordial pressed to my burning lips, and said faintly, 'Thank God, the Christian Commission has come,' as I fell into another faint. When I woke again I was inside our lines, in the hospital, my wound dressed, and my life saved!"

The boy was still resolved to find his regiment, but after anxious and venturesome searching he had to give up the task. On the edge of the town the ground was covered with wounded men, among whom now the nurses, surgeons, and ambulance corps were at work, but beyond them not a man could be seen in the gathering darkness. The firing had ceased, the troops were lying in concealment in hollows and behind barricades; the night had settled down. In the darkness it was too late to find the regiment, and Jack, with a heavy heart, sank down on the earth and pulled his blanket over him and fell into a troubled sleep, waking once in a while shivering with the cold and horrified with the groans of the wounded all about him. He awoke early Sabbath morning and found the situation more quiet. The Union army had been defeated the day before in each attempt to carry and hold the heights. In sight of each other the two armies now lay in line waiting for something to happen.

"THANK GOD, THE CHRISTIAN COMMISSION HAS COME."

Jack, after taking a bite of meat and a hard cracker, made up his mind to start out across the open space in the effort to find his comrades. He did not know their exact position, and could not ascertain whether they had been moved or not since going out. He had to guess at the whole matter. Venturing forth, he could look out over the plains to the hills a mile away, from which the rebels the day before had poured such a galling fire upon the Union troops. He could see no Confederates at

THE HEIGHTS OF FREDERICKSBURG.

all, not even a picket, and he fancied that it would be possible for him to get out to the place where he supposed the command to be. Wrapping his blanket up in a roll and throwing it around him, and cautiously noting his position, he started. He had not gone twenty yards when he came to a fence. As he climbed this he heard a sound that set his heart to beating more rapidly than usual—zip! zip!—and two minie balls struck the fence near where he crossed. He dropped on the earth and lay flat down for a few moments. Again came the hiss of another bullet, and its dull, thudding sound as it went into the ground near his head. He durst not stir for a little while lest he might draw the fire of the enemy again.

By and by he rose, determined to make another trial. He ran at full speed for some distance, but he saw at once on the picket line of the enemy puff after puff of smoke, and heard the reports of a dozen musket shots, and saw the bullets strike all about him in the ground. Some of them whizzed past his ears in a way that made his blood run cold. He dropped again. He was now in a quandary. He could neither go forward nor back. It was impossible to get to the regiment, and almost impossible to return. He lay on the earth hugging the ground, a bullet striking near his head whenever he made the slightest motion. He accused himself of being a fool for trying to get across the plain and venturing into such a fix.

By and by, summoning all his pluck to the front, he swiftly rose, darted off whence he came, back toward town, mounted the fence, dropped to the ground behind it, escaped the bullets, and waited for the night to come or for the regiment to return.

If the boy had been a little older and wiser he would not have made such a crazy venture. He afterward learned that General Carroll, the commander of the brigade, one of the most daring and heroic of leaders, had not been able even to send a messenger for more ammunition across that bullet-swept space, and that in the nighttime General Whipple, who led the division, answering the request that had reached him in the darkness for aid, had sent out Lieutenant Eddy, ordnance officer, and Lieutenant Weise, of the ambulance corps, to ascertain the position of Carroll's troops, and that these gallant officers, in their efforts to get to the front line, had been captured or shot; at any rate, they had not been heard from when General Whipple made his report

HE LAY ON THE EARTH HUGGING THE GROUND.

of his work in the battle. But the boy was in his teens, and had not yet learned that discretion may be the better part of valor.

In the dusk of evening, as the boy crossed the plain in search of the Eighty-fourth, he discerned it coming in. With gladness he ran and reported to Colonel Bowman, and told him he had been trying to come out to the regiment all day and had been driven back.

"I wonder you did not get a bullet in your hide," said the colonel, " for making such a rash attempt. You had no right to expose yourself. We were safely hidden there behind the bank, and you could not have been of the slightest service under the circumstances. You must learn as a soldier not to run such risks when there is nothing to be gained by the exposure."

On Monday both armies rested. Burnside wanted to attack again, but his generals would not let him, and meanwhile the rank and file lay on their arms awaiting orders to advance.

That night the regiment was ordered out on picket. The boy was on duty on the picket line from sundown until about ten o'clock. Then, relieved of work for a few hours, he went off into the corner of a yard, threw himself down on the withered grass, not yet entirely killed by the frost, and went to sleep. About midnight it commenced raining, and, roused a little by the drops falling on his face, he pulled his rubber blanket closely about him, rolled over, and went to sleep again. By and by he felt some one shake him violently. Then he heard a loud whisper:

"Lieutenant Sanderson! Wake up! We are going to

"WAKE UP! WE ARE GOING TO RETREAT!"

retreat! Orders have come to evacuate the town. I have been hunting you for half an hour. It is a lucky chance you were not captured. Five minutes more and you would have been left behind. Come!"

Jack got up in a hurry. The company was in line; the rain was coming down with violence, the mud was over shoetop, and the night dark as pitch.

The regiment was among the last to leave. Gradually the troops had been withdrawn during the early part of the night. Everybody went softly, trying to make as little noise as possible; indeed, before Jack was awake the bulk of the army had retreated. Down the steep bank they went, stumbling, splashing through the mud, keeping an eye to the rear all the while, and anxiously wondering whether any suspicion of their movements had been awakened in the Confederate commander's mind.

Word was quietly passed to the outposts of the picket line, and these cautiously withdrew to the river. Here the pontoon corps was in waiting, and when the last man had gone over the boats were loosened, the Fredericksburg end of the bridge was unfastened from the bank and allowed to swing with the current around until it reached the other side. By this time dawn was appearing, and with the dawn appeared also the Confederate pickets. They came into the town, reached the river bank, saw with mingled satisfaction and disappointment that their prey had escaped them, and had nothing to do but rejoice that they had got rid of the Yankees so easily.

The army went back and settled down into winter quarters. It had been once more baffled, repulsed, defeated. Heartsick and discouraged, it felt that it ought not to have been sacrificed to appease public opinion, which just at that time demanded a forward movement; and it felt, too, that some one had blundered.

THE HEIGHTS OF FREDERICKSBURG.

Worn out, anxious, and disheartened, it went to work to make log huts and mud houses, and settle down for the winter.

Among the wounded was one of the jokers of the regiment, who in his own waggish way kept all about him in good humor; and while his drolleries were not sufficient to cure his own hurt they served as medicine for many near him in the hospital, who were rallied and recruited from the very verge of death by his fun. One day a worthless, long-faced fellow, in whom no one had any confidence, exhorted the wounded man to pray. At once the irrepressible wag, wounded even unto death, warded off the admonition by a characteristic reply. "O," said he, assuming an expression of forlornness and despair, "there is no use in my praying. It is a hopeless case."

"You are certainly mistaken," was the answer. "You can surely offer up a prayer. Begin now."

"Why, mister," said the almost breathless wag, "don't you know that the Lord will not hear a soldier's prayer unless it is forwarded through the regular military channels, and has the indorsement of the secretary of war?"

This thrust "brought down" the hospital, and nurses, surgeons, and patients alike joined in the laughter and shouts that arose, in the midst of which the would-be exhorter was glad to beat a retreat.

CHAPTER IX.

THE ARMY OF THE POTOMAC IN WINTER QUARTERS.

THE army, driven back from the bloody field and impregnable hills of Fredericksburg, settled down into camp life with a sad and heavy heart. There was nothing in the situation to encourage even the most courageous soldier; while there were many things to depress and demoralize everybody. The boys all knew that a blunder had been committed; that the attack against the steep and frightful heights on which the hosts of Lee were securely fortified ought never to have been made; and although General Burnside gallantly took all the responsibility upon himself for the plan and the movement, and the soldiers were ready enough to see and appreciate his magnanimity in the case, yet there sprang up as a consequence of the ill-starred defeat a brooding spirit of discontent, restiveness, and surly discouragement, which soon spread throughout the entire army, from the high private in the rear rank to the generals in command of corps and grand divisions.

Soon after the battle the following address from President Lincoln was read to the soldiers, but the demoralization had set in too deep to be arrested by any such means:

"EXECUTIVE MANSION, *Dec.* 22, 1862.

"TO THE ARMY OF THE POTOMAC: I have just read your commanding general's preliminary report of the battle of Fredericksburg. Although you were not successful the attempt was not an error, nor the failure other than an accident. The courage with which you, in an open field, maintained the contest against an intrenched foe, and the consummate skill and success with which you crossed and recrossed the river in the face of the enemy, show that you possess all the qualities of a great army, which will yet give victory to the country and the cause of popular government.

"Condoling with the mourners for the dead, and sympathizing with the severely wounded, I congratulate you that the number of both is comparatively so small. I tender to you, officers and soldiers, the thanks of the nation.

"ABRAHAM LINCOLN."

This order was read to the regiment on dress parade one evening by the adjutant, in a resounding voice, and it was received with hearty cheers; but as the officers dispersed after the display was over there was an undercurrent of comment and criticism which would have given the President some light on the situation if he had overheard it.

"So the President can only congratulate us on escaping from the clutches of the Johnnies with ten thousand dead and wounded. Well, it was lucky there were not three times that number. If old 'Burny' had had his way, from all accounts, there would have been fifty thousand left on the field instead of ten."

This was the comment of one of the officers. Another replied:

"Does Father Abe want us to believe he thinks the 'attempt was not an error?' Maybe he does fancy it was not, viewed from Washington City, but if he had been with us ten days ago, and seen the slaughter-pen into which we were hurled to be butchered by the thousand, he would have concluded that there was something like a blunder somewhere."

AN UNDERCURRENT OF COMMENT AND CRITICISM.

Another officer continued: "Our failure was an 'accident,' was it, Mr. President? The Lord deliver us from any more such accidents! The worst 'accident' that has befallen us is to have a commander at our head who is not able to lead us to victory. 'Little Mac' would never have dreamed of hurling men against such a stronghold when nothing was to be gained by it but certain defeat."

"O, no," said another; "'Little Mac' would have kept you ditching till the ditches were your graves. He did not know when to order his army forward into the works of the enemy, and Burnside did not know when to call them back from inevitable disaster."

And so, far and wide, the spirit of complaint and depression extended, until the whole army was infected by it.

One of the headlines of the *New York Tribune*, a few days after the battle, read, "No Discouragement or Demoralization," purporting to set forth the condition of things at the front; but those who were there knew better. The army had lost heart and hope and confidence, not in itself or in its cause, but in its leader. It did not believe that Burnside, however patriotic and self-sacrificing and brave he might be, was able to command the Army of the Potomac. And in moody, surly, and ominous silence, mingled with occasional low growls of discontent, and with many doubtful shakes of the head, and a good deal of anxiety for the future among both officers and men, the heart-sick army settled down into winter quarters.

Among the fatally wounded in the battle of Fredericksburg was one of Jack's beloved schoolmates and lifelong companions, Corporal John H. Styer, of Berwick, Pennsylvania, an overgrown, rollicking, well-reared stripling, who, enlisting in Lieutenant Clarence G. Jackson's squad a few weeks before, had, with eager loyalty, joined the regiment at the front. In his first fight he manifested steadfast courage; severely hurt, he lingered for some time, and then heroically passed away, one of the youthful martyrs of liberty.

The colonel of the Eighty-fourth Pennsylvania, to which Lieutenant Jack Sanderson now belonged, issued orders to the command under him to make itself comfortable, and while it was not definitely announced that no further movement against the enemy was to take place until spring, yet a general impression to that effect soon pervaded the army of Burnside. How the boys availed themselves of this impression and made good use of it a few words will set forth. The weather had been very cold, and the regiments that had simply camped down in their shelter tents had suffered severely. Here and there were shrewd, farseeing commanders who had taken the responsibility on themselves of preparing huts and other shelters for their troops, but many regiments had been living thus far in mere tents in shivering discomfort. Now everybody went to work to build winter habitations.

Let us take a look at these men of war and the shelters which they have made as places of refuge during their period of hibernation. The commanding officers of the divisions and army corps we find quartered, here and there at least, in the houses of the former residents, who have for the most part gone South for the winter, if not for the war. Brigade and regimental officers have large wall and hospital tents erected for their use, with portable stoves, cots, floors, and other appliances of comfort, and some tokens of luxury at hand and in use. Company officers for the most part live in log huts, roofed over with shelter tents, pieced together. Do you know what a shelter tent is? It is a rude shelter, made of three or four pieces of canvas which are cut out and fitted so as to button one to the other, and afford space enough underneath for two or three men to sleep in a pinch. On the march each man carries one piece of canvas rolled up on his knapsack, and at night he and his mate find two notched sticks and a crosspiece, button their bits of canvas together, and forthwith their habitation for the night is complete. During the season of winter quarters these sheets of canvas, duly buttoned together, made a fairly good roof for a mud house or a log hut.

It was singular what comfortable places the boys built for themselves. Here in a side hill we find a dozen officers quartered in a cavern dug out of the earth. A chimney has been excavated and a big fireplace carved out of the earth, and here, warm, dry, cheerful, and jocose, the occupants bunk together on the ground, on which has been thickly spread a covering of rubber coats, blankets, overgarments, and other bed material. Or, perhaps, we find bins and bunks arranged about the interior, with a table, rude benches, a camp chair or two, and other odds and ends. Now and then a picture is hung up; sometimes the walls are covered with cuts taken from *Harper's Weekly* or *Frank Leslie's Illustrated Newspaper*, both of which had a large circulation in the army, while in almost every tent or other habitation we find in use some knickknack or handy trifle of comfort, sent from home. Dugouts, log houses, mud huts, structures made of bushes, earth, and canvas, all mingled together in a curious mongrel fashion—if one can fancy these and other like structures, each with an individuality of its own, and reflecting the personality of its occupants and inventors, and along with them a various collection of soldiers, covering a large stretch of country, twenty odd miles in length along the Rappahannock, and nearly that distance in breadth, and embracing a population of over a hundred thousand men—with no women or children, except a few nurses and drummer boys to give variety to the picture—if one can fancy this agglomeration of rough, rude, uncouth, and at the same time picturesque habitations, he may form a fair idea of the army in its comfortable winter quarters.

In pleasant weather each day was quite well filled with its various duties. The early roll call opened up the tasks of the day. Jack was disposed at first to try to get a little more sleep than the law of camp life allowed him, and so he began to indulge himself in a morning nap once in a while rather than get out of bed at reveille to respond to his name and attend the usual assembly of the company to which he belonged, about half past five on a wintry morning. This happened three times, and no more. It was the duty of the orderly sergeant of each company immediately after roll call, to take the report of the company to the headquarters of the adjutant, where the adjutant's assistant, the sergeant major, summed up the various reports and gave them in at once to his superior, who reported the result to the colonel or other officer in command, who could tell at once how many men he had ready for duty, how many were sick, and how many were absent without leave or otherwise unaccounted for. Jack, I say, had enjoyed three morning naps, absenting himself thereby from early roll call. On the fourth morning, after hearing the bugles sound out their clear and stirring notes, and listening in his snug bed to the orderly sergeant calling the roll, he had turned over under the blankets to get some more sleep, in a very comfortable frame of mind. Before he could settle back into sleep there came an alarm at the tent door. "Who is there?" called Lieutenant Sanderson. "The sergeant major," was the reply. "What do you want? Why do you wake me at this hour? Go away; don't disturb me," was the salutation of Jack as he rubbed his eyes. The tone of the sergeant major, as he made answer to the lieutenant, was not very jocose. He said, "Lieutenant Sanderson, Colonel Bowman wants to see you at once in his tent." "Why, what is the matter? What does he want at this hour, six o'clock in the morning?" "I do not know," was the serious reply of the noncommissioned officer. "I have given you his message."

Jack dressed in a hurry, puzzled and anxious to know what was brewing. He hastened out into the frosty air, and in a few moments tapped nervously at the headquarters tent of the colonel commanding. "Colonel," said the lieutenant, "I was told to report to you, and here I am."

The boy saw that the colonel was angry, and that something was the matter. "Yes," said Colonel Bowman, "I see you are here now; but where were you half an hour ago, at the time of roll call?"

With tremulous tongue and stammering speech the boy answered, as his eyes fell under the stern and penetrating look of the colonel, "I was in bed."

"And where were you yesterday morning at roll call, and where were you day before yesterday morning at roll call, and the day before that? Tell me now, where were you?" thundered the colonel.

"Well, colonel, I was in bed, trying to get a bit more sleep."

"Is that the business of a commissioned officer, to snooze in bed when his men are up attending roll call? Is that the way you are going to set an example to your command and obey orders as an officer? I have a notion to order you under arrest at once and take away your sword from you, to let you see what punishment is due for such an offense. Go back to your quarters, sir, and let this be the last offense of this sort you are guilty of while you are an officer in my regiment! You ought to be thankful that I have let you off so easy. You can go to your tent and meditate for a while."

The boy made haste to obey, thoroughly awake now and realizing what a predicament he had got into. He had presumed that because he was a relative of the colonel of the regiment he might take a privilege, now and then, denied to others. He had no thought that he would be brought up with a round turn by the colonel for this delinquency, and, stung to the heart, ashamed of himself, mortified beyond measure, and glad that no one else was present to hear the reproof that had been given him, he beat a retreat, wishing for the time that he could

> Fold his tent like the Arabs,
> And silently steal away.

One dose of such strong medicine as was administered that morning was enough for the boy, and he never had occasion to take another. He was glad enough to escape with one such interview with Colonel Bowman on the subject of being present with his company at roll call.

One of the most affecting scenes of camp life at this point, Stoneman's Switch, as it was called, was a funeral which occurred one wintry day. One of the boys in the hospital, who had been wounded in the battle two or three weeks before, began, after an interval of suffering bravely borne, to droop. In his delirium he fancied himself within reach and call of the loved ones at home, and he frequently called for his mother and his sister to attend him. One day the surgeon gave in the verdict that the brave boy must die, and before night the hero had met and conquered the last enemy. The next day a burial party, formed of the company to which the dead soldier had belonged, with other comrades from the regiment, lovingly bore or followed his body to the grave that had been dug not far away in a commanding site on a neighboring hill. Through the snow and the slush, led by the band, which played as a dead march the familiar air called the Portuguese Hymn with melting and penetrating effect, the boys marched out and reverently stood by the open grave. No chaplain was then serving with the regiment, and there was no burial service read, but, as the boys stood in silence at the side of the pit that had been dug, one of them, with tremulous utterance, began to sing,

> "Rock of ages, cleft for me,
> Let me hide myself in thee."

"ROCK OF AGES."

Soon another voice chimed in with the first, and then another joined, until, by the time the closing stanza of the glorious old hymn had been reached, all the boys, in the cold, bleak January weather, with uncovered heads and tearful eyes, with tenderness and pathos, thinking of the dear ones far away, and wondering whose turn next would come to die of sickness or wounds, in the camp or hospital or on the field, were singing,

> "While I draw this fleeting breath,
> When my eyes shall close in death,
> When I rise to worlds unknown,
> And behold thee on thy throne,
> Rock of ages, cleft for me,
> Let me hide myself in thee."

Such serious and solemn occasions were not allowed, however, to check the merriment, the jollity, and the good cheer of camp life, and for the most part the soldiers led a jovial, careless, and rollicking career, which even wounds, privations, deaths, and battles were not allowed for any great length of time to overshadow with gloom. As one means of recreation and sport a minstrel troupe was organized in the regiment, and often in the evening the camp resounded with the sound of fiddle, banjo, and bones, while the air reechoed with the stale jokes which Christie and his fellow-minstrels were just then retailing on the stage throughout the land.

On the 20th of January the army was roused from its winter quarters by marching orders, and the various corps were soon on the move. The Eighty-fourth Regiment was drawn up in line and with some display and a good deal of enthusiasm the following proclamation by the commander of the army was read:

"*General Orders, No. 7.*

"The commanding general announces to the Army of the Potomac that they are about to meet the enemy once more. The late brilliant actions in North Carolina, Tennessee, and Arkansas have divided and weakened the enemy on the Rappahannock, and the auspicious moment seems to have arrived to strike a great and mortal blow at the rebellion and to gain that decisive victory which is due to the country.

"Let the gallant soldiers of so many brilliant battlefields accomplish this achievement, and a fame the most glorious awaits them. The commanding general calls for the firm and united action of officers and men, and under the providence of God the Army of the Potomac will have taken the great step toward restoring peace to the country and the government to its rightful authority.

"By command of   MAJOR GENERAL BURNSIDE.

"LEWIS RICHMOND,
  "Assistant Adjutant General."

The Third Corps, under General Stoneman, formed a part of the Center Grand Division commanded by General Hooker, and the troops, with such leaders, moved out briskly and blithely, yet hopelessly, from their camps, like Abraham, who "went out not knowing whither he went." One of the most splendid exhibitions of soldierly loyalty and pluck which that army ever displayed was its action on this occasion in marching forth with alacrity and cheerfulness under Burnside's command just after that officer had made a stupendous failure at Fredericksburg. The wounded from that battle were most of them still in hospitals; the dead were hardly buried, the men had scarcely recovered from the fatigue, exhaustion, and demoralization of that struggle, and were still oppressed with a sense of the utter hopelessness of success under the leadership of Burnside, who had confessed his incompetency for such a post; and yet at his bidding, with the belief that an awful struggle with the Confederates was before them, they obeyed their chief, and without a murmur, but with a good deal of courage and buoyancy, hoping against hope for the best, they went out to attempt once more the overthrow of Lee.

The weather on the first day was cold, bright, and exhilarating, and it alone proved a tonic for the boys who had been in camp for a month. The movement was performed as quietly as possible at first, so as to take the rebels by surprise, but doubtless they were apprised of what was going on. The command moved down the river, hiding behind the hills and meeting long trains of pontoons heading up the river. They camped on the frozen ground for the night and then started on a backward trail, this time directing their steps up the Rappahannock toward Banks's Ford. That day it began to rain and blow and finally storm. The troops had to halt and cover themselves for the time by their shelter tents, which were found of little avail in the pouring torrents of water which pelted them. In the very midst of the movement everything was brought to a halt. General Burnside said to himself: "We will stop a few hours till the rain is over, and then we will resume our advance against the foe." Then he stopped, and the wagon trains stopped, and the infantry stopped, and the cavalry stopped, and the artillery stopped, first, of all, indeed, because they soon found it impossible to budge. They were stalled by the mud. The bottom had dropped out of the entire region. Mud is no name by which to describe the sticky, miry, pitchy, unfathomable, and unexplorable semifluid beds of stuff which filled and overflowed the roads, every one of which was transformed into an abysmal slough of despond. That army was literally "stuck in the mud;" infantry mired, cannon bogged, horses stalled, wagons sunk axle-deep in the squashy clay, everybody calling for help and no one able to render any, and the whole force of a hundred thousand men as absolutely helpless as though the rebel army had come upon them when asleep and bound them hand and foot. Here is a cannon, deep in unknown depths of viscous and gelatinous slime mixed with an undercurrent of quicksand. A score of horses are hitched to it, and they flounder and sink to their bellies in frantic and ineffectual exertions, some of them drowning in the mud, and trampled under the feet of the others, which with desperate tugs and struggles strive to keep a footing in the mire and do the bidding of their drivers, who urge them vainly out of the gulf of mud in which they have become inextricably mired. A strong rope is now hitched to the gun, and fifty men tug at it without taking an advance step. The gun does not move. Another detail of fifty men is added, and the whole hundred pull with all their might and main, and with the same result. Still another detail is brought, and a hundred and fifty soldiers, brawny and stalwart, with shouts and curses and cheers and utmost endeavors, unite in the effort to pull the cannon out of the mud, but it will not budge. And there it stood, and there the army stood, bemired, covered with mud, enduring the storm, chilled to the marrow with the sleet and piercing wind, out of rations, and only six or seven miles from their camps, and no way to get food, literally " stuck in the mud." Pontoons, caissons, cannon, horses, riders, footmen, generals, staff officers, all were in as desperate a plight as could be well imagined, simply because the rains had come upon them midway in their movement and the marvelous capacities of Virginia mud had become exemplified in their experience.

It was in view of the recollections of this campaign, in after years, that a Union veteran, answering the inquiry, in a casual conversation with a stranger, " Have you ever been through Virginia?" replied: " Been through Virginia! Yes, I have—in several places!"

What did they do? They did nothing but wait till enough of the mud subsided to allow them to struggle out of it, and then the whole army marched back again to camp, sick, hungry, exhausted, woe-begone, dirty as the ground, and wretched as can be imagined. This was the famous "mud march" of General Burnside, and the last movement he engineered in the Army of the Potomac; for shortly afterward, within two days, indeed, of the return of his army to its winter quarters, President Lincoln relieved him from command and appointed another in his place. The new leader was one of the most gallant men that ever lived, one of the most distinguished-looking officers who ever led an army into battle, full of personal enthusiasm, and of magnetic, impetuous, and dashing qualities, which, embodied in his previous deeds of courage and daring, had earned the *sobriquet* of "Fighting Joe Hooker." What the new commander undertook to do with the splendid army that came under his leadership we will tell in later chapters.

CHAPTER X.

OUT ON THE PICKET LINE.

SOON after returning to camp from the "mud march" one evening Captain Bryan came into the canvas-covered log house that served as the headquarters of Company B, and said to Lieutenant Sanderson, Lieutenant Smith, and Orderly Sergeant Simmons, who were there together:

"Boys, I have good news for you. It will make you fairly dance and kick for joy when I tell you. You will roll over on the ground in your glee."

"What is it, captain?" said all three of them in a breath. "Have you leave of absence? Has any one secured a pass for you to Washington? Has the sutler got a new stock of goods? Is Quartermaster Kephart going to give another blow-out? Have you heard of a chance for promotion? Are we to be excused from company drill to-morrow morning? Are we ordered off on recruiting service for the winter? Are you on the track of a soft snap somewhere in the service, where there will be increased allowances, better pay, a chance to show off a new uniform, and no danger of being ordered into battle? Is there an extra ration of 'commissary' to be issued? Is Captain Zinn going to be promoted to be major? What is the news, anyway. captain? Do not keep us in suspense so long."

Meanwhile the captain stood twirling an official paper in his hand before the sheet-iron camp stove which served both for cooking and heating purposes, the howling wind outside sending the smoke in suffocating volumes into the tent, making everybody cough and sneeze, while at the same time the freezing and bitter weather inclined them all to get as near the source of heat as possible.

When Captain Bryan had excited the curiosity of the boys sufficiently he replied: "You are not good guessers. You are all wide of the mark. We are not going home on recruiting service, nor going off on a pleasure trip to Washington, nor to a party at Kephart's. We are going out on picket, and we have to start at daybreak to-morrow morning. It is snowing, blowing, and freezing now, and what it will do by morning the Lord only knows. We must take three days' rations with us, and we won't have much chance to cook them out along the picket line. So bustle around lively, boys, and make your arrangements for a six-mile trudge through the slush and snow and a three-day stay out in the country along the Rappahannock."

This information was somewhat of a damper to the little company, for the command had just got in from its dreadful experiences in the mud with Burnside, and had barely got itself lodged in its new huts and nondescript tents for the winter, and it was not pleasant to think of being so unceremoniously ousted from them. But in a little while the boys were cheerfully packing their knapsacks, drawing their rations, cooking their pork, and stowing away their load of ammunition for the jaunt into the country.

"Reveille at four o'clock, boys," was the captain's final order; "breakfast at five, and everybody ready to 'fall in' at six." And with this prospect before them the members of the Eighty-fourth lay down in their bunks, or before the fireplaces in their cabins, and went to sleep to be roused on time, get their coffee, sling on their burdens, get into line, and start out in the teeth of the raging storm for the picket line, six miles or more away.

Arriving there, they found the regiment which was to be relieved by them in an uncomfortable plight. The sleet and rain and snow had been beating upon them for thirty-six hours; the fires had been of necessity few and far between, and no tents could be erected; so that everybody was drenched, shivering, hungry, tired, and glad to get relief and start back to camp. They cheered as they saw the Eighty-fourth coming to their relief; the officers in charge gave the necessary instructions, imparted the countersign for the day, indicated the points to be securely guarded, and the roads that needed most vigilance in the neighborhood, and then, happy that their tour of duty on the picket line was over, eagerly anxious to get into shelter and secure a change of flannels and dry their soaked garments, they started back to the encampment, leaving the Eighty-fourth, and the other regiments that formed the detail for picket duty in that portion of the line, in charge.

The work assigned for the time was to guard a part of the bank of the river, and also to inclose with a cordon of pickets that portion of the rear of our army which touched the Rappahannock, on the right flank of the Army of the Potomac. It required a couple of hours to get the pickets stationed, to arrange their beats, to give them proper instructions, and to make the rounds, to see that each man was in his place and attending to his duty. The boys along the river sheltered themselves from observation, as far as possible, behind trees, bushes, rocks, and high banks, in such fashion as to keep their eyes on the other side of the stream, which was lined in like manner by the Confederates. By mutual arrangement it was agreed on both sides that there should be no firing between the pickets, and sometimes there was a friendly interchange of greetings, news, and other things more substantial, one side being eager to get coffee, and the other willing to trade, with tobacco as the currency in the transaction. Now and then, in spite of the officers, a conversation like the following would take place:

From the southern side of the river a voice would be heard, "Halloo, Yank! What are you uns doin' over thar? Are you still stuck in the mud? Don't you want us to come over and help you out?"

One of the Union pickets, first assuring himself that no officer was near, would cautiously reply, "Halloo, Johnny Reb! Still alive, are you? Had any news from Vicksburg lately? Aren't you tired yet? Got any rations? Pretty near starved out, ain't you? Why don't you come over on this side? Give us a call some morning. We will treat you just as well as you did us the other day when we crossed over into Fredericksburg."

Silence for a few minutes and then another voice:

"Say, Yank, have you any papers to exchange?"

Answer.—" What have you over there?"

Rebel.—" The *Richmond Enquirer* and the *Charleston Courier*. What have you?"

Union Picket.—" The *New York Tribune*, the *New York Herald*, and the *Washington Chronicle*."

Rebel.—" Got any news in your papers? What is going on?"

Union Picket.—" Lots of news. Sherman has taken Vicksburg, the *Alabama* has been captured, England has refused to let any more pirate ships be built in her yards for the Confederacy, and Butler is going to advance up the Mississippi from New Orleans and open the Father of Waters. Lots of news, Johnny Reb!"

"Yank, you're telling a pack of lies."

Then came some unreportable objurgations against Greeley and Butler, and then a proposition to exchange newspapers, which was accepted. When the water was low enough, and the weather allowed, a picket from each side met in midstream and exchanged coffee or tobacco and Northern papers for Southern ones. Sometimes this was done by a boat, and sometimes floats were sent forth from one side to the other, and so skillfully managed that the exchanges were made by this means. When the Confederate papers were received they were passed from one to another until they were worn out, as the report of the condition of things in the South was read and pondered. Sometimes these dailies were found to be printed on wall paper, and very often on the coarsest sort of wrapping paper, the blockade and the lack of manufacturing facilities and establishments in the Southern States cutting off almost entirely the supply of printing paper.

Meanwhile, half a mile or so back from the river, where the picket line crossed the road, headquarters had been established. At noon an alarm came from one of the outer pickets stationed out farther along this road. When the sergeant of the picket guard went to respond to this alarm he found a squad of cavalry halted—half a dozen men—who had been out on a scouting expedition. Receiving from them the countersign, they passed in. Soon afterward an officer rode up, outward bound, and was halted. "What did he want? Where was he going? What right had he to pass through our lines?" One of these questions was answered, and the others were held in abeyance by the document which the officer showed, signed by General

A PICKET FROM EACH SIDE MET IN MIDSTREAM.

Hooker, permitting him to pass all sentries, outposts, picket lines, by day or night, until further orders. So he was allowed to ride on his way unmolested, the boys meanwhile puzzling their wits ineffectually to guess his mission. " Is he an independent scout? Is he a Union spy? Is he going across the river on a secret mission? Why is he venturing out alone? Won't he fall into the hands of Fitz-Hugh Lee or Jeb Stuart before he returns?"

At nine o'clock Jack went on his round as officer of the picket guard, taking the pickets one by one, and finding them alert and cheery enough in spite of the snow in which they were tramping and the sleet which was driven into their faces by the howling winds. He supposed the night was going to pass without any incident of note, and had turned to go back to headquarters from the end of the line, when Corporal Sones appeared, and, after saluting, said: " Lieutenant, I have an idea that something is going on at that house on the hill. I was up there to buy some bread a while ago, and I thought the folks looked skeery-like, as though they'd been interrupted in some sort of deviltry. They'll bear close watching. I have no confidence in any of these people."

Jack, his attention thus directed to the house, took a stroll in that direction, the corporal walking by his side. The building was a fairly comfortable one, and stood a quarter of a mile from the bank of the river, on an eminence overlooking the slopes that led down to the steep banks of the stream. The people living in it had secured a guard from the provost marshal of the army, and had not been molested, under the strong protestation that they were not allied in any way with the Confederates on the other side of the river. It was now drawing near midnight, and the two soldiers, after considerable watching and waiting, were about to turn back to the picket line, thinking that perhaps their suspicions were ill-founded; but while they stood debating the matter they saw a light appear at an upper window in the house. It flashed there but a moment and was gone. While they still stood in the cold, wondering whether the light meant anything or not, it appeared once more, and then twice in succession. Then the curtain was drawn and the light went out or was turned down. As this window was in plain sight from the other side of the river it was evident that signals might be exchanged and communication carried on without much risk of detection, if the work was shrewdly done. Once more a light appeared, was hidden, and then appeared twice again. Of course it might be that all this happened so; perhaps some one was sick, and it was necessary for one of the inmates of the house to carry a light into and out of that room quickly; but Jack and his fellow-soldier began to surmise that something more than all this was going on, especially as they saw a curtain going up to the top of the window and then slowly let down, this time shutting out the light finally.

Jack said to the corporal, " I am sure we are on the right trail. Those folks are making signals to the rebels, and may be harboring Confederate spies. Let us report this to Colonel Bowman and see what he thinks about it."

Forthwith the two marched back toward headquarters to consult with the commander of the regiment as to this case.

Colonel Bowman, with lawyer-like penetration and soldierly instincts, leaped at once to the conclusion that the people in the house in question were rebels, and it was not five minutes until a party had been detailed to watch the premises and arrest the inmates if any further suspicious work were done. As this party approached the house, which was outside the Union picket line and protected by a Union guard, they saw a figure stealthily creeping along through the garden, hiding among the bushes and clearly making for the river. The men had hardly taken

OUT ON THE PICKET LINE. 183

a single step in the direction of the dark object when it leaped out from its hiding place and made a bee line for the woods and the river bank. "Halt!" said the officer in charge of the party; "halt, or we will shoot." The order was quickly given to fire, and half a dozen bullets sped in the direction of the fleeing man, for such it seemed in the darkness to be. The men followed as speedily as they could travel over the frozen, snow-

A FIGURE STEALTHILY CREEPING ALONG THROUGH THE GARDEN.

covered ground, but there was no moon, and the region was unfamiliar, and the man soon got under cover, where he was safe for the time, no longer chase being possible at that hour of the night in the thicket.

They knocked at the door of the house, and after considerable waiting they gained admittance. The guard assigned by the provost marshal department of the army had been so well treated that he was fast asleep, and knew nothing of anyone having been on the premises other than the regular inmates, who professed to know nothing whatever of the man who had got away.

The woman of the house avowed that she did not know that there was a man about other than her husband and her little boy, who also made protestation that they were true-blue Union people, and had no thought of helping the enemy.

"Didn't we see the signals you made to the rebels to-night? We understand your tricks. We saw the light flashing back and forth and the curtain going up and down. You are both nothing but rebel spies, and before you are through with this you will wish there never had been a Southern Confederacy," said the officer in command of the arresting party as he took possession of the premises, put the pickets on duty about the house, and placed the family under arrest.

Next day the people thus arrested were sent to the provost marshal general's headquarters, and information was duly given of the suspicious circumstances that had been noted against them. What became of them after that the boys never found out, but for the time being at least the signals that had been going on between that house and the rebels on the other side of the Rappahannock came to an end.

CHAPTER XI.

A CONTRABAND'S WONDERFUL DREAM.

WHILE Jack that night at the picket-line camp-fire was trying to get a little sleep he was roused by a commotion, and waking up and emerging from his blanket and rubber poncho (which he had thrown about him in order to keep as dry as possible while he lay on the ground with his feet toward the blazing logs) he rubbed his eyes and sat up to find out what was going on. He had come off duty an hour before and was wet, tired, and cold. He looked about him and found seated at the bivouac fire, the center of an interested group of officers and men, a unique specimen of the African race, an old man, with a grizzly gray beard, a bent form, a crooked leg, and, as soon appeared, an inexhaustible fund of native humor, wit, pathos, and quaintness. He was wet to the skin, having swum across the river, eluding the pickets on the other side, and making his escape safely into the Union lines. A slave all his life, this was his first breath of freedom. Under the Stars and Stripes he was secure and at liberty.

"Can you cook, uncle?" was the inquiry of one of the officers.

"Yas sah, yas sah, I kin cook; but I hain't had much chance, sah, lately, for purwisions is mighty scarce where I come from. I'se mighty hungry now, sah."

At once there was a proffer of coffee, hard-tack, and pork for the old man, who, after his appetite was appeased and his clothes were dried, began to feel more at home.

THE CENTER OF AN INTERESTED GROUP.

"What do you think of the war, uncle?" was the question of Jack to the old refugee.

"I can hardly tell what to think, sah. I still has hopes, sah, dat the old flag is gwine to win."

"Of course it is, uncle; it is sure to win; but how does it come that you have hope of it, coming from the South, where the rebels are rejoicing over their late victories? They expect to beat us and wipe out the Union from the map, and tear up the Stars and Stripes, and make the Stars and Bars the great flag. How comes it that you have hope of Union victories?"

"To tell de truth, massa, it is 'cos of a dream I'se done gone had long ago."

"A dream, uncle? let's hear it!" shouted the chorus of voices about the fire.

It was a picturesque scene—the log fire, with eager and attentive officers and soldiers grouped about it, the flickering flames casting weird shadows over their faces, the snow and sleet falling about them, and in the midst the patient, craggy, wrinkled, withered face of the old Negro, who, in a cracked voice, and with a pathos born of years of suffering, unspoken longings for freedom, disappointed hopes, and many sorrows, told his story.

"I'se bin a slave, massa, eber sence I was bahn, and I'm now about a hundred yeahs old, I reckon."

"Hold on, uncle, none of your chaff, now," was the interruption of Jack, as he broke in on the old man's reminiscences. "You are not a hundred years old, by any means. You are not over eighty, anyway. When were you born? Who has the family record?"

The old man, thus brought up with a sudden check, assumed a meditative aspect, as though he were trying to recall the past and settle the question in dispute, and in a moment resumed: "Nobody knows when I was bahn, it's so long ago. I'se mighty old, I tell you, honey. We's got no fambly record among de cullud people, and sometimes we can't recollec' de exac' time when de chillens was bahn, but it was a long time ago; I'se suah ob dat fact. I was neber a plantation niggah, but was always a serbant in de house. I was owned by some ob de fust famblies ob Virginny, sah, some ob de berry fust. I hab been de body serbant ob Major Stewart, ob de artillery, and he done gin me charge ob his tent, and his uniform, and his money, and his valuables ob ebery sort all de time. When de battle comes on he say, 'Now, Sam, you take good keer ob dese mattahs, an' if I do not come back from de fight you see dat de missis gets 'em all right.' My massa, Major Stewart, was a fine gentleman; he was a kinsman to de Fitchews, and de Lees, and de udder fust famblies ob de State. He was berry good to his cullud people, and we had a right smaht chance ob a good time at his house, and nobody knew much about trubble dar. I allus say to de niggahs on de place, 'You dunno how good you got it heah. Neber min', you dunno what trubble is. You neber had no trubble.' When de little piccaninnies done gone die, and de mudder would cry, and carry on, I used to say, 'Neber min', honey, you dunno what trubble is. Dis heah is not trubble. De little lamb is gone wid de good Shepherd to de big sheepfold o' glory. De little lamb's safe dar. No wolf catch 'em dar, no dogs get arter 'em dar, no thorn bushes dar to tear de fleece and hurt de tender flesh; no dark mountains dar to get lost in, no pits to fall into, no rocks to bruise 'em, no big debbil to worry 'em. De little lamb is safe foreber. Honey, you dunno what trubble is.' An' when one ob dem sassy boys and gals on de place would get a good flogging fur impudence and laziness I'd say, 'Neber min', you dunno what trubble is; you neber had no trubble yit. Keep your sassy tongue still, and put a bridle on your mouf, as de Scriptur' say, and don't be stubborn like de hoss or de mule, an' you won't get so many lickin's. If you don't min' better you'll know one ob dese days what trubble is. Trubble, sure enough, wid a lighted pine knot in one han' and wid a big whip in the udder, will hunt you up, and you will fin' out den what he is.'"

"Well, uncle, how about your dream? You have not told us that," said one of the group, as he put a fresh log on the bivouac fire and lighted another pipe of tobacco.

"Yes, honey, I'se comin' to de dream pretty soon. Let me go my own gait, an' I'll get dar by an' by, as de tarrapin say once 'pon a time. I was talkin' about trubble, an' I hab seen trubble in my life. Trubble done gone fin' me out, and come to my cabin.

"DAT WAS DE DAY TRUBBLE COME TO OUR CABIN."

and squat down at my fire, and say he gwine to stay wid me all my days. I fin' out what trubble is to my heart's content. Nobody can't tell me about him now any more 'an I know myself. One day a stranger come to massa's house, and we fin' out dat trubble come wid him. He was a trader fum Georgia, and come to buy slaves to take 'em down South. Dat was trubble fur us. We fin' out pretty soon after he come dat ole massa's in debt—dat was Major Stewart's father—and unless he could pay some o' his debts by selling off some o' his slaves he would lose de ole place. He neber had done such a thing befo', and it almos' broke his heart, and de heart ob ole missis, but it had to be done all de same. Dar was our Sally; she was our daughter, honeys, and we had watched her grow up sence she was a baby. We set lots o' store by her. She could read, Sally could, and she got presents from missis and from de fambly, and wen she opened her mouf to sing it was like all de birds in de air a-singin' in de springtime in de mawnin' in de woods. Ah, we had music in our cabin when Sally was dar. Dis yer trader fixed his eyes on our Sally de moment he got inter de room whar she was. He saw her trippin' about de house and doing her chores, and heard her singin' in de kitchen, and watched her as she run on errands for ole missis, and nothin' would do but Sally for him. He would not make any offer for any udder boy or gal on dat place onless he could hab Sally wid de rest on 'em. Dat was de day trubble come to our cabin, wen we found out dat ole Massa Stewart had done gone and sold our Sally, an' dat she was gwine down into de South, and dat we'd neber see or hear from her again. My ole woman neber got ober dat. When she was down sick, and a-dyin', she would rise up and cry out, 'Don't ye hear dat singin'? Is not dat her voice again?' An' den she would moan and toss and call for Sally until nobody could stand it widout cryin'. Dat was trubble, to see your own flesh and blood dat you lubbed better dan yer own life taken out ob yer home and put into a wagon and sold out ob yer sight, an neber hab no chance to fin' out war she is, and neber hab no hope dat she will eber come back, and lie awake all night long picturin' to yerself de harm dat's come to her, and de sorrow and de shame dat she is in, and de pain dat is obertakin' her, and de enemies dat is oppressin' her, and de distress dat she is endurin', an' wonderin' all along wedder she will get so far off de track dat de Lord can't fin' her and bring her to de long home at las'. O, honeys, dat is trubble. I done gone fin' out what trubble is in my life. He stan' ober my cabin and flutter his dark wings, and he bring clouds and tempest and sorrow right off!"

"But your dream, uncle, tell us that. It is getting late, and some of us have to go out on picket along the river pretty soon," said the officer of the guard as he rose and buckled his belt, and drew his overcoat about him, and looked out into the storm. "Hurry up the dream part of your story."

The old Negro wiped his brow and eyes and mopped his weird and furrowed old face with his bandanna, and then, without noticing further the interruption, went on:

"De udder trubble dat I'se been in is dis yer wah. I'se bin wid Major Stewart for more dan a yeah, and last summer, sah, at de battle ob Antietam, de major, sah, got hisself hurt in de fight. He had chawge ob de cannon, and was helpin' in de battle, when a ball struck him and kerried off his arm smoove up to de shouldah, sah. I was at de hospital helpin' de surgeon when dey brought him in to hab de wound dressed, and de major saw me, and he say, 'Sam, I'se done for now. Take good keer of de things and take 'em back home.' An' den de doctor gib him something to put him to sleep, and he neber woke up arter dat. An' I took his sword and his uniform and his pistols and his watch back to ole Virginny, and gave 'em ober to my old missis;

and when she saw 'em she almos' went crazy. An' den when I see dat ole lady, my ole missis, crying wid a broken heart, and callin' de name ob her boy, and askin' if he would neber come back to her again, and gwine on all night long and all fru de day about de major, her deah boy, and lookin' down de long abenue ob trees, and going out to de gate and strokin' de mane ob de big hoss he used to ride, and ravin' wid her grief, den it all come back to me how my ole woman took on when our Sally was sold off from us into de South, and I said to myself, 'Dis yeah is trubble, suah enough. Now my deah ole missis is got her share ob de trubble?' O, de wah brings trubble wid it. When I was in dat hospital at Antietam, and saw de doctors cutting off de arms and legs one arter another, and throwin' 'em out de windows until dey was piled up clean to de window sill, a big heap of 'em on de ground, den I say, 'Dis is trubble. Dese men what lost an arm or a leg, and is gwine to die and leave deir frens behin', trubble is come to dem, sure enough!'"

The officer of the guard at this juncture took out his watch, snapped it open and shut, and then said:

"Old man, if you have any dream to tell let us have it. I am going in just ten minutes. Maybe we will find some other old contraband down by the river who may want to be welcomed into the Union lines, and we must keep watch for him. I am beginning to think you never had any dream."

Thus challenged, the old man now brought his wits to a focus and replied:

"O yes, honeys, I has dreams ebery night o' my life. I sees visions and I dream dreams, as de Bible says. Dat ar dream dat I has now in my min' come to me one night in de camp, arter a big battle. Dat day I see lots ob soldiers, and hosses, and wounded men, and cannons, and flags, and blood, and dust. I was anxious about de major, my master, and I was sorry fur de wounded, and I was skeered about myself, and de awful noise ob de battle almos' drove me crazy. An' den when de night come, and de wounded began to groan all ober de fiel', for a long time I could not sleep, and I jis lay and tossed and shivered and prayed on de ground. And den I had dis yeah vision dat I'se been tellin' you about. Dat was de time when I had dis yeah dream." And with the words the old man's head fell forward on his hands, and it seemed as if he were about to take another journey into the land of visions and dreams.

Meanwhile the restless officer of the picket guard, noting the time of night, and about to start on his 'grand round,' broke in again with eager voice, "Wake up, old man; give us the dream. It is time for me to go. Don't drop off to sleep now."

The old man raised his head, and his eyes were seen to be full of a strange and pathetic luster. He was like one who was seeing afar off, beholding things that are invisible. His voice was tremulous, and his words sent a kindred tremor into the souls of those who stood about the camp-fire listening to him speak.

"Dat ar dream," he proceeded, "was about an army. I saw it in my vision, comin' fum de ends ob de airth, wid flags and guns and bugles. My Master! but didn't dey make the airth shake and tremble when dey come passin' befo' me in de night! I could see deir black faces *shine* as dey went marching by."

"Black faces?" inquired one of the officers. "Was this a *black army* that you saw in your dream?"

"Yes, honeys, dat was an army ob black men dat I saw. Ebery man ob dat army, from de general down to de drummer boy, was black as your hat, an' de way deir eyes did shine, and deir faces, too, as dey marched to de battle, was de meracle ob it. Dey marched ober de mountains and down into de plains, and dey made de berry hebbens full ob de music ob deir bugles. An' by and by when dey began to sing, den de mawnin' stars seemed to stan'

A CONTRABAND'S WONDERFUL DREAM. 195

still and listen to de melody. An' den I saw a tall, pale-faced, sorrowful-lookin' white man ridin' on a white hoss, and he come out to see de army. It seemed as if dat army was his and dat dey was willin' to min' what he would tell 'em. An' when he come out he had a torch in his hand, and he said sumthin' to dat army dat make 'em shout and sing, and den he reached out his hand wid de torch in it, and he touched de baynet ob de fust soldier dat was near to him, and dat baynet took fire from de torch, and den dat fire passed all 'long de line ob dat regiment, and puhty soon all de swords and baynets of all de men in it was on fire. An' den he passed on to de nex' regiment, and he sot dem on fire too! And de fire spread fum dat to the nex', an' so on. I looked till I see, as far as dat army spread itself out on de plain, it was all on fire! Ebery sword was burnin', and ebery baynet was blazin' like a pine knot. An' den, wid dat white man in de lead, and wid ebery man in dat big army o' black men pressin' on behin', and wid ebery sword and ebery gun all blazin' in de night, dey marched out to battle. An' den jus' afore I woke fum my sleep I looked to de east, and I saw dar de mawnin' star a-shinin' in de sky, and de fust rays ob de risin' sun was beginnin' to 'pear. An' den I woke up to sleep no mo' dat night."

When the old man was done no one had a word to say. The boys were strangely moved by the tale. None of them had ever been "abolitionists," and they had as yet no clear idea of the actual relation which slavery had had or was coming to have to the conflict. Just before that Mr. Lincoln had issued his proclamation of emancipation, which of course could be of no account except as it became effectual by the victorious march of the Union army; even in the army many had been bitterly opposed to it. But it is safe to say that nobody at the camp-fire that night who listened to that strange withered-up and bent-down old Negro tell his story ever doubted from that hour to the end that the issue of the war would be victory for the Union and freedom for the slave. The vision of an army of black men, with their bayonets all set on fire from the kindling torch of the President, told in tremulous tones by an old man who felt all that he said, seemed like the utterance of a prophet foretelling the coming of a day of jubilee for the world.

The story of the old man was hardly done, and the boys were still wiping their eyes on their rough coat-sleeves and blowing their nasal organs in a violent way, and saying to each other that they believed they had really caught cold in that northeast storm that had been raging, when there came ringing from one picket guard to another all along the line the alarm, "Sergeant of the guard, alarm at the outpost, No. 3." Following that came a musket shot, and then all was alertness and attention. Voices in the darkness, the clatter of cavalry, the noise and splashing of hoofs in the slush and snow, put everyone on the *qui vive*. The picket reserve was at once arrayed in line, and stood with their arms ready to use if need be. In a moment the mystery was solved by the appearance of a squad of cavalrymen and two men in citizens' clothing. The officer in command of the cavalry explained the situation by saying that he had in charge a farmer living near the Union lines who had been harboring a deserter and aiding him to get away. They were gloomy and taciturn, and had nothing to say.

This latter incident multiplied a thousandfold will indicate what went on day after day in Burnside's army before General Hooker took command of it. Many thousands of desertions had occurred, and the people in the neighborhood of the army had aided and abetted the plans of those who were trying to elude detection and find their way back into the North. General Hooker soon remedied this state of things, and by his fine executive ability, by a generous system of furloughs, and by giv-

PEN AND INK SKETCH OF PRESIDENT LINCOLN.

ing his command plenty of work to do in the shape of drills, reviews, picket duty, and parades, he brought it up to a high state of efficiency, until it was really what he claimed it to be, " the finest army on the planet."

On a bright and beautiful day in February General Hooker arranged for a grand review of his whole army, which it was announced the President would attend and witness. With that announcement everybody was at his best in appearance and behavior. On a spacious plain not far from the Lacy House, where ample room was afforded for maneuvering the troops, the display was made. Many miles of marching were necessary in order that all the army should be marshaled at one point, as their camps were scattered over a large extent of country. It was a sight sufficient " to stir a fever in the blood of age " to see that great army all massed in one place, seven corps of infantry, one magnificent corps of cavalry, and a great body of artillery. From far and wide they came, their bands of music mingling in patriotic strains in the glowing, buoyant air, the generals in splendid uniforms and showily mounted on prancing horses, who seemed to enjoy the display as much as their riders, the artillery coming into line with the precision of machinery, at a gallop, the cavalry dashing across the plains, the staff officers gayly loping their horses hither and thither with their orders and messages, and, in brief, the whole mechanism of an army, handled with skill, ease, grace, and military pomp, amid intense enthusiasm and ardor.

At last the whole army stood in line of battle, General Hooker, with the President and other noted visitors from Washington, in the midst of a brilliantly dressed body of officers, posted in front of the center of the line. When the troops had presented arms, and the banners had drooped, and the bands had united in a piercing blast of music, the commanding general and troops passed in review, proud, hopeful, exultant, confident in their leader, and believing in their beloved President, "Father Abraham." During that visit the President made a hasty visit to many of the camps of the soldiers, galloping from one encampment to another, greeted with hearty cheers, showing his long, ungainly, awkward figure to poor advantage on horseback, making a very brief address now and then to "the boys," and leaving his image—the picture of patience, fidelity, political shrewdness, and indomitable gentleness and human kindness—indelibly printed in their hearts. Years have gone since those days of danger and political turbulence; other great figures have come to the front, and the country has within recent years recalled the memory of the fathers of the republic with increased veneration; but among them all, not excepting the one who stands first in war, and first in peace, and first in the hearts of his countrymen—among them all no wiser statesman, no nobler spirit, no loftier character, no abler leader has appeared than the emancipator and martyr, Abraham Lincoln.

"FATHER ABE."

CHAPTER XII.

ONCE MORE ON THE EVE OF BATTLE.

DURING the tour of the regiment on the picket line the camp had been guarded by a few convalescents and left in charge of an amiable, patriotic, middle-aged officer of the command — Captain Dash — a most estimable gentleman, full of the milk of human kindness, intelligent, affable, and well posted on all subjects except those belonging to his temporary calling of a soldier, but who had a sort of "alderman-of-his-native-village" air about him, a magisterial dignity, a pompous sense of military authority, which (when taken in connection with the fact that the gentleman not only did not know anything about war but he did not even "suspect" anything, so invincible was his ignorance of the usages and customs of camp life and of the technical duties of a soldier) became excruciatingly funny to those who saw the situation. An amusing instance of this set the whole regiment to laughing when it returned to its winter quarters. The boys found that during their absence the doughty and dignified captain had kept up all the forms and ceremonies of the camp. He had ordered the meager command out on dress parade, using a few sick musicians who had remained behind in hospital to extemporize music for the occasion; he had insisted that all the men in camp who could walk should turn out in full uniform; and thus with a score or more of men he had gone through with the ceremonies of parade, guard-mounting, and other occasions of martial display with a serene and beautiful consciousness of the possession of full military power for the time lodged in his own majestic person. Posted in full sight on the bulletin board at the headquarters tent which he occupied was an order, in which were duly set forth some of the special instructions intended to govern the camp during this exigent period in which its brief command was intrusted to him, signed by himself in a way that indicated a deep sense of the authority which had invested him for the time being: "A. Dash, Captain Company ———, Officer of the Day and Officer of the Guard, Commanding Post."

In the due course of time, after really showing genuine bravery on the battlefield and enduring with fortitude the privations of active campaigning for some months, this captain, on account of illness that made him unfit for duties at the front, was transferred to the newly formed "Invalid Corps." He remained to the very last unsophisticated, gentle, affable, polite, and never learned that his knowledge of men and things and of human life at large had not been in the slightest degree attempered with the least bit of intelligence concerning military matters. On the other hand, he rejoiced with a sweet spirit of simplicity in the delusion that he had made of himself a strategist and tactician of high attainments, as his own modest confession evinced on one occasion when he met an officer of the regiment in Washington on Pennsylvania Avenue. The captain was dressed in the light blue uniform that indicated the officers of the Invalid Corps, was shaven clean, and was clearly enjoying life in his new command. After cordially greeting his old friend he said to him in a burst of confidence, " Major, this work is just the thing for me. During my sickness in the hospital I feared that when I resumed active military command I would not feel at home again, but I find I am inured to the vicissitudes of military life. Indeed, all my knowledge of tactics is coming back to me !"

With this glimpse of our old friend Captain Dash he passes out of sight, although his memory is still cherished by many who saw in him some sterling qualities of manhood, while at the same time they laughed heartily at his infirmities as an officer.

On the morning of February 22 there was a heavy snowstorm, and the howling winds and sweeping tempest made outdoor life irksome and uncomfortable even to contemplate. The bitter storm had roused the camp early, and the soldiers were in the midst of preparing for breakfast when there was heard in the distance the sound of a cannon. It sent a thrill of wonderment and anxiety into every mind. "What did it mean? Was it an omen of trouble? Did it portend a skirmish or a battle? Would the army have to venture out into this dreadful storm in order to withstand the foe?" While they asked these questions, lo, there came another booming echo, followed by a third ominous and resounding report of the firing of artillery. In the headquarters tent of Company B, getting ready for a breakfast of beefsteak and hard-tack, the three officers of the company were huddling about the old sheet-iron stove, trying to get warm. Captain Bryan looked serious, Lieutenant Smith put on a gay, jaunty, and swaggering air of "don't care a tuppence if it is a fight—I'm ready for it," while Lieutenant Jack Sanderson exclaimed, jocosely, " Let's quit soldiering and go home! The weather is too cold for outdoor adventures."

Suddenly the tent flap was lifted and Sergeant Major Johnny Rissell poked his head inside and cried out, apparently in great alarm, "Captain Bryan, get your men ready for battle at once. Our outposts have been attacked by Lee. Don't you hear the cannonade?" And while the ruddy-cheeked, cheery boy, whom everybody loved, spoke the words there came another boom, boom, of the artillery as if to ratify the warning. Captain Bryan quickly seized his belt and buckled on his sword, the two lieutenants following his example. Orderly Sergeant Simmons hurried from tent to tent with the excited cry, "Fall in, boys; we are attacked; there is going to be a big battle!" Breakfast was forgotten, muskets were hurriedly taken down from the rack and inspected, and the company was about to form line, many of the boys unnerved by the sudden alarm and the apparent advent of a terrific engagement. But before the boys were actually drawn up into line, and duly dressed and all ready to march out to the field, Captain Bryan began to notice that none of the other companies were "falling in," that no long roll had been sounded, and that the other camps did not appear to be disturbed. The situation was perplexing, and the sounding of the cannon again in the distance did not relieve the perplexity. All at once a happy thought struck Jack, and before any orders had been given for the company to march out from their company parade ground he whispered to Captain Bryan: "Are we not sold? I do not believe this is an attack at all. This is the 22d of February, and this firing is only a salute in honor of Washington's Birthday!" Some of the men caught the words, and began to laugh and then to cheer. "Who gave this alarm?" was the instant question. "Sergeant Major Johnny Rissell brought the word of an attack," said some one in reply. "Where is he?" shouted a dozen voices; "Where is that rosy-cheeked joker?" "Put him under a snowdrift!" "Head him up in a pork

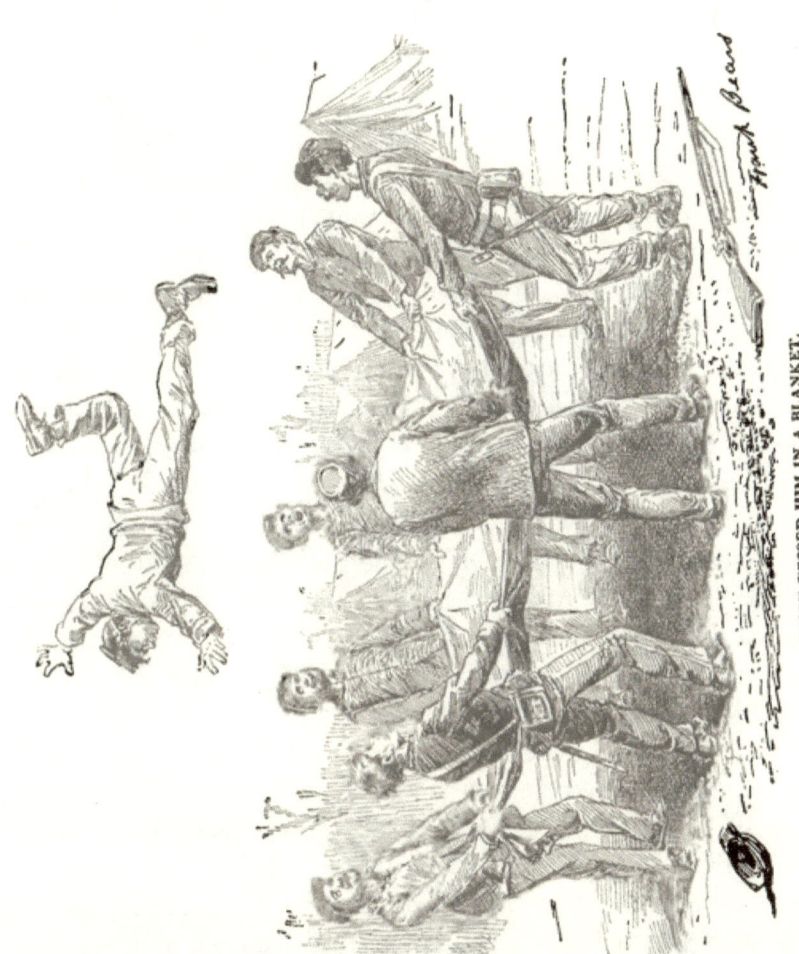

THEY TOSSED HIM IN A BLANKET.

barrel!" "Pack him in a cracker box!" "Ship him off to Camp Convalescent!" "Drum him out of camp!" "Put him on half rations!" "Send him down to Acquia Creek Landing and dump him into the Potomac!" were some of the eager, jovial shouts of mock revenge that came from a hundred voices. Some one at this moment caught sight of Johnny at the other end of the camp, hunting for cover, and cried out, "There he is; there is the champion joker! Catch him before he hides!" And with the words a score of men were running, plunging, stumbling, shouting, as they dashed through the blinding snow and the sweeping winds to find the object of their sport. They overtook the jocose fellow, washed his face with snow, plunged him in a snow bank, and tossed him in a blanket in their rough sport, and then finished their game with three cheers for Washington's Birthday. I need not say that everybody in the company was greatly relieved to find that there was no attack and no danger of battle, but that instead of an engagement there was a national holiday.

A few days after this adventure the camp was gratified with the news that their gallant commanding officer, Colonel Bowman, had been promoted to the head of the brigade, their former leader, the dashing and courageous General Carroll, having been transferred to another part of the army. The boys rejoiced at this recognition of the capacity of their colonel, and hurrahed over the announcement with hearty vigor. A day or two afterward Jack was surprised by having the following order handed to him by the adjutant of the regiment:

"HEADQUARTERS, SECOND BRIGADE, THIRD DIVISION, THIRD ARMY CORPS,
"CAMP NEAR STONEMAN'S SWITCH, VA., *March* 1, 1863.

"*Special Orders*, No. 34.

"Lieutenant Jack Sanderson, Company B, Eighty-fourth Regiment, Pennsylvania Volunteer Infantry, is hereby announced as aid-de-camp on the staff of the colonel commanding the brigade. He will be obeyed and respected accordingly.

"By command of COLONEL S. M. BOWMAN,
"Commanding Brigade.

"CHARLES W. FRIBLEY,
"Acting Assistant Adjutant General."

This order and promotion almost took away the boy's senses. It was too good to be believed at first. To serve on staff duty— to have a horse to ride; to share in the authority and display and parade of brigade headquarters; to have an opportunity to get acquainted with the officers on duty with the generals commanding the division and the corps; to get an insight into the upper circles of military life; to bear dispatches on the battle-field and really serve as an aid—whew! the boy could hardly draw his breath as he tried to take it all in. Congratulations poured in upon him from the gallant fellows who made up the Eighty-fourth, any one of whom would have been glad to accept a similar post of duty, but none of whom were jealous of Jack on account of the promotion. The boy, however, did not really take in the situation as actually true until he had reported at the headquarters of the brigade and asked Colonel Bowman in person whether it was all a dream, or whether he was actually to consider himself on detached service as an aid-de-camp. The colonel laughed at the boy, shook his hand heartily, and said:

"Lieutenant Jack Sanderson, you are really to serve on my staff. I expect you to show yourself a quick, alert, helpful officer in this position. I will trust you and lean on you as long as you prove trustworthy. We are going to have another big battle one of these days, and I want you near me when it comes off. Now you are at liberty to go to the brigade quartermaster with this requisition and pick out a horse for yourself and have him duly equipped for actual service. You may move your personal baggage down into this adjoining tent and adapt yourself speedily to the new situation."

The boy made a military salute, and, feeling very proud and wondering what sort of a record he would make in his new position, went forth to assume the duties of an aid-de-camp.

Let us follow him and get a glimpse of the brigade. It is made up of three veteran regiments—the Eighty-fourth Pennsylvania, now commanded by Lieutenant Colonel Milton Opp, one of the manliest and most gifted young men in the service, slain a year later in the wilderness; the One Hundred and Tenth Pennsylvania, with the gallant Colonel Crowther at its head (these two regiments having been like twins from the date of their entrance into service); and the Twelfth New Hampshire, commanded by Colonel J. H. Potter, a modest, brave, experienced officer, a West Point graduate, who had seen years of active campaigning in Mexico and on the frontier before the opening of the civil war. This latter command was fuller than the two older regiments, which had been longer in service and had been greatly reduced by the accidents of battle and by sickness. Here then we find Pennsylvania and New Hampshire striving together for the supremacy of the Union.

The quartermaster of the brigade, to whom Jack now directed his steps, had charge of the wagons, the animals, and, in general, the clothing and transportation of the command. Near him was the brigade commissary of subsistence, whose office it was to provide victuals for the men. In camp he had for them plenty of fresh bread, supplied by the brigade bakery, fresh beef, potatoes, and other vegetables; while for the march he shut down his supplies until they included only hard-tack, salt pork, coffee, sugar, and other matters of that kind which could be packed away in small compass and which were not liable to spoil on the way. This officer also gave his name to a stimulating fluid which was in almost universal use in the army, which body was by no means a temperance society, although there were good and stanch men in it who went through service without tasting liquor of any kind. Nevertheless the use of whisky was so common that the officer who kept it for issue, and who was permitted by the rules of the army to sell it as well as other provisions and articles in his custody to officers at actual cost, by common consent gave his own title to the beverage in question; and so for four years whisky was called by everybody in the army nothing but "commissary." "Fill my canteen with commissary," was the order for whisky.

Among the good things that General Hooker did after he took command of the army was to reorganize this commissary department, so that the boys were fed better than ever before. On more than one occasion he gave orders that the private supplies of some of his generals should be halted until the wagons containing rations for the men were allowed to get through the muddy roads. In answer to the remonstrances that reached his ear he replied, "My men shall be fed before I am fed, and before any of my officers are fed." "Fighting Joe Hooker" knew how to win the hearts of his men to him—by filling their stomachs with food, by granting them furloughs, by keeping them down to work in multitudinous drills, reviews, and dress parades, and by other wise devices, by which the army was kept busy, contented, and inspired at the same time with new hope and courage. Its old sores were healed, its former defeats forgotten, its malcontents rooted out of place, and its former vigor and ambitious ardor were restored.

A visit of Colonel Bowman and his military family to the headquarters of General Whipple, who commanded the division, and to

THEY SET OUT TO MAKE THEIR CALLS OF CEREMONY ON THEIR GENERALS.

the corps headquarters, where Major General Sickles was in command, was a pleasant thing for the new members of the staff. The colonel and his half dozen staff officers, including Jack, put on their best uniforms, had their horses groomed with extra care, their belt plates and swords polished until they looked like so many mirrors; and thus completely accoutered they set out to make their calls of ceremony on their generals. General Whipple, a modest, cultivated gentleman, a West Pointer, greeted the party with cordiality, introduced his staff, and then bade them good-bye as they rode off again toward General Sickles's headquarters, a mile or two away. Here everything was on a high scale of display. Gayly decorated officers in fancy Zouave uniforms, an imposing array of orderlies and staff officers, elegantly ordered appurtenances, all betokened that the headquarters mess did not live on overmeager fare. General Sickles himself was a man whose appearance is best described by that overworked adjective "dashing;" he wore a military mustache and goatee, had a sharp, quick eye, and was a man of personal daring. His political and social history had given a considerable sprinkling of the romantic to his history; and thus far during the war he had shown himself, while ambitious, at the same time a capable, resolute, and enthusiastic leader, possessing a good deal of personal magnetism and somewhat of dare-devil recklessness. He was vivacious and sprightly in his greetings; and the room where he received his visitors was quite full of all grades of officers, among whom were several brigadier generals, with their stars shining on their shoulders. The boy, standing for the first time in his life in the midst of an assemblage of such dignitaries, felt his head in a whirl, and seemed to be in a vision, overwhelmed with awe at the sight of so many officers of high degree. At the close of their visit General Sickles tapped his bell, and a colored servant appeared with decanters and glasses for those who would take liquor; those who drank paid their respects to their host, and then all took their departure. It was quite an event for the new staff officers to see and talk with two live generals all in one day!

It was not long after this that the boy saw the cavalry corps start out on an expedition across the Rappahannock. This, everyone said, meant an onward movement. It so happened that about the time they crossed the river a terrific storm came on, which turned all the streams into swollen and foaming torrents, and thus hindered any coöperation on the part of the rest of the army. As soon, however, as the storm passed away the men felt that a forward movement was near at hand, and even before the orders came they began to prepare for it.

One night a group sat at the bivouac fire, where all manner of fun had been transacted. Comrades had been smoking their pipes, telling yarns, reading the latest papers from home, gossiping over the news that had come from abroad that France and England were making threats of recognizing the Confederacy, and singing "John Brown's body lies moldering in the grave." Finally, just before tattoo sounded, an officer said:

"Boys, we are going to have another battle in a few days."

"Why," said one of the officers, "captain, how do you know? Have any orders come yet to move?"..

"No," was the reply; "we have no orders yet, but this fine weather makes an advance inevitable. Hooker is not going to fool away any more time with grand reviews, parades, and all that. The roads are dry, the river is low enough to cross, either by fording or on pontoon bridges, and you might as well keep your knapsacks within reach, for one of these fine mornings you will be roused in a hurry."

"All right," said the other, "let the orders come; the sooner the better for our cause. Let us whip the rebels this time, and then go home. O, that will be a glad hour when we have peace once more and I can see 'the girl I left behind me!'"

Some one struck up in rousing notes at this juncture, "When Johnny comes marching home again;" and scores of voices joining the refrain made the welkin ring with the stirring music.

Before the song was over Adjutant Mather stood before them, his face serious, and a paper in his hand.

"Boys," he said, "we march at five to-morrow morning. Five days' rations, men in light marching order, sixty rounds of ammunition, and no headquarters baggage wagon."

"Hurrah!" shouted the boys; "that means business. We will whip them this time. Joe Hooker is our leader, and we will follow him on to Richmond!"

The group soon separated, and for an hour all were busy in the camp packing knapsacks and haversacks and putting things in order for the march. Then, the bands on every hillside playing patriotic airs, "the watch-fires of a hundred circling camps" sending strange lights and fantastic shadows across the fields and through the streets of tents, came tattoo, with its penetrating strains, and now and then before "taps" a song, a laugh, a shout, or perhaps the tones of a hymn; and at last the great army settled down to take its rest before it started out to grapple again with its deadly foe among the thickets of Chancellorsville.

CHAPTER XIII.

THE THICKETS OF CHANCELLORSVILLE.

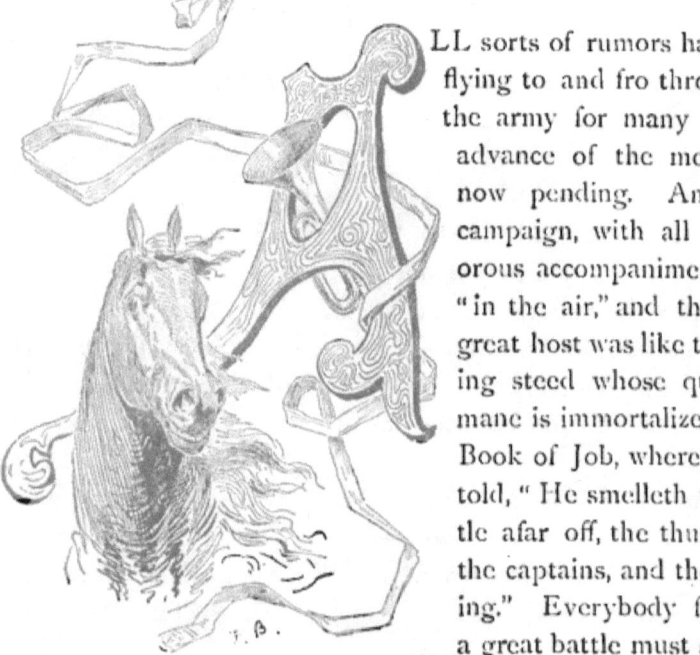

ALL sorts of rumors had been flying to and fro throughout the army for many days in advance of the movement now pending. An active campaign, with all its vigorous accompaniments, was "in the air," and the whole great host was like the pawing steed whose quivering mane is immortalized in the Book of Job, where we are told, " He smelleth the battle afar off, the thunder of the captains, and the shouting." Everybody felt that a great battle must soon be fought; that the now opened and settled spring weather brought with it the necessity for another movement " on to Richmond." The troops had been so thoroughly reinvigorated, disciplined, drilled, and heartened by their winter reviews, recruitments, and rest that they were at last eager for the encounter and in magnificent fighting condition. With a dashing leader at their head, with skilled and courageous generals marshaling the subordinate commands, accoutered completely with the best equipments that Uncle Sam's treasury, overflowing with greenbacks, could provide, the Army of the Potomac heard with quickened pulse and flashing eye the command issued in the closing days of April, 1863, " Forward across the Rappahannock!"

The Third Corps, in the movement which resulted in the battle of Chancellorsville, was held in reserve during the first two or three days of the campaign, marching first down the river, as though it was to join the troops which were making a feint against the right flank of General Lee to the east of Fredericksburg. If we join the bivouac of the Eighty-fourth Pennsylvania and listen to the boys as they retail the flying rumors of the moving camps we may the better appreciate the situation. Men all day long have been marching eastward, and then, behind the hills, have faced about and countermarched to the west again, while camp-fires have been built in all directions along the bank of the river in the neighborhood of the pontoon bridges which have been laid. It is clear that General Hooker wants the rebels to believe that he is going to cross in force to the east of the town, but the shifting and hurrying troops which march in the other direction under cover of the hills tell that the real stroke is to descend in some other place.

The coffee has been made, the fires are lighted, the shelter tents are fixed for the night, and the boys have an hour for gossip before the sound of tattoo. Let us listen to their conversation.

"Captain," says one sturdy soldier, carving a beef-bone into a scarf-pin or other ornament to send home, "what's the news? What does this all mean? Where are we going to cross? When is the fun going to commence?"

"Well, Tom," was the reply, "you will have to ask General Hooker, if you want all your questions answered satisfactorily.

He knows all about it, I suppose, and we will be wiser inside of a week than we are now. One thing I heard to-day, however, that is of interest. Stoneman's cavalry has been waiting for two weeks at the fords up the river to get a chance to cross over and make an attack on the rear of the rebels. The waters have been so high that they could not cross till yesterday; some of them ventured over before the rains last week and were overtaken by the floods, and could hardly return; they barely got back again. Now they are all on the other side of the river, and by this time they have wakened up Fitz-Hugh Lee and Jeb Stuart, and between those dashing fellows on that side, and Pleasonton, Gregg, Kilpatrick, and Buford on ours, there will be some

'Racing and chasing on Cannobie Lee.'"

A staff officer, Captain Fribley, the acting assistant adjutant general of the brigade, who had just then come up from Colonel Bowman's headquarters, was at once beset for information. Giving his military mustache a characteristic twist, he said:

"Boys, the musical part of this performance will be up the river. We march in that direction at sunrise. Most of the army is there already, and the maneuvers have been so skillfully conducted that our men have crossed over on the pontoons at the United States Ford, and at the other fords above that, without firing a shot or losing a man, except in some brilliant cavalry skirmishes. All this parade down here on our left, below Fredericksburg, is a little bit of military fuss and feathers. We have made a crossing here and thrown up some works to protect our pontoons, but we are not going to make any direct attack here just now. The heavy business will be off to the right, on the left flank of the Confederates. Thither we march in the morning."

The announcement was greeted with hearty cheers, which

spread from camp-fire to camp-fire, and from tent to tent, until the sky was full of glad echoes, the resounding exultations of the eager and expectant soldiers, who were anxious to strike an effective blow for the flag, and who rejoiced that the preliminary movements had been so remarkably successful.

On Thursday, April 30, the Third Corps, under Sickles, marched up the river to join the troops which had already made a successful crossing into rebeldom. They rested near the United States Ford that night, and early next morning crossed on the pontoon bridge and marched into the woods and in the direction of Chancellorsville. On the way they halted for a while, and the following order was read to them from General Hooker:

"HEADQUARTERS ARMY OF THE POTOMAC, *April* 30, 1863.

"*General Orders, No.* 47.

"It is with heartfelt satisfaction that the commanding general announces to the army that the operations of the last three days have determined that our enemy must ingloriously fly or come out from behind his defenses and give us battle on our own ground, where certain destruction awaits him.

"By order of MAJOR GENERAL JOSEPH HOOKER.

"S. WILLIAMS,
    "Assistant Adjutant General."

The enthusiasm with which this ringing and exultant proclamation was received by the troops cannot well be described. The woods resounded with the cheers of the various regiments as they heard the jubilant words of their sanguine commander repeated far and wide. Soon after the order was read General Hooker himself rode down the road on his splendid white horse, attended by brilliantly dressed staff officers, and again the cheers ascended to greet him. He lifted his hat, bowed, smiled, and addressed a word of hearty cheer to those nearest him. It was clearly to be seen that he was in "high feather," and expected to make short, quick, skillful work in the battle which had already opened, as the cannonade and musketry in various directions now showed. A staff officer, who had talked with General Hooker, stopped at brigade headquarters and said to Colonel Bowman: "General Hooker is in a gleeful and exultant mood. He thinks he owns the Confederacy, and has a mortgage on the whole of Lee's army, and he is going to foreclose and claim his own property. He said in my hearing, 'I have the rebellion in my breeches pocket, and God Almighty himself cannot take it away from me.'"

This remark sent a cold chill into the hearts of some of the listeners. Brave as they were, and profane as some of them had been, this boastful utterance of General Hooker made them shake their heads in doubt and brought an ominous look of foreboding and alarm to their faces. One officer said:

"I do not like that sort of talk on the eve of a battle. There is no sense in defying the Almighty while you are fighting General Lee. I think General Hooker's face is too red. If he carries his canteen with him on this campaign we will be in a sorry fix before its close."

Bowman's brigade bivouacked in the woods that afternoon, in sight of the line of battle in the distant thickets, where a struggle had been going on all day between the front lines on either side. It was trying to one's nerves to sit still under such circumstances, once in a while a shell hurtling among the trees and exploding in the air or on the ground, now and then a bullet whistling close to the ear or striking a limb above the heads of the troops, who were holding themselves in readiness to march out to the edge of the battle at a moment's warning. The thickets were dense, the undergrowth was rank, and only at rare intervals was a road to be found penetrating the wilderness. When the brigade to which Jack belonged arrived they found the troops already on the field, scattered in the midst of this thorny, tangled, impenetrable forest, where it was impossible to see five rods into the jungle, and where maneuvering, in any proper sense of that word, was impossible. What the outcome of this situation might be no one could dream.

Friday night, May 1, passed away without the brigade whose fortunes we are following being called into action. The boys woke early next morning and found an ominous silence pervading the lines of battle. "What was up? Were the rebels retreating? Were they getting ready for an attack? What would the day bring forth?" These were the questions which rose to the lip as the boys made their coffee, toasted a bit of pork on the end of a stick, and broke off a bite of hard-tack wherewith to attemper their morning meal.

It was about nine o'clock that the sound of a cannon was heard in the woods off to the south of where brigade headquarters were temporarily established, and then came a few musket shots, and then a stray shell or two harmlessly bursting in the air. Then came galloping by, later in the morning, a scout with news that electrified everybody. "Hurrah!" he shouted, "the rebels are in full retreat; we can see their wagon train in the distance moving off toward Gordonsville. We are sure of victory now. That's what General Hooker said, they 'must ingloriously retreat.' Hurrah!" And off he rode with the good news. Soon General Sickles came dashing by on his horse with several staff officers. Stopping to say a word with Colonel Bowman, the brigade commander, it was ascertained that he was sure that the rebels were retreating and that the Third Corps were to follow up and press their rear. The First Division, commanded by Birney, marched out and deployed in the open fields.

and then in a few moments they disappeared in the forest. It was not long until word came for Berry's Second Division and Whipple's Third Division—to which Jack's brigade belonged—to "fall in" and follow through the woods after the rebels, who were supposed to be in full retreat. The boys thought, as they obeyed orders and formed line and began the march into the woods, "We have the Confederates now in a trap. They are 'skedaddling,' sure enough. All that we need to do is to press them with earnestness, and we will bag 'em every one. This is the end of the rebellion. We have the Johnnies on the run, and we will keep them there until they are caught!" And with this gleeful confidence of a sure and speedy victory the brigade deployed into the edge of the woods.

They had gone but a few paces when Colonel Bowman said to his staff, "We must dismount and send our horses to the rear; the undergrowth is too thick for anyone to ride through it." The officers were very willing to dismount by this time, for the thorny branches had been catching their hats and scratching their faces, and the animals were, accordingly, sent back to the rear in charge of the orderlies, who were glad enough to escape from the perilous edge of battle in that way.

Then came a scramble on foot through the thicket. It was the same region in which the awful "Wilderness" battles occurred under Grant a year later, a tangled, dense, almost impervious forest of vines, brambles, thornbushes, and scrub oaks, without a path or an opening except two or three roads that branched in various directions from the region of the Chancellor House, where Hooker's headquarters had been established. Into this jungle the troops marched with high hopes, and soon they were lost to sight even of each other. No line could be maintained in such a thicket; in fact, nobody could see more than a few yards ahead or to either side of him.

"Hurrah, boys!" shouted Captain Fribley; "now I understand that old bit of rhyme from Mother Goose:

> 'There was a man in our town
> Who was so wondrous wise
> He jumped into a bramble bush
> And scratched out both his eyes.'

Here is the spot, surely, where he did the deed, and we are pretty sure to imitate his heroic example unless we are very careful!"

Bending down to the earth, crawling under the scrub oaks, jumping over the tangled masses of vines, the men slowly made their way through the dense and howling wilderness. Now they came to a creek with steep banks, winding sluggishly through the jungle. Just here the bullets of the enemy began to whistle.

"HALLOO, MAJOR, HAVE YOU NOT LOST YOUR ALIGNMENT?"

"Steady, men; guide right; keep up your alignment!" shouted Major Zinn, of the Eighty-fourth, as he swung himself down the bank and nearly lost his footing in the creek below, barely able to save himself a ducking by clinging to a grapevine that grew close to the edge of the water.

"Halloo, major," replied Jack, as he followed down the steep and slippery bank, "have you not lost your alignment, or your balance, or something?"

Just then a shell exploded in the air, and the pieces dropped miscellaneously here and there in an unpleasant manner; and a battery farther to the front, in the direction in which the boys were pressing their way through the thicket, replied, while word was passed down the line: "The rebels are abandoning their wagon train and are in full retreat! We are shelling their rear now! Press on!"

This was good news, and forward the boys urged their way, until they had gone perhaps two miles into the undergrowth, with torn clothes, scratched and bleeding hands and faces, and now and then a wound, but with no enemy in sight. Farther on the men confidently expected to find the rebels in the shape of a rear guard. One charge on that, and the battle, it seemed, would be over. In fulfillment of this expectation news came from the front, where Sickles was pressing forward: "Lee's army is retreating. We have shelled their wagon train and scattered their rear guard and taken five hundred prisoners! Victory is before us; hurrah, boys, press on!" And with each dispatch of that kind that reached the lines in the woods the boys shouted with excitement and enthusiasm and strove with greater eagerness to scramble through the thorn bushes and get out into the clearing beyond, if there was any to be found.

By this time the afternoon was waning away, and the troops were halted in the forest to re-form their lines. It was about five o'clock; the enemy had disappeared, and Sickles was wondering what had become of him. His trains had vanished; his rear

THE THICKETS OF CHANCELLORSVILLE. 227

guard had gone; perhaps he was trying to draw our men out a little farther, in order to get them into an ambush. Suddenly, in the rear of the line, back in the direction of Chancellorsville, two miles or so behind the men of the Third Corps, like a thunderstorm bursting without warning from the azure depths of a summer sky, came rattling volleys of musketry, with the booming of cannon and the sound of distant yells. Every heart stopped beating for one dreadful moment. What did this mean? Sickles and all under him supposed the rebels in full retreat southward, when, all at once, they were astounded and alarmed with the indications of a severe engagement which had burst forth in their rear, where the Union lines, taken by surprise, had given way, the Confederates having made an overwhelming attack upon Hooker's right flank, where no preparations had been made to repulse them!

Immediately the lines were faced about, and back through the forest the Third Corps pressed its way toward the point it had left at noon, the battle growing more frightful in all its dreadful omens as they neared the field. News came to Sickles as he galloped down the road: "Jackson's corps has made a flank attack, has broken in the whole Eleventh Corps, has captured our rifle pits, and is pressing on to our center. The whole army is in imminent danger, and your own corps is almost surrounded. Multitudes are flying from the field in panic and dismay. Bring back your corps at once, or you will be cut off from the rest of the army!"

And, as the words were spoken, the noise of the struggle to the northward of the Third Corps became still more terrible. Stonewall Jackson, the great and intrepid fighter, all day long had been silently leading twenty thousand men around the Union army through the forest, with the intention of falling upon its right flank, Howard's Eleventh Corps, where no attack had been deemed possible. He had formed his men in line, and at about five o'clock had led them in an irresistible onset against the unprotected Union line, taking it by surprise, on the flank, from a direction in which no one had expected danger to lodge. Thousands had been stricken with dismay; pack-mules, wagon trains, and artillery had been mingled in a dreadful plight of entanglement and disaster, and for an hour it appeared as though the army would be panic-stricken throughout and driven in utter confusion to the fords of the Rappahannock.

It was during this awful period of impending ruin that General Pleasonton, with his artillery and cavalry, stemmed the tide of defeat. Galloping to the front at the first sound of danger, he saw ten thousand men charging in magnificent line against the right flank, a great on-coming wave of bayonets sweeping down the road, which led directly to Hooker's headquarters and the center of the Union line. If they capture the hill on which our guns are posted all is lost. Something must be done to gain time and save the day; something must be done to afford opportunity to post the cannon and give a chance to load. Close by stood brave Major Keenan, with four hundred Pennsylvania cavalrymen. "Charge that advancing line with your men; do what you can to stem the tide till I can plant these guns and fire a volley of grape into the face of the enemy." The gallant young officer, well knowing that he was about to gallop to certain death, made a military salute, and replied, " I will do it, general," and put spurs to his horse, cried. "Forward, charge!" and, leading his gallant men, swept down the road, four hundred mounted men in the teeth of ten thousand bayonets. Sabers crossed bayonets, horse and rider tumbled to the earth in the close encounter; but the impetuous shock of the heroic cavalry charge could not be withstood, and the onset of the rebels was checked for a few moments, while Pleasonton planted his

"FORWARD, CHARGE!"

twenty guns on the hill and gave command to his artillerists to fire. Their grape swept the road in the front, and by this time much of the panic had been stayed, and a line of infantry had been formed which sufficed to man the breastworks and afford defense to the endangered line.

While this was in execution the Third Corps was urging its way back through the woods, not knowing what was going to occur or whether it would be able to rejoin the rest of the army or not, the sounds of the battle becoming more frightful and appalling as the troops drew nearer to the scene. The night put an end for a while to the engagement; but about midnight Sickles ordered another attack, finding that the rebels occupied a part of the line which it was of urgent importance for him to regain. For an hour the darkness of the forest was lighted up with the glare of musketry and flaming explosions from the cannon, and made to echo with the fierce yells of the two armies. Sickles's experiment was a success, and after an hour of battle the tumult subsided, and, exhausted, anxious, and terror-stricken, the soldiers sought respite in sleep. Wounded men groaned here and there in the underbrush, surgeons went to work to relieve their distress, nurses and hospital stewards cared for all who could be reached, but multitudes lay bleeding and dying between the lines where no help could be afforded them. Among the wounded on the Confederate side was Stonewall Jackson himself, who in the nighttime, between the lines, reconnoitering, was mistaken along with his staff and his array of orderlies for a party of Union cavalry and fired upon by his own watchful men. His wounds proved to be fatal, and he was taken to the rear, and thence to Richmond, where, a few days after the battle, his heroic spirit passed into eternity. What he might have done next day, if his life had been spared, no one can tell. He was Lee's right hand, and that great commander was maimed and crippled from this irreparable loss throughout his after course. Stonewall Jackson, the Cromwell of the Confederacy, ended his military career in the infliction of the most terrific blow he had yet aimed at the Union cause, when he incurred his death wounds at Chancellorsville.

Meanwhile everyone wondered, "What shall be on the morrow? How shall we get out of this wilderness? Who will lead off in the attack in the morning? What will be the issues of the fight? How about the inglorious flight of the rebels which Hooker so sanguinely foretold? Are we to repeat the experience of Fredericksburg, and march back again to the other side of the river, whipped again?" With these inquiries and forebodings the Union army lay on its arms to get a few hours of sleep before the further battle on the morrow.

CHAPTER XIV.

A BATTLE SUNDAY IN THE WILDERNESS.

AFTER the exciting and exhausting experiences of the dreadful day and the fearful night just glimpsed, the fight continuing at intervals until after midnight, Jack tied his horse, and, giving him a munch of hay and a bite of grain, wandered a few paces to one side under a tree and dropped off to sleep. He did not know in the darkness that he had strayed aloof from brigade headquarters, and so utterly exhausted was he that the sounds of picket firing in the early morning did not rouse him. He still slumbered on, and would have wakened a prisoner had it not been for the friendly service of a fellow-officer on staff duty, Lieutenant Norton, who, after diligent search, shook him roughly and shouted in his ears, "Lieutenant Sanderson, wake up; Colonel Bowman wants you at once. The fight has opened; the brigade is in line of battle; the pickets have begun firing; we may have to retreat from this point in a little while. Wake up, and get your horse and yourself out of this!"

The boy could hardly rouse himself out of the stupor of complete exhaustion into which he had fallen even with these goading words sounding in his ears; and it needed another shake from his mentor's hand to effectually bring him to a sense of the situation.

"Wake up, Jack, the bugles are sounding the 'assembly.' We have no time even for coffee. Get up and saddle your pony, or you may be captured. Yonder is the brigade in line, and the rebels are in strong force in our front. Quick, or it will be too late."

At last Jack was awake. He jumped to his feet, shook his clothing to get rid of dirt and leaves, threw the saddle and bridle on his horse, and, speedily mounting, hurriedly galloped to the point in the field below, not far away, where he saw the brigade headquarters flag, at which point now was his post of duty as an aid-de-camp. The battle now, apparently, was to be, not in the thicket, as the day before, but in an open space, where officers on staff duty could use their horses.

"Well, my boy," said Colonel Bowman, with a mixture of satire and humor in his voice and manner, "I hope you have had a good night's rest and are awake for all day. You will need now all your waking faculties on the alert. We are going to have a battle Sunday. Yonder in our front the Twelfth New Hampshire is already hotly engaged under its brave commander, Colonel Potter. Off to our left you see our men hurrying forth, and here to our right is a battery wheeling into line. You would feel better, probably, if you had breakfast, but we have no time for that this morning. We are up now for all day, and the fight has begun, as you see."

Jack looked about him unnerved and in some trepidation.

In every direction were the increasing sounds of tumultuous battle—aids galloping over the hills, batteries hastening into position, infantry marching to and fro in the woods in front, and off toward the left the continuous rattle of a hot musketry engagement. The boy began to soliloquize:

"I wish I had a cup of coffee or something to steady my stomach. If I had a bite of cold pork and hard-tack it would help me out. My hand trembles and my knees are shaky. I do not like a battle anyway, and to go into one before breakfast and without a cup of coffee is trying to weak nerves. The battle in front grows hotter and hotter, and in a little while we must march up into that front line in the woods and face that awful cannonade and that sweeping musketry fire!"

As the boy thus spoke under his breath, in a shiver of dismay, he saw a stream of wounded men coming out of the woods and rushing to the rear, many of them barely able to walk, and all anxious to find the hospital. His unstrung nerves became still more shaky at the sight, which emphasized the thronging perils of the hour, and he continued his self-cogitations:

"Must we move forward into that slaughter-pen? Have we pluck for the trial when it comes? I am all in a tremble, and my horse shivers with fear, as though he understood also the terrible danger. How long must we stand here in silence and take the fire of the rebels in the second line, bullets flying, shells exploding, men falling, and no chance to give a blow in return?"

Just then, to his alarm and dismay, he saw the troops to the left of Bowman's brigade driven from their rifle pits and their low line of earthworks, behind which they had been firing at the rebels. The Confederates had been enfilading the Union line, and the fire had been so hot as to drive our men out. It was a perilous hour. The retreating men left a gap in the Union line which was about to be occupied by the advancing Confederates, whose threatening line showed, eager and desperate, in the fringe of woods beyond. It was an hour on which much depended. The boy wondered for a moment if all was not lost, and whether the disaster was not irremediable, and then glancing at the brigade commander, Colonel Bowman, he was reassured. No sign of fear was visible there. His eye flashing with contagious fire, his sword waving high in air, his voice sounding like a trumpet, he sent the inspiration of his own courageous example into the whole brigade as he shouted, " Eighty-fourth Pennsylvania, left, face! Forward into the breastworks! Double quick, march!"

With the command came new life for Jack. Till that hour he had been in danger of a panic, now he felt his face flame and his blood boil and his soul all astir. Putting his spurs to his horse he rode eagerly on toward the vacated position, which the regiment, urged by the example of its brigade commander and incited by the heroic conduct of Colonel Opp and Major Zinn, was hurrying to seize. There was a race for a few moments between some of the advancing rebels and the Eighty-fourth to see who would get there first. Some of the Confederates, in their rashness, pushed a little too far ahead of their comrades to escape from the clutches of our own advancing troops, and before they could turn back and retrace their steps they fell into the hands of the hurrahing regiment, which was now safely ensconced behind the barricade that had been hastily thrown up the day before along the foot of a short ravine, constructed of fence-rails, saplings, and other material of that kind, and covered with a thin scum of earth. Light as it was, it afforded shelter and a chance to defend the Union line of battle, and thus sufficed for the time being. The Eighty-fourth was followed closely by the intrepid One Hundred and Tenth, under Colonel Crowther, with exultant shouts; and these two regiments, hav-

A BATTLE SUNDAY IN THE WILDERNESS. 237

ing secured their post, were at once engaged with the enemy in front and off to the flank, the earthworks soon becoming a very hot place for its occupants. Jack, in glancing about him, saw some rods away to the rear one of the men, who had dropped behind a stump on his way to the front, and there he was lying

"DO NOT SKULK HERE."

panic-stricken, pallid, cowering with fear. The boy remembered the panic which had but lately passed like a thundergust over his own soul, and rode back to the spot, which was, indeed, more exposed to the rebel fire than the earthworks below at the foot of the hill, and spoke to the shivering soldier: "Do not skulk here.

Hurry up and join your company. This will be a bad record to make if you stay here." As he spoke both of them afforded a good mark for the rebels on the other side of the ravine, and the bullets began to whistle about their heads and to strike the stump behind which the man was seeking to hide.

"Hurry up and get to your post!" shouted the boy. "You are in greater danger here than you would be with your company down there."

Thus encouraged, the man rose and made a break for his post, and there did valiant service for the hour, which was to be fraught with momentous issues for the whole command.

Still the bullets showered on the hillside and descended into the vale, and in all directions the struggle became desperate. Stonewall Jackson's men, now in command of the valiant Jeb Stuart, were making heroic attempts to drive in the Union right flank, against which they had directed their awful charge the evening before.

Looking off to the left of the position, in the woods across the little valley, the boy saw something moving. Peering intently in that direction with keener gaze, he thought he saw a suspicious movement among the forest trees and in the underbrush. Turning to Lieutenant Norton, of the staff, he said, "Lend me your glass. I believe the rebels are moving to our left through the woods yonder." Taking the field glass, and steadying himself for a moment, and trying to keep his restless horse, agitated by the terrific sounds of the battle, quiet for a moment, Jack was horrified to find, by means of the telescope in his hand, that the woods at which he was looking were crowded with troops in gray and brown, moving by the flank, in a direction which would insure from their guns an enfilading fire on the position which the brigade had but lately assumed. Colonel Bowman was not far away, and to him in great excitement Jack shouted: "Colonel, we are being flanked. The rebels are crossing through the woods yonder in heavy force. You can see them now in the edge of the underbrush. If they get around to our left we will be taken in front and on flank, and may be surrounded."

The brigade commander looked in that direction, and instantly replied: "Jack, ride with all speed to General Whipple's headquarters, yonder where the battery on the hill is stationed, and tell him of this movement. We will be flanked unless that matter is checked."

Jack needed only a word, for he saw the danger that threatened the troops, and digging his spurs into the flank of his horse he galloped across the field, now swept with bullets and covered with smoke, to the place where General Whipple and General Sickles were stationed. Dashing up to one of the staff officers there, he saluted and shouted: "Captain Dalton, the rebels are moving by the flank right across our front yonder through the woods. They are there in heavy force, and unless they are stopped the men who are in the trenches yonder will be flanked."

The officers looked in the direction indicated, and then quickly turned to the battery commander, after a word with General Whipple, and ordered some shells sent into the edge of the forest where the movement was being carried on under shelter of the trees and underbrush.

Even from division headquarters the movement of troops could be discerned in the distance. One shell after another was fired into the forest, and the movement seemed to be arrested, when Jack galloped back to his post. As it turned out afterward, the Confederates did not stop in their course, but simply veered off into the woods to escape observation, and in half an hour more accomplished the purpose which they had been keeping in mind and which had been foreseen by those who discovered the movement. Jack, returning to the advanced line, found that brisk fighting had been going on, as the cheering, the rattling and heavy musketry fire, and the clouds of smoke all indicated. On arrival he found that two Southern battle flags and a dozen prisoners had been captured by the regiment. Colonel Bowman said to the boy: "Take an orderly and present this captured flag and these prisoners to the division provost marshal with the compliments of our brigade, and then join us again."

Jack was quite proud to be the bearer of this message and to have charge of such an embassage and such a trophy, and proceeded with all haste to carry out his orders. In order to escape the terrific fire of shell and grape that was now sweeping the plain from the rebel guns the little party took to the woods and proceeded under the cover of the trees to the place appointed in advance as the rendezvous for prisoners and for trophies of the battle. Even in the woods, however, the effects of the firing were dreadful, limbs falling to the earth, cut to pieces by cannon balls and in some cases by bullets, shells dropping here and there and exploding as they fell, and the earth quaking and the air resounding from the frightful concussions of the battle, which was plainly getting more fierce every instant. The faces of the prisoners, weary, pallid, haggard, affrighted, as they pressed on under guard, and hurried to get away from the bloody scene, glad to get out of the battle, even as prisoners of war, made an impression on the boy's memory that time has not yet effaced. Now the captured flag caught in the undergrowth and had to be extricated, and now a battery hurrying into position stopped up the path, and anon a wounded horse, with a leg cut off by a cannon ball, was hobbling off in agony to die, while hundreds of bleeding men on foot or on stretchers were hurrying to the rear or being borne off to the hospital.

Arriving at the edge of the woods and looking back, the boy saw a terrific picture of tumult and slaughter. While clouds of smoke covered the scene, yet here and there the curtain lifted and disclosed the Union lines in imminent danger. The attack on them was being pressed with desperate vigor. Jeb Stuart was clearly doing his utmost to show that he was equal to the emergency created by the departure of Jackson from the field. Before Jack could deliver up his prisoners and the captured flag and return to the brigade the advanced line occupied by it had been forced back. The rebels had made their flank movement, had driven in a portion of the Twelfth Corps, and had come in upon the very rear of the gallant Eighty-fourth and the One Hundred and Tenth. While the boys were occupied with the force in their front they were amazed to find themselves suddenly attacked on the left flank and in the rear, and looking around they heard a hundred voices shout, "Surrender, lay down your arms; you are prisoners."

The companies farthest from the Union lines in the angle of the fortifications had nothing else to do but surrender, and they did so in indignation and wrath, some of the bravest of them, however, refusing to yield, and being shot down at their post.

Others, nearer the Union line, clubbed their muskets, made a desperate resistance, and with wounds, and by the skin of their teeth, fled from the captured trenches and escaped into the retreating ranks.

Meanwhile Jack was cut off from his command. He had delivered up his prisoners, had handed over the flag, and was now free to return to his post. Where was it? The command had been driven out of their intrenchments. To attempt to return thither was to rush into the jaws of certain death. What position had the corps now taken?

Suddenly, in his bewilderment, in the crowd of rushing troops and amid the wheeling batteries and the galloping staff officers, he discerned a familiar face, that of Captain Fribley, the assistant adjutant general of the brigade. "Captain," Jack shouted, "where is the command? Where are you going? How can we get back to the boys?"

The captain, with features that could hardly be maintained in composure amid the fluctuating emotions that overran them, at first could not speak; then with effort he replied:

"Well, boy, you barely got out of the worst snap you were ever in. That batch of prisoners and that flag saved your life. Just after you left for division headquarters the fire became hotter than I ever saw it before. The Confederates that you saw moving around to our left poured in an awful shower of bullets on our line, taking us with a raking fire which enfiladed our ranks, but we stood it like men. At last Colonel Bowman sent me to say to General Sickles that we must have help or we could not hold that post. I had barely delivered the message when, looking back, I saw our boys almost surrounded. I hurried toward them, but it was too late for any help to be given. Captain Peterman was shot in the head, Lieutenant Jackson was taken prisoner, and maybe two hundred others are dead, wounded, or in the hands of the rebels. I galloped over here to the headquarters of General Hooker to see if reinforcements for the Third Corps could be had, but I found that General Hooker was knocked senseless by a falling pillar of the Chancellor House, and his staff are in bewilderment and no one knows what to do. Two or three other army corps are lying about in the woods without firing a gun, and Sickles has to bear the brunt of the whole morning engagement."

"HOW CAN WE GET BACK TO THE BOYS?"

Jack listened with pallid face to this sad story and gulped back a tear as he thought of his comrades whom he had left a half hour before, now dead, wounded, or in the hands of the rebels and doomed to captivity in Southern prisons.

"How about Colonel Opp, and Major Zinn, and Colonel Bowman, and Adjutant Mather?"

"They are safe, and we will find them by and by, I reckon; where the new line of battle is I am sure I cannot tell, but we will search for it."

And on through the thicket, shunning the open field which was still swept with a murderous fire from the rebel guns, the two picked their way to the front. Soon they came to an open space that was clearly too dangerous to be crossed without urgent reason, and they halted in doubt.

"Jack," said Captain Fribley, "we cannot get over this field now, and I am going to have a bit to eat while we are detained. Here is a bale of hay for our horses, and we can make a cup of coffee in ten minutes, and by that time this disorder may be checked and we may be able to find our brigade. The whole line is on the retreat now, and it will be some time before they can be placed in proper position."

With the words the two dismounted in the edge of the woods, gave their exhausted horses a bite of hay, and proceeded to prepare a meager meal for themselves. The day was scorchingly hot, the woods were full of suffocating smoke from the battle, and the tension of their nerves had been since dawn strained to the utmost limit of endurance. They felt as though they must have a bit of nourishment or drop in exhaustion. The coffee was hardly made before signs of increasing danger, and of disorder among the troops, were seen to be multiplying. The army was being forced back from the hill occupied by Sickles and Howard the night before; how far they would be driven was now a question.

246 WHAT A BOY SAW IN THE ARMY.

The boy, in his anxiety, exclaimed: "Captain Fribley, don't you think the whole line may be forced back? Is there any danger of our men being driven back to the river? This looks like such a movement."

"O no, boy!" was the reassuring response of the captain;

THEY PROCEEDED TO PREPARE A MEAGER MEAL.

"never fear, we will get out of this all right. Hooker has enough men to whip Lee if he will only use them. That line of earthworks in rear of the Chancellor House that we saw a while ago is the post to be occupied by our men as they fall back. The rebels cannot break through that. It would be a good thing for us if they would try to drive us to the river. It is not often that Lee attacks us; if he only presses this attack far enough and makes Hooker fight we will whip the rebels out of their boots!"

Just then an officer rode by, coming from the direction of the river. Upon being hailed and asked for news, he replied: "Sedgwick has taken Fredericksburg, and is in the rear of Lee, pushing this way. All that Hooker needs to do now is to use his troops, and the thing is settled!"

This news was heartening and glorious indeed, and, in spite of the dismal surroundings, and the terrific slaughter, and the temporary retreat, the officers felt encouraged. As they were about to mount their horses again, having lunched with appetite incited to omnivorous proportions on hard-tack, cold meat, and coffee, and feeling renewed for the work before them, Captain Fribley suddenly cried out, "The woods are on fire! Look yonder; the underbrush is burning all along our front."

With horrified faces the two stood for a moment, appalled with terror and dismay and an overwhelming sense of helplessness. They were not in danger themselves, but the sight before them meant death by slow torture for multitudes of wounded men in the bushes. Far and wide the flames extended, here and there checked for a while by the exertions of the troops on both sides, who dug trenches and whipped out the fire with bunches of weeds or rude brooms, made of switches of birch or beech bound compactly together; but in spite of these exertions the fire spread for miles through the forest, finishing the work of destruction begun by the two armies. Hundreds of wounded men, rebels and Union soldiers alike, helpless, bleeding, choking with heat and smoke, struggled for a few desperate moments to get out of the furnace of fire which surrounded them, watched in dismay and ghastly despair the crackling flames approach them, wondered if they were to be abandoned to die in this fashion.

and then, in bitter anguish, were slowly burned to death. War is always a dreadful thing, but on this battle Sunday in the Wilderness it assumed aspects of terror and brought with it visitations of anguish which crowned it with a climax of unutterable horror. To be wounded and left to die on the field, to suffer the intolerable pain of fevered thirst which inevitably follows, and have no water to drink, and then to be slowly tortured to death by forest fires, surely this doom can hardly be surpassed in the annals of war.

The officers had hardly mounted when Jack cried out, "The rebels have captured General Hooker's headquarters at the Chancellor House! Our army has been driven nearly two miles this morning already! It is about time to hear from Sedgwick if he is going to do anything for us to-day."

The plain in their front was still swept by the incessant artillery fire of the enemy. Masses of troops, miscellaneously mixed together, without order, in confusion and distress, their ammunition exhausted, their wounded left on the field, their cannon captured, were slowly and sullenly flying across the fields before the rebels, who were pushing after them. In half an hour, however, the troops were stationed behind the new line of breastworks that had been thrown up by direction of Hooker in the rear of the first line, covering the roads that led to the river, and here they felt they could hold their place against the Confederates.

"The Chancellor House is on fire!" suddenly cried out Captain Fribley, as they rode slowly through the retreating troops trying to find the Third Corps and join the command to which they belonged.

"It was used as a hospital, and was full of wounded men. Alas for the boys now!" was the reply of Jack, as his heart was transfixed with this new phase of the battle.

By this time they had reached the breastworks in the edge of the woods, where the remnant of the brigade was found. The battle had spent its force, and there was a lull for a while, the silence of which was rudely broken by the sounds of an engagement raging down toward Fredericksburg.

"Hurrah, boys!" shouted Colonel Bowman, with exciting tones, "do you hear that music? Sedgwick is attacking Lee in the rear. He is on his way up the river to our aid. That movement ought to insure a decisive victory in spite of our reverses to-day and yesterday."

The boys listened with flashing eyes and throbbing pulses, reflecting that the battle might open again at any moment all along their present front. What was their amazement, however, when that whole afternoon passed away without any order to advance. The line of earthworks was made stronger; trees were cut down and piles of logs were erected in military fashion by the engineers as a shelter for the cannoneers, and the fortifications were soon considered impregnable. But, meanwhile, the heft of Lee's army was concentrating on gallant Sedgwick six miles away, and no counter attack was ordered by Hooker, whose energies, in some strange way, suddenly suffered a complete collapse. Sedgwick was driven to the river, and escaped, after a desperate struggle, across the fords and bridges, without a gun being fired on that terrible Sunday, or on the following day, to relieve him from an attack which was overwhelming. No further fighting occurred along the line except an occasional skirmish. The two armies lay at bay, watching each other like two wild beasts which had torn and crippled each other in a savage encounter, and were each waiting for the other to make the first move.

The division commander of the Third Corps, the noble and brave General Whipple, was a victim of the battle on Monday.

A sharpshooter in a tree half a mile away in the rebel line got range of our men and picked them off, at his leisure, one by one. Among those who were wounded was General Whipple. The rain was falling drearily, and at the foot of a tree the gallant soldier lay, where he had fallen, with a bullet through his body, wounded unto death. A few of his staff gathered about him, and a Catholic chaplain was sent for to administer the sacrament of extreme unction, the service for the dying, to the bleeding officer. When he arrived the scene was pathetic in the extreme — the tearful and stricken officers mourning the expected death of their beloved general, the prayers of the devout priest ascending to heaven for the salvation of the dying man, the sinking and almost breathless figure of the general himself, his battles over, his work done, his end drawing near, the pallor on his brow, and the chill of death at his heart—all this made up a picture which those who saw it can never forget.

On Tuesday night, May 5, a rainstorm set in which caused the river in the rear of the Union army to rise suddenly and threateningly. That night, one by one, the regiments of the Union army were withdrawn; nobody was allowed to sleep; it was intimated in all directions, "Boys, we are going to retreat again to our old camps at Falmouth. Keep wide awake, or you will be left behind."

Drenched to the skin, sinking into the mud at every step, the way barricaded by wagon trains and artillery and ambulances, the roads chock full of troops, retreating step by step through the darkness and tempest, the weary army made its way through the woods again back toward the United States Ford. Here the pontoons had been broken by the rising river, and delays occurred in order to repair damages. The strain on the nerves of the boys under such circumstances can perhaps be imagined. No one wanted to awaken the suspicions or even draw the

A BATTLE SUNDAY IN THE WILDERNESS.

attention of the rebels in front. The horrors of a night engagement and the danger of a panic must be avoided. Keeping their eyes turned toward the rear, watching lest the advancing skirmishers might suddenly open fire from the woods, grieved with unutterable sorrow that so many lives had been thrown away and an opportunity wasted that promised a great victory, and wondering when this cruel war would be over, the troops went through the mud and rain toward their old winter quarters camp at Stoneman's Switch, waiting for the next move in the game of war.

It would be hard to tell which side was most relieved that day when finally the Union army stood intact on the left bank of the Rappahannock. The rebels were so glad to get rid of their foes that they did not make any attack or, by even the firing of a gun along the picket line, disturb the Union army on its retreat. And the soldiers in Hooker's rear guard that morning, who watched the successive portions of the army cross the pontoons, in suspense for hours lest at the last they might themselves be captured, surely knew what it was to draw "a free breath" when finally the order was given to step on the bridges, and in a few moments they found themselves escaped from the thickets of Chancellorsville!

CHAPTER XV.

"ABOUT, FACE! NORTHWARD, MARCH!"

"WHAT next?" was a familiar, oft-repeated question for a full month after the reverses at Chancellorsville, in the tents, log huts, and mud houses of the Army of the Potomac. It was uttered along the picket line, pondered at the bivouac fire, and turned over and over at the mess table. "What next?" said General Hooker to himself and to his most intimate staff officers and to his corps commanders, perhaps, when he counseled with them. "Who is to make the next move in the game? Will the Union army march across the Rappahannock again? Shall we change our base of operations, seeking to approach Richmond from another quarter and in a new direction? Or will General Lee try to attack our line, or make a flank march against us, or venture to strike us in the rear?"

"What next?" was the anxious question spoken in perplexity, and almost in dismay, at Washington, by the burdened Lincoln, and the scientific Halleck, and the fretting, fuming, impatient Stanton. "Who will secure us a decisive victory at the head of the Army of the Potomac? Who will prove himself master of the situation, and marshal our hosts so as to win?"

And so in the army itself, by the swollen waters of the Rappahannock, out over the hills of Stafford, and across the wasted fields, from which crops, fences, outbuildings, and all things movable had been taken away, was heard the same puzzling inquiry, "What next?" Even the contrabands took it up and puzzled their woolly heads with the difficulties of the military situation, wondering, "What is Massa Hooker done gwine to do wid dish yer big army?" And while the question was being asked the weeks went by and the early days of leafy June arrived. Then the question was settled and definitely answered by General Lee himself, who concluded that he would not wait for another attack from General Hooker; that he would not stand on the defensive any longer, but that he would invade the North.

The Army of the Potomac had been warned, throughout the whole of May, after the battle of Chancellorsville, to be ready for any sort of work that might develop; but nobody thought there was any hurry in the case, until one day couriers were seen flying in all directions, with orders to march in two hours with sparse baggage and plenty of ammunition!

That stirred up everybody into a condition of consternation and bewilderment. "Whither are we going? What is up? What is all this hurrying about?" And in response there was no other explanation but: "Pack up, men; we have no time to lose. Leave all your winter quarter paraphernalia, all your comforts, all your furniture, all your knickknacks, here in the care of the quartermaster department. We have no room on the wagons for stoves, mess chests, dishes, cots, and other litter of that sort. Ship all such stuff to Washington for storage. Leave it here in charge of the post quartermaster, and you may get it again sometime hereafter. *But hurry and get ready!* We march in a little over an hour. We will not be back here again! *Hurry!*"

In the midst of the exciting scene came other news that discommoded Jack not a little. The brigade was to be rearranged. Colonel Bowman was to command his own regiment, and General Carr was to take the brigade. The brigade staff was not needed by the new commander, who had his own assistants already designated. The officers, Jack included, who had luxuriated in the possession of horses to ride, and other perquisites of staff duty, were remanded to their companies, where they had to go afoot. That was a sore disappointment to the boy. His company had its gallant captain, Bryan, and its brave second lieutenant, Smith, already on duty with it, and there were not more than thirty men in it, so that it seemed like a waste of raw material to assign three commissioned officers to service with the company.

However, he had to submit, and with a sore and sinking heart he gave up his horse, which he had ridden so gayly and proudly for four or five months on parade, on review, and in battle, and tried to make up his mind to accept the foot service now before him with due resignation.

The hurry and commotion, the stir and haste, the excitement and effervescence of the scattered camps of the Army of the Potomac that day may be fitly likened to the fermentation occasioned in a wasp's big nest when stirred up by a long pole. Wagons were driven hurriedly from the place where they had been parked and were loaded with desperate haste; tents were torn down in a jiffy; the stuff that had accumulated through the winter-quarter stay in front of Fredericksburg was sifted out, some of it thrown away or burnt, and that which was valuable packed up for shipment to Washington; knapsacks were rolled up and thrown into a pile ready to be slung on the multitudinous shoulders of the great army; staff officers and generals were to be seen galloping in all directions, arraying their troops in marching order; a final ration of fresh beef was stowed away in the wagons for immediate use on the march; the few cattle on the hoof that remained uneaten were driven off to the North, guarded by the cavalry, sure to be killed and devoured before many days rolled by; bugles were sounded in all directions, and in a flutter of excitement, in a fever of wonderment and trepidation, aglow with curiosity and kindling with military ardor, nearly seventy thousand men set out on their march northward along the left bank of the Rappahannock River.

Amid the preparations for the march, and in its early stages, there was but one word that was emphasized, "Hurry up." Everybody felt that the business that was in hand required haste—urgent, instant, imperative haste. Nobody seemed to know anything about the situation except that Lee was making a move that must at all risks and with all possible speed be checkmated.

In three hours after the marching orders were distributed the army began its journey away from its quarters in front of Fredericksburg, the long trains of baggage and ammunition wagons, flanked, preceded, and followed by guards, taking the safest roads; the cavalry trotting in the distance ahead of the other troops (most of that arm of the service, indeed, having set out in advance several days before, had already crossed the river and uncovered Lee's movements); the artillery wheeling into line and lumbering along the dusty highways; the generals, with their brilliant array of staff officers, riding proudly at the head of their commands; and the long lines of blue-coated infantry, laden with well-filled haversacks, knapsacks, and cartridge-boxes, and girded about with their blankets and carrying their muskets "at will," sallied forth, taking up the line of march and proceeding in utter uncertainty across the hot and dusty plains.

The boys were sorely tried by that first day's march, and still more severely tested by the days and nights of weariness that followed. They had made no long marches in haste for months; the campaigns in front of Fredericksburg had not imposed any strenuous tax on their pedal extremities, and it took some time to limber up their legs and put them in first class marching trim.

The day was in part spent before the Third Corps made much headway on its journey, so that night overtook it on its route of march. "Close up, boys," was the order that ran along the ranks from time to time, sounding in the ears of the faint, the weary, and the straggling troops like goads to urge them on with more rapid pace.

The roads were dusty, the day was hot, and no chance had been afforded for rest or meals, and the march was becoming irksome and worrying. "Are we going to march all night?" growled one of the boys. "Is there to be no let-up to this business? Do they think our legs are made of cast-iron?"

"Cheer up, boys!" was the hearty reply of Captain Bryan. "We must keep up with Johnny Reb. It won't do to let him get ahead of us. Uncle Joe Hooker would not hurry us up in this fashion if it was not necessary. Where are we going to camp to-night, major?" continued the captain to Major Zinn, as the latter rode along by his side.

"We do not know yet," was the reply. "It seems that we are to keep our eyes on the fords of the river and keep the rebels from crossing over this way if they show any sign of wanting to do such a thing."

Just then a staff officer rode by and gave directions to Colonel Bowman about the matter under discussion, and "Hartwood Church" was announced as the destination for the night. It was now dark, and several miles were before the regiment yet before any supper or sleep could be secured, and additional

THE ROADS WERE DUSTY, AND THE DAY WAS HOT.

directions had been received to make all possible speed on the march. "Crowd your troops. Let there be no lagging. Press them forward with all possible haste," were the orders, and the tired soldiers doggedly persevered in their journey, knowing that if they dropped out by the way they were likely to be taken prisoners by the rebel cavalry.

At Hartwood Church a brief chance was afforded for rest, but before daylight came the bugles sounded anew, and, after a swig of coffee and a bite of breakfast, the boys started on again, still pressing cheerily up the river (understanding that the guns of General Lee might presently be heard thundering against their left flank), on the alert for an attack at any moment, and meanwhile in total and perplexing ignorance of what was really going on in connection with the whole movement. The general officers, of course, and some of their staff, had a larger view of these operations, and understood what the various marching columns were intended to do and what Lee was attempting on his part; but the men themselves saw only a very small part of the movement, and perhaps at the time knew much less of what was going on than the people at home who read the papers, and thus, by means of army correspondence, kept track of the campaign.

Dust, filling the air, stifling the lungs, and begriming the faces of the boys in blue, rose high toward the sky, forming tall and conspicuous columns whereby the movements of the men were plainly indicated from afar. The "branches" and springs were almost dried up, and it was difficult to find good drinking water anywhere along the route of march, so that the sufferings of the army from thirst became torturesome as they marched over the barren region along the Rappahannock River, which had been scathed, stricken, peeled, and smitten by both armies ever since the beginning of the civil war, the Union and the Confederate troops successively overrunning every inch of its soil, sweeping away fences, destroying crops, burning up outbuildings, until no bloom, no spear of grass, no horse or cow or sheep or fowl, no garden or fenced inclosure, and not a single adult male inhabitant was to be found anywhere over the desolate territory.

After a terrific march in the heat, the soldiers who had been stricken into helplessness by the oppressive rays of the burning sun being laden on the ambulances until these were more than full, the command arrived at Bealeton Station, on the Orange and Alexandria Railroad. "Colonel," was the direction of General Humphreys, at the head of the division, to Colonel Bowman, "take your men to Rappahannock Station, guard the bridge, resist any attack that may be made from that direction, and burn the bridge if necessary to keep the rebels from crossing to this side."

Exhausted already by their onerous march, the grimy and hungry men had to turn their faces toward the river and march several miles along its banks on picket duty, not knowing when a whistling bullet or an exploding bomb might signify the opening of another great battle. A day was spent in this service without discovering any signs of immediate danger, and then the march was resumed, the column heading northward.

On Saturday night, June 13, a message came from General Humphreys directing the detail of a lieutenant for duty at headquarters of the division, as assistant provost marshal of the command. Scanning the regiment for an officer, it was found that Jack Sanderson could be spared from his company, as there were three commissioned officers on duty with it, while the most of the other companies had but two present for duty, which was as many as any of them needed, in view of the depleted number of the command. What, therefore, was Jack's amazement and anxiety that night when, just as he was about to sink down on his rubber blanket and subside into the sleep of a weary soldier, he received an official document containing the following assignment:

"HEADQUARTERS SECOND DIVISION, THIRD ARMY CORPS,
"NEAR RAPPAHANNOCK STATION, VA., *June* 13, 1863.

"*Special Orders, No. —.*

"First Lieutenant Jack Sanderson, Company B, Eighty-fourth Pennsylvania Volunteers, is hereby detached from his regiment for special duty at division headquarters as assistant provost marshal. He will report to the brig.-general commanding at once on receipt of this order. He will be obeyed and respected accordingly.

"By order of   BRIGADIER GENERAL A. A. HUMPHREYS.

"CHARLES HAMLIN,
 "Assistant Adjutant General."

"What does this mean?" was the exclamation of Jack as he read with astonishment the order, rubbing his eyes to get them wide enough open to comprehend the situation.

Sergeant Major Rissell, with his usual roguish twinkle in his eye, replied: "I guess it means just what it says. You may get a horse to ride and have a chance to hurry up the stragglers and look after things about division headquarters, and all that sort of thing. Sorry to lose you, lieutenant, but glad that we are going to have one of our boys on duty up there. Maybe you can serve a fellow a good turn one of these days." And away ran the light-hearted fellow, ruddy of cheek, cheery of heart, and inaccessible to fatigue, melancholy, or fear.

Jack betook himself at once to the colonel, and asked him about the matter. "I cannot give you any further light on the case. General Humphreys wanted a trusted officer to serve as commander of his provost guard, and you have been chosen, and you are to go. So get ready."

"But, colonel, must I go away off to division headquarters at this hour of the night. I am just about ready for bed, and I am fagged out. I must pack up my traps and get ready, so that what little baggage I have can be taken along with me. Will it do if I report for duty the first thing in the morning?" This was the utterance of the boy as he pondered the case over and over.

"Yes, go to division headquarters as soon as it is dawn. We march to-morrow, early in the morning, and you must be there to take charge of your new command. Good night."

This was a turning-point in the history of the boy, although he did not dream of it then. This assignment to the new duty at division headquarters, as it finally turned out, gave him an unusual opportunity to see the battle of Gettysburg. On detached service he accompanied the division to that great field and shared in the experiences of that critical struggle, while the regiment, the day before the battle opened, was assigned to guard the wagon trains of the command, thirty miles from the scene of the desperate conflict. If he had remained with the regiment he would never have been a participant in the dreadful combat which proved to be the turning-point in the history of the nation and the pivotal struggle in the life of the government. As the boy accepted the assignment and proceeded to arrange for a change of quarters, and racked his brain and knitted his brows in the vain effort to make out beforehand whether he would like the new post or not, he little thought that much of his future life would in reality be shaped by the turn which events were at that moment taking. It may suffice here for the moment, in passing, to say that the boy's after life to a very great extent was shaped, in many regards, and in far-reaching aspects and relations, by the fact that he was a participant in the battle of Gettysburg, a matter that was determined by this order detailing him for duty at division headquarters.

Early next morning Jack reported for duty to General Humphreys, a well-proportioned, military-looking officer in middle life, with a keen, searching eye, a face in which mingled signs both of the soldier and the scholar, and an air of quiet dignity which betokened possibilities of power held in reserve, stored away for use in any emergency that might occur. This was General Humphreys, one of the ablest men in the army, and a remarkably self-poised, benignant, and considerate gentleman.

Lieutenant Sanderson was introduced to a party of nearly a hundred men and put in immediate command of them, Captain Russell serving as his superior. "These men are to serve as headquarters guard. Sometimes you will lead the march and sometimes you will act as rear guard. You will detail men to put up and take down our tents on the march, station sentries when we camp, and be ready for whatever other duties may develop as we proceed on our journey." With this injunction Captain Russell rode away with the other officers of the staff, giving directions to Jack to bring up the rear of the division, keeping the ranks well closed up, arresting all stragglers, and keeping his eyes open in view of a possible attack on the marching column.

What a day of oppression, of taxing toil, of exhausting and utterly prostrating labor that was for the boy and for those under his command! The division began its march early in the morning, and did not halt, except for a few moments at odd intervals, until it reached Manassas Junction, the scene of the first battle of Bull Run. Jack had to follow toilfully in the rear of the division, urging up the bummers, arresting those who were bent on straggling, cheering on the faint-hearted, helping the sick to the ambulance corps, prodding on his own men who were giving out, and wondering amid the heat, the dust, the fatigue, whether the day would ever come to an end. He found it impossible to keep up on foot, and no horse as yet had been furnished to him; and so it happened, toward the close of the day, that he found himself, with a little squad of men—all that was left of the rear guard—miles in the rear. The march had been delayed at times by bad roads, slough-holes where the artillery horses floundered and stuck; and then when the troops got across these bad places they were hurried forward by sharp and imperative orders to "keep closed up," so that they were on a nervous strain all the while from dawn till darkness. When night finally closed in Jack and his little band of exhausted men were far in the rear, trying in vain to bring up stragglers, and to frighten or otherwise hasten forward those who had fallen out of ranks on the march. "Come, men, don't linger here; the rebels are following us up, and you may be caught. Press on a little farther. No stragglers are allowed to remain behind. We have positive orders to bring up every man and leave none in the rear." With this word on his lips he and his noncommissioned officers were busy all day long increasing the number of miles traversed by the meanderings which they had to make to carry out instructions and close up the ranks. "Liftenant," said the Irish sergeant, McBride, who served with the provost guard, as the day wore away, and increased rather than lessened the labors that taxed the little body of men, "it is not the length of the road that I mind so much as the width of it. Sure I've got cross-eyed already to-day thrying to kape my two eyes on both sides of the road at once on the watch for stragglers. The two legs o' me have both got twisted up after the same fashion. This sort of work is worse than Jersey tanglefoot to give a man the blind staggers. I've been shovin' one man and shakin' another man, an' hurryin' this one and chasin' that one, till I can hardly stand. Now, liftenant, one thing I'd loike to know."

"Well, sergeant, what is it? Speak quick, there is a bummer yonder waiting for a little encouragement from you. He is about to make a cup of coffee, and if he stops to do that the gray-backs will have him sure, for they are following close on behind. Speak out your question, and then keep on at your work."

This was the response of the now overtaxed and exhausted Jack.

"Well, liftenant, what I'm puzzled about is this: We have orders to kape the division well closed up, and to put all the stragglers under arrest. Who is goin' to kape us closed up? Who is goin' to act as rear guard fur us and bring us into our camp? We've been laggin' behind for two hours, and one afther another has fallen out and bin picked up by the ambulances, and now they're gone on, and we are lift behind, and who is goin' to close us up? That's what's in my mind." And away he hurried to gently prod with his bayonet a bummer who was minded to resist his authority and to remain behind, whether or no.

SERGEANT McBRIDE.

After that, as night grew dense and thick, the boy's mind

became numb and hazy. During the crossing of Bull Run on a narrow bridge, impeded by a gully or something of the sort at the farther end, while a crowd of soldiers were jammed on the planks, he fell asleep on his feet and almost tumbled into the stream below half a dozen times while on the bridge. Then he kept on, his senses benumbed, his brain exhausted, his tongue parched, having only enough sense left in his almost distraught condition to keep in the path that had been followed by the troops ahead, wondering at every step whether he had strength enough to take another, urging himself on for a while by thought of the dangers that might lurk in the rear if he should drop out and fall asleep, until even this refuge failed him. He forgot his command, his perils, his surroundings, everything, and with just enough wit remaining in his exhausted noddle to prompt him to take a few steps to one side of the road, where he would escape being run over or trodden upon if wagons or artillery should by any chance follow on behind, he dropped in the stupor of complete exhaustion to the earth, and knew nothing more until the morning.*

* General Humphreys, the division commander, a veteran, accustomed to weigh every word he used, and not given to exaggeration of a soldier's privations and hardships, said in his report, concerning this day's march, "The suffering from heat, dust, thirst, fatigue, and exhaustion was very great."

CHAPTER XVI.

"MARYLAND, MY MARYLAND!"

AFTER a few hours of stupor the boy began to stir out of the dust in which he had been lying since midnight. Slowly emerging from the region of exhaustion into which he had taken his venturesome journey, and rubbing his eyes in order to clear from them, and from his face as well, the extra quantum of sacred soil which had accumulated there during the march, he looked about him. None of the army had yet begun to move; the pressure had not been put on the troops yet for the day; the machinery had not yet started. In a moment he was gladdened by the sight of the headquarters flag of the division not far away from where he had been lying in the dust. Without knowing it, he had caught up, in the darkness, to the head of the column, and had there dropped, faint, worn out, and exhausted, to the earth. Here and there a sentry was in sight, and scattered in all directions were thousands of men, stretched on the ground in all sorts of ungainly attitudes, without tents or baggage, the most of them having dropped down upon the earth without ceremony as soon as the dreadful march of the previous day, which happened to be the Sabbath, and which had proved to be anything but a day of rest, had come to an end.

Sentries were keeping watch over the sleeping host here and there ; horses, roused by the flies which were commencing to nip them in the early dawn, were beginning to squirm and kick and switch their tails and squeal, while in the east the cloudless sky and the increasing light foretokened the approach of another sultry day.

While Jack was trying to pull himself together after the dilapidation which he had suffered he heard a cheery voice close by, which proved to be that of one of his noncommissioned officers, Sergeant McBride, who had stuck close to him throughout the trying duties of the long and arduous march.

" The top of the mornin' to ye, liftenant. What do ye think of the Bull Run Hotel where ye've been stoppin' for the night? Will ye plaze to order yer breakfast, and it shall be served in yer room. If ye don't like yer quarters here ye can go on a little further and make yerself at home at the Manassas Junction House, where the accommodations are aiqually deloightful. Shpake yer moind, liftenant."

" Good-morning, sergeant. I'm glad to find your tongue still able to wag. It will be a sorry hour for this provost guard when anything happens to put a quietus on your powers of gab. Have you any news yet? Are we going to march any farther to-day? How are you pleased with your surroundings? Do you see anything very bright and hopeful in the situation ? "

Thus much Jack managed to speak in spite of his parched tongue and his throat, which were as dry as punk. He wondered where a little drinking water might be found, while he waited for the next observation of the effervescent Irishman.

"Sure, liftenant, I have in my moind, if I have any of it left to me this mornin', the words of a countryman of mine in the Emerald Isle, where a wonderin' tourist made some slightin' remark about the pig bein' allowed the run of the cabin, an' at once he spoke out and said, 'Isn't there ivery accommodation here that a hog could wish?' Who am I that I should complain whin I am enjoyin' the convaniences and luxuries that Gineral McDowell and his brave officers and min had to themselves two years ago in the nixt month at the first battle of Bull Run, and whin I am stoppin' at the same place where Gineral Pope stopped at the second battle of Bull Run, a year ago the comin' August? An', sure, here at our very feet is a relic of those pleasant days." And as he spoke he dug with his bayonet into the dusty soil and unearthed the whitened bones of a human hand. "Here," he proceeded, "is the first sign of welcome I've seen in this region. One of the former guests that stopped at this same hotel reaches out his hand and says, 'Yer welcome! Make yerself at home. Shake!'"

"Cover up those bones, sergeant. Between you and the owner of that skeleton hand I am all upset. Let us have something to eat and drink, and not disturb any more of the former guests of this establishment."

And forthwith they proceeded to imitate the example of the troops, who were by this time beginning to stir from their dusty beds and skirmish after something to eat. A rousing cheer was sent up as the commissary sergeant, with his assisting squad of men, was seen at this juncture coming into camp with some fresh beef that had just been killed. By the time this was cut up, distributed, broiled on sticks, and greedily devoured the wearied men had resumed their spirits and recruited their strength, and were ready for whatever the day might bring forth. The march was not severe or long that day—from Manassas

Junction to Centerville, over the grounds swept and trodden down by the two armies at frequent intervals during the whole preceding part of the war. The outer fortifications of Washington were now to be seen here and there, and it looked as though the Army of the Potomac might be hemmed in behind them by the movements of the Confederates. Another day brought them to Gum Springs, in Virginia, a part of the country that had not hitherto been scourged by troops from either side. In a pleasant orchard, with delightful shade and plenty of good water, the division encamped, enjoying for several days a refreshing rest. This part of the campaign was a picnic, literally, compared with that which preceded and followed. Milk and butter, chickens and eggs, fruit and vegetables, could be bought and secured in large quantities by foraging expeditions.

"Major," said Jack, during this stay at Gum Springs, to the adjutant general of the division, Major Charles Hamlin, "why are we halting here? What is the outlook for the campaign?"

"We are simply waiting here," was the reply, "for developments and for orders. Lee was behind yonder mountain wall a few days ago," continued the major, pointing to the Blue Ridge, "watching for a chance to pounce down on Washington. Thus far we have foiled him. Hooker has put his army at full speed to place them between Lee and the capital. Now we shall see whether Lee will try to attack us here or what he will do. We may be here for a week, and we may get orders to march in an hour. All depends."

"What are the probabilities, do you think?" proceeded the boy, curious to know whatever might be known about the movement in contemplation.

"My opinion is," said the major, "that Lee is going to cross the Potomac. His cavalry are over there in advance now. He needs food for his horses and men. He must have supplies, and he may secure them in Maryland and Pennsylvania. Then he expects to recruit his army in 'Maryland, my Maryland.'"

"Surely, he will not get many recruits there. Do you suppose he will?"

"No," emphatically replied the officer, "he will not. There are a good many rebels in Maryland, but nearly all of those who are willing to fight for the Confederacy have already crossed the border and joined the Southern army. Lee will be disappointed in that regard; and he will be disappointed, too, in another respect. He fancies that the peace party men, who have been opposing the draft, and shedding crocodile tears over a broken Constitution, and abusing the President, will join his invading army when he makes his appeal to them on Northern soil. He will find that they will not rally about him as fast as he now imagines. Lee's presence on the other side of the Potomac will arouse the North as it has not heretofore been stirred. Instead of dividing our ranks it will unite them. I have no patience, at any rate, with the croakers and copperheads at home who are keeping up a fire in our rear all the time, and it would be a good riddance if they were all conscripted by Lee into his army and carried off to the South. They will not volunteer, you may be sure of that; and yet if they are 'loyal,' in any sense of that word, to anything, it is to the South; but they have no stomach for fighting. Once in a while they will 'hurrah for Jeff Davis,' but they will not fight for him nor for his Confederacy."

As the two conversed they heard in the direction of the mountains the booming of cannon. "Ah," said the major, "the cavalry are at work in the gaps of the mountain. Pleasonton, with his cavalry corps, is out yonder at Aldie Gap, and when he and Jeb Stuart meet together there is sure to be music. Our sabers will guard the passes that open up toward Washington, and Lee will not think of trying to come this way."

Just then a newsboy came galloping by laden with the dailies from the city, the *Washington Chronicle*, the *New York Tribune*, and the *Philadelphia Press*, with other papers. He was eagerly beset and, as usual, sold out his stock in short

A NEWSBOY CAME GALLOPING BY LADEN WITH THE DAILIES.

meter at a dime a copy, without protest. The news from the city of New York was read aloud with eager interest, and its reading was interrupted with hearty cheers. The boys shouted over the tidings that the militia regiments of that State and of Pennsylvania were being concentrated with haste at Philadelphia and other central points, *en route* to Harrisburg, where General Couch was to organize them against the invaders of the North.

On June 25 the division turned its face and its toes northward again, marching all day, until late in the afternoon they saw before them the beautiful waters of the Potomac spread out through a delightful landscape, and beyond the river the green hills of Maryland. Shouts and cheers were given with a will as the sight was afforded. The river was spanned by pontoon bridges, over which the advancing troops, with song and shout and enthusiasm, were pouring into Maryland. It was almost night when Humphreys's division crossed the boat bridge and found itself assigned to the towpath, with orders to march fifteen miles that night yet to Monocacy Junction. It had already been raining for an hour or two, and at nightfall the rain grew to a storm, which pelted relentlessly the marching column. It was a dismal, monotonous, wretched, and irksome experience which the boys had that night. Again Jack was in the rear, bringing up the stragglers, urging forward the weary, and trying to cheer up the sick and keep the troops closed up. It was a vain, a thankless, and an impossible task. No human being could have kept that division closed up or have prevented straggling that night. The storm was in their teeth, the towpath was slippery and narrow, and now and then, in spite of care, a heavily laden soldier would topple over into the canal and scramble out or be fished out by his comrades, sputtering, cursing, drenched, and dripping. Above was the dense, murky, impenetrable darkness, through which came no hint of moon or star behind the clouds big with rain and storm. The four thousand men who made up the command were stretched out at irregular and fitful intervals that night, reaching clean from the crossing at Edwards Ferry to the intended destination of the troops fifteen miles away. About two o'clock in the morning Jack dropped in the grass at a point where the towpath widened into a bit of a meadow, and here, with the rain pelting him and the water trickling down his back, striving to keep the worst of the tempest off by a rubber blanket, he sank into the deep sleep of complete exhaustion. Waking at dawn, he found himself with a little squad of his provost guard in wretched plight, aching in every muscle, wringing wet, soaked to the skin with the drenching rain, and shivering with cold.

What a change in the aspect of things was caused by a single cup of coffee! Enough wood was splintered up to make a fire, and about it the boys gathered in details of three or four, as many as could find accommodation for their tin cups, filled with good strong coffee, which, when well boiled and drunk hot, black, and sweet, served as a tonic and an invigorator and a reconstructor of notable value.

By and by the sun came out, and the boys began to cheer at the sight of his rays, and still more so at the new and unwonted scenery which greeted their vision. For months they had been accustomed to see only the fenceless and defenseless region of battle-blasted Virginia, swept clean of almost all traces of animal or vegetable life, trodden under foot by two great contending armies—gardens utterly wiped out, fields rendered a barren waste, boundary lines all destroyed, farms completely desolated and most of them abandoned, and the whole country from the Potomac to the Rapidan turned into an uninhabited waste. Out of this barren and war-stricken territory they came now into a garden of opulence and of bloom. The rolling hills of Maryland, with fair and fertile valleys intervening, abounding with teeming orchards, exuberant grain fields, green and glorious meadows, abundant gardens, and dotted with smiling towns and happy hamlets, appeared in all their beauty before the eyes of the soldiers of the Army of the Potomac like a vision in fairyland.

The hearty greeting given to the soldiers in this march into

and across Maryland gladdened the army. In Virginia the
Army of the Potomac was considered a ruthless invader; the
few inhabitants that were left in the land looked on with
scowling sullenness and ill-concealed bitterness as the boys in
blue passed by their homes; now, however, the atmosphere rang
with cheers, the Stars and Stripes were everywhere floating on
the breeze, men, women, and children vied with each other in
their exhibitions of loyalty and zeal in view of the arrival of the
tried army that was about to meet Lee and his men again on
the field.

One of the most affecting and pathetic incidents of the campaign occurred soon after marching across into Maryland. Jack,
with his company, was ordered that day to take the lead, and
just behind them came one of the regimental bands, while ahead
of them rode General Humphreys and his staff. As the division
marched along they passed by a country schoolhouse in a little
grove at a crossroad. The teacher, hearing the music of the
band at a distance, and expecting the arrival of troops, had dismissed the school to give them a sight of the soldiers. The
boys and girls, before the troops came in sight, had gathered
bunches of wild flowers and platted garlands of leaves and
secured several tiny flags, and now, as General Humphreys rode
up in front of the schoolhouse, a little girl came forth and
presented him with a bouquet, which he acknowledged with
gracious courtesy. Then the group of assembled pupils began
to sing, as they waved their flags and garlands in the air. The
song made a tumult in every soldier's heart that day in the
whole command, and many strong men wept as they looked on
the scene and thought of their own loved ones far away in their
Northern homes, and were inspired with newborn courage and
patriotism by the sight and the song. This is the song which
rang forth that day from that country schoolhouse, and which

soon afterward echoed and reëchoed throughout the battle in many a soldier's ear and heart, miles away, on the bloody field of Gettysburg:

> "Yes, we'll rally round the flag, boys, we'll rally once again,
> Shouting the battle cry of Freedom;
> We'll rally from the hillside, we'll gather from the plain,
> Shouting the battle cry of Freedom!
>
> "We are springing to the call of our brothers gone before,
> Shouting the battle cry of Freedom;
> And we'll fill the vacant ranks with a million freemen more,
> Shouting the battle cry of Freedom!
>
> "We are marching to the field, boys, we're going to the fight,
> Shouting the battle cry of Freedom;
> And we bear the glorious stars for the Union and the right,
> Shouting the battle cry of Freedom!
>
> "The Union forever, hurrah, boys, hurrah!
> Down with the traitors, up with the stars,
> While we rally round the flag, boys, rally once again,
> Shouting the battle cry of Freedom."

As Jack passed with his company he turned to his men and shouted, "Boys, give them three cheers and a 'tiger!'" The command was obeyed with a will, and the example was imitated by the regiments that followed; so that amid the singing of the children and the cheers of the soldiers and the beating of the drums the occasion was made memorable to all concerned.

On Sunday, the 28th of June, the command marched through Frederick, made historic by many interesting facts in the story of Maryland, but embalmed in verse by the incident of Barbara Frietchie, which is said to have occurred in the previous autumn, one day during the Antietam campaign. Jack thought of the old lady and her devotion to the flag as he trod the same streets with his provost guard that Sunday, but he thought of other things besides. His shoes had given out, and no horse had as yet been available for his use during the campaign, and he must be shod. He found a shoestore open and bought a new pair of shoes, and marched thirty miles in them before the sun had set next day—a process in the operation of which he found himself as well as the new shoes pretty thoroughly " broken in " by the time that day had expired.

Next day the army was stirred with a bit of important news. It was announced that General Hooker had resigned his command because of some conflict with General Halleck, at the head of military affairs at Washington, and that Major General George G. Meade had been promoted from the command of the Fifth Army Corps to be the leader and commander-in-chief of the Army of the Potomac. What a buzz that made throughout the ranks of eighty thousand men when the news was known! How the boys chatted and wrangled in a good-natured fashion, and wondered what the upshot of it all would be, and continued on their northward march, confident of victory on Northern soil if they were only handled with passable ability and given a fair chance to get at the invading army !

As the boys marched they talked over the case, headed northward and approaching the Pennsylvania line.

" Well, I am sorry to see Fighting Joe Hooker leave us now. We will meet the rebels and have a big battle in a day or two, and he would better have stuck to us a while longer. I always felt my backbone stiffened and the rousements go all over me like a nervous chill when he rode up on that big white horse of his, his eye flashing and his face all aglow, and his example worth a whole division to any army. I wish Joe Hooker had stayed with us !" This was the ejaculation of one of Jack's chums as they marched along.

Another messmate replied : " I hardly think it makes much

matter to us who is at the head if he is able and true. We have surely learned by this time that McClellan, for example, is not the only military man in the world. I do not sympathize with the cry that used to be heard more or less clamorously in our ranks, 'Give us back our old commander!' He had his chance, again and again, and lost it. I like, rather, to recall a little poem printed in the *Tribune* a year ago as the cry of the nation and of the army. Listen, boys, and see if this is not your sentiment as well as the poet's:

"'Give us a man of God's own mold,
   Born to marshal his fellow-men;
One whose fame is not bought and sold
   At the stroke of a politician's pen.
Give us the man of thousands ten,
   Fit to do as well as to plan;
Give us a rallying cry, and then,
   Abraham Lincoln, give us a man!

"'Is there never, in all the land,
   One on whose might the cause might lean?
Are all the common men so grand,
   And all the titled ones so mean?
What if your failure may have been
   In trying to make good bread of bran,
Of worthless metal a weapon keen?
   Abraham Lincoln, *find* us a man!

"'O, we will follow him to the death,
   Where the foemen's fiercest columns are.
O, we will use our latest breath
   Cheering for every sacred star.
His to marshal us nigh and far;
   Ours to battle, as patriots can,
When a hero leads the holy war,
   Abraham Lincoln, give us a man!'

"There, boys, that has the right ring to it. Maybe Father Abe has found us a man in General Meade. He looks like a professor rather than a dashing leader; but he is genuine metal, clean through, without any veneering. He has no spread eagle about him, and not much of what you call 'style.'"

And while the words were on his lips, lo, and behold, along rode the new commander, with twenty or thirty finely mounted officers attending him. He was tall and spare, he wore glasses, his shoulders were a little bent, and his face betokened a good deal of anxiety and care, as well it might in view of the responsibilities that had been suddenly thrust upon him. The boys cheered, of course, but not with much enthusiasm. It was clear that they accepted the new commander on trust; no one knew whether he could command an army or not. But the army was so well disciplined, so thoroughly loyal, so anxious to win the day on Northern soil, that in spirit they said: "Whether it is Meade or Hooker, Burnside or McClellan, we are the same tried and true soldiers. We will do our part whoever may be at our head. But we *do* ask to be led with courage and skill against the foe. We pledge our lives that we will in any case show ourselves worthy of our cause, and will quit ourselves like men."

On the march, after leaving Frederick, and just after the change of commanders had occurred, a staff officer from corps headquarters came riding by one day and said to General Humphreys, "General Meade captured a prize yesterday at Frederick."

"What was it?" was the instant reply of the general.

"A man in citizen's clothes was arrested at the picket line trying to pass out with some frivolous excuse of having to go to a neighbor's on an errand. It happened that he could not be identified by any of the neighbors, and on searching him dispatches were found on his person from Jeff Davis to General Lee. It seems that Lee had planned to have Beauregard follow after him and threaten Washington by the overland and direct route from Richmond, while he himself should occupy the attention of our forces in the North. Now, it appears that the South is entirely stripped of troops, and Beauregard can make no movement at all, and Davis, moreover, is apprehensive that Richmond, by the James River route, may be attacked while Lee is away."

General Humphreys was silent for a moment, and then, referring to a map of the border counties of Pennsylvania and Maryland, and noting the various roads and points of connection as located thereon, he said: "It is a problem, as yet unsolved, what General Lee intends to do. He is over yonder in the Cumberland valley, advancing upon Harrisburg, and attacking also the region about York. Maybe he will turn back and meet us in battle when he finds we are threatening his flank and rear in our advance toward Pennsylvania. He must keep his communications open with the South by way of the Cumberland and Shenandoah valleys, and our position now endangers that line of possible retreat which he must maintain. We are now groping in the dark to unmask the movements of the rebels, and in a day or two at farthest we will probably meet them somewhere along the border of these two States. General Reynolds is in command of three corps to lead the advance and reconnoiter with this end in view. Where the first blow will be struck no one can tell just now, but the time must be close at hand."

Just then the advance, which was led that day by the division whose fortunes we are following, met a citizen with whom General Humphreys had some conversation:

"Have you had any visit from the Confederates at all in this vicinity within the last week?"

"None of their troops," was the reply, "have come through our territory. The people, however, have been in alarm for days, and many of them have driven their cattle and horses away to the mountains for safe-keeping. The Cumberland valley, over the mountains yonder, has been overrun by the invaders, and great damage has been done. Farther north a day or two ago a rebel column of infantry, under Ewell, marched across the country through a little town called Gettysburg to York, and they have been spreading havoc and confusion among the farmers there. They wanted a thousand barrels of sauerkraut from the Dutchmen there, and were very wroth because the Germans said they had none this time of year, supposing that the rebels were ridiculing their favorite dish, when in fact the Confederates wanted the kraut as a relish and an antiscorbutic, to keep off scurvy."

On the march that day, June 30, General Humphreys said to his staff: "General Meade sends us to Emmitsburg to investigate the lay of the ground there. We are liable at any moment to run into the advance of Lee's army, and any hour may bring on a great battle. General Meade wants to know the character of the country round about and be ready to meet Lee wherever and whenever that general may turn up."

That night they camped near Emmitsburg, Md., and the next morning the great battle of Gettysburg began, twelve miles away to the north. How the division of Humphreys got there, and how they fared in the battle, another chapter will reveal.

CHAPTER XVII.

SMELLING THE BATTLE AFAR OFF.

ON the 30th of June Jack's regiment, the Eighty-fourth Pennsylvania, was assigned to duty with the wagon trains, to act as their guard and convoy, miles away in the rear. Lieutenant Colonel Opp, now in command of the regiment, urged General Carr, the brigade commander, to change the order and send some other regiment on that tour of service. "A battle is impending, general, and we prefer the front, and not the rear. Let us go with the brigade, and send another regiment to the rear with the trains." This was the plea of the courageous colonel in behalf of his officers and men.

General Carr said in reply: "No, colonel, this order must stand. The Eighty-fourth must go with the trains. You may find it no easy task to guard them, however, as Jeb Stuart is in our rear, trying to make his way clear round us and join the rest of Lee's forces. He may attack you before night."

Nothing was to be done but submit, and reflecting on Milton's words, "They also serve who only stand and wait," Colonel Opp, with a heavy heart, led his regiment out of the line at Taneytown, and at their head directed them to Westminster, where they were during the battle. So it happened that Jack, detached from the regiment, shared in the engagement because he was on duty at division headquarters, while the regiment, just as brave and thorough soldiers as any in the army, were convoying the trains thirty miles away, doing their duty at that end of the great line of battle.

That night, June 30, everyone in the scattered army corps of the bivouacking hosts, from the commander-in-chief down to the anxious teamsters with the wagon train, felt the pressure of suspense, perplexity, and uncertainty, and they asked with anxious hearts, "What will the morrow bring forth?"

Early on the morning of Wednesday, July 1, Humphreys's division of the Third Corps marched from Bridgeport to Emmitsburg, a few miles distant, in a northwest direction, where they were ordered to throw up earthworks and make a line of intrenchments that would serve for protection in case of an attack. It was still uncertain where Lee might be, and in the march feelers were thrown out in all directions to avoid surprise. The regiments were deployed in their various positions, which had been chosen with care in view of the possibility that an engagement might occur at the very point where they were digging and intrenching themselves, when suddenly there was heard to the northward an answer to the question which had been asked for a week or more by everybody in the Army of the Potomac. From the commander down to the high private in the rear rank all had been uttering the conundrums, "Where is the rebel army? What is Lee going to do? What is he aiming at?"

A decisive answer to this series of perplexing questions was now heard booming through the air from the hills to the north in the shape of artillery firing, each cannon shot saying: "Here is the Army of Northern Virginia. We are arrayed for battle. You have been looking for us; now we report our whereabouts. We are at Gettysburg, equipped for fight. Come and meet us, if you dare!"

Every man in the command heard the sounds of the opening battle with quickened pulse and with bated breath. He knew it meant a summons for him shortly to hurry to the field, and he felt, furthermore, that the struggle would be one of the fiercest ever fought in the annals of war. If ever the Army of the Potomac was put on its mettle, and felt that it had to do its utmost in behalf of the flag and land it loved, it was in view of this conflict now just commencing at Gettysburg.

General Humphreys, listening to the cannonade, which soon became hot and quick and was reinforced by the sounds of musketry, said at once: "That means an engagement. General Reynolds has with him the First and the Eleventh Corps and is out on a scout, but he has clearly run into the advance of Lee's army, and the decisive battle may be on at this hour. We must be ready to march at an instant's warning. And yet we must keep up our preparations here, so that if we are taken in flank, or if we have to retreat from Gettysburg, where that firing is, I suppose, we may not suffer from an attack on the road."

The morning waned away, and the division still stayed at Emmitsburg, busy with the spade, alert with its pickets, watching the roads entering town from the west, and waiting for orders and for news.

Everybody wondered: "What is the issue of the fight? Who is winning the day? Is this a skirmish between a couple of divisions, or is it a regular battle, and will it prove to be the prelude to the great engagement which has been inevitable since Lee crossed the Potomac?" About noon a few frightened refugees arrived from near the town of Gettysburg with all sorts of frightful tales to relate. "An awful battle is going on up yonder. General Lee has his army all there and is driving our men. We were glad enough to get away." This was the dismal tale that was told with many embellishments and additions by the alarmed people who had fled from the scene. So the morning passed, the battle in the distance growing hotter and fiercer as fresh troops were apparently led into the fight on either side. General Sickles, the corps commander, restive and eager in spirit as he listened to the cannonade, and his men, like hounds held in by the leash with the prey in open sight, were chafing and impatient for permission to march to the field; yet his orders were peremptory to hold and fortify Emmitsburg, lest it might be seized by the advancing Confederates and occupied by them to threaten our line of communications.

About three o'clock an officer was seen urging his horse at full speed toward the troops, coming from the direction of the firing. He halted at General Sickles's headquarters and delivered his message:

"General Howard sent me to you, General Sickles, with the suggestion that you come at once to Gettysburg. A hot battle has been raging there since nine this morning. At ten o'clock General Reynolds was shot dead by a rebel sharpshooter. Howard got there in time to take charge of the field, but he is hard pressed. Only two corps, the Eleventh and the First, are on the field. Our men were holding their ground when I left, but fresh troops were arriving on the rebel side, and reinforcements are needed at once. Your men will have to march about ten or eleven miles to get there. General Howard simply makes a suggestion; he hardly feels justified in giving you an *order* to come, but he has sent the same message to Slocum, down at Two Taverns, east of Gettysburg, and he hopes he will respond."

General Sickles, always eager for a fight, needed but a suggestion in order to prompt him to march. Birney was not far away, at the head of the First Division, and he was ordered to lead off. Two brigades were left behind to guard the position for the time, and an officer was dispatched to General Meade, whose headquarters were at Taneytown, ten miles eastward, with news of the movement and the reason for it; and off the Third Corps started on the march for the fight, Sickles galloping eagerly ahead with his staff in order to survey the field and be able to locate his troops intelligently when they should arrive.

General Humphreys's division was ordered to take a roundabout course by a road two miles distant from the main route, lying to the west of it, and somewhat rough and untraveled. Soon after leaving Emmitsburg the general began to receive news of disaster and trouble that had overtaken our troops in Gettysburg. Fugitives now and then appeared with stirring stories of defeat, which soon became too one-sided to make it possible for them not to have some solid basis of fact. "Reynolds is killed; our men are whipped; the rebels are there in overwhelming force; the day is lost!" This was the occasional rumor that beset the advancing division.

Lieutenant Colonel Hayden, inspector general of Sickles's staff, had been sent back by General Sickles to guide the division to its place in the line at Gettysburg. He was confident that he had been ordered to bring them in to Gettysburg from the west, by way of the Black Horse Tavern, on the Fairfield road, three miles west of Gettysburg, but as General Humphreys and his men marched swiftly along they were continually warned to look out for danger in that direction.

At one point in the march a citizen of the vicinity said in

alarm: "You are getting into dangerous quarters. The rebel army is advancing from that direction. That part of the country is overrun with Confederates! The woods are full of 'em! Look out!"

General Humphreys knew he must be approaching the enemy's lines, and sent word to the buglers to utter no sound, and directed that as little noise as possible be made by the men in marching. In accordance with these orders canteens were strapped up close, the artillery went with caution, the horsemen rode with care, and everyone marched as though stepping on eggs. Further on in the way toward Gettysburg about nightfall a staff officer of Howard met the column and expressed surprise that they were being led through the byroad and in a direction that would bring them to a point west of Gettysburg. "None of our troops, General Humphreys, are anywhere in that vicinity. That region is full of Confederates. You are liable at any moment to receive an attack on your left flank if you keep on much further. Our men have been driven pellmell through the town. Gettysburg itself is held by the rebels, and our forces have fallen back a full mile and a half from the point where the battle began this morning. You are going into a dangerous region. We are all stationed on Cemetery Hill, to the south of the town. There the rebels may attack us at any time, but you are going right into their jaws if you keep on in that direction."

Colonel Hayden replied to this warning: "My orders from General Sickles were to bring this division by way of the Black Horse Tavern, on the Fairfield road, and until those orders are countermanded we shall keep right on, rebels or no rebels."

The night, meanwhile, closed in, and the sound of the battle, which had come to an end about four o'clock, had been succeeded by an occasional scattering fire, seemingly from the skirmishers. The troops hurried their steps in order to reach their bivouac, wherever it might be, and get some rest before the work of the morrow. After marching over rough roads, traversing gloomy woods, and wading through a creek or two, the men were suddenly halted. They rested for a moment, glad to get a breathing spell, and then a quiver of excitement passed through the ranks, and the "goose flesh" was made to run up and down everybody's spinal column in spasmodic and frequent currents by the news that was passed from man to man in a hushed and anxious voice: "About, face, boys! we have to countermarch! We have run into the rebels! Get out of this as quickly and as quietly as you can. Make no noise. We are in the rear of the Confederate army."

The general and his staff had reached the tavern while the troops were halted a short distance away; when they arrived in sight of it, and had ridden up to its long, inviting, old-fashioned porch to alight, Colonel Hayden said to General Humphreys, "Here is a roof to sleep under to-night, and to-morrow morning we will march into Gettysburg."

It happened that a wounded Union soldier on parole from another part of the army was at his home in the neighborhood. He was on the watch for our men lest they might be drawn into an ambush. Safe himself from any assault or ill-treatment on the part of the Confederates, he was anxious lest our men might be caught in a trap, and on catching sight of the advancing column of Humphreys, led by their general, he came out from his hiding-place and spoke with amazement to one of the staff. In a hushed tone of voice, and trying to hide his anxiety, he said in a surprised and quizzical air, "Colonel, don't you know you're inside the rebel lines?"

Colonel Hayden, with indignation and amazement, thought at first that a trick was being played upon him, and he retorted in his rough way, "Do you not know that you can be shot for

"COLONEL, DON'T YOU KNOW YOU'RE INSIDE THE REBEL LINES?"

lying?" The man was silent for a moment, and then, seeing that he was misunderstood, and knowing that this was no time for any long harangue or elaborate explanation, he replied, "Well, colonel, if you cannot smell the brimstone here look yonder and you can see it a-burning!"

The officer and those who were with him took a hasty glance across the creek, and, to their unutterable astonishment, they saw on the slopes of the hill the smoldering camp-fires of the rebels. Not a quarter of a mile away, across the creek and out the road, westward, was a party of Confederate pickets; and within five minutes after General Humphreys had been warned of the situation and made his preparations accordingly twenty or thirty of Longstreet's men arrived at the tavern and stopped there for the night.

General Humphreys, with utmost self-possession, without any indication of anxiety or disturbance, sent his staff quietly back to the troops where they stood at ease along the road expecting orders to go into camp for the night, with the command: "Send word along the line to countermarch. Tell the regimental commanders to keep their force in hand ready for a night attack, if any should occur. Let no noise be made in the retreat. About face at once, and march back to the Emmitsburg road, and thence we will be guided to our place in the line of battle." Need I say that these orders were gladly obeyed? That division was in the rear of the rebel line of battle at midnight, and four or five miles away from any other Union troops. They felt lonesome, and they allowed no grass to grow under their feet as they made swift and silent steps back to the road they were now directed to take. As rapidly as was consistent with the dignity of the Army of the Potomac and the reputation of the Third Army Corps they made their way out of that hornets' nest. Why, even the very horses seemed to catch the spirit of the occasion, and they went along as though their feet had been wrapped in cotton. Nobody even breathed hard, and like an army of ghosts that division glided through the forest and across the fields and through the creeks, intent now only on getting back inside the Union line of battle! And when at last, about one in the morning, streaming with perspiration, nervously exhausted from the strain they had been under, the men arrived upon the hillside whereon they were to throw themselves for the remainder of the night, no words can describe the feeling of relief with which one said to another, " Boys, say, I never want to stop at the Black Horse Tavern again! Too many ' secesh ' in that neighborhood! I prefer to keep inside the Union lines!"

Over the hills of southern Pennsylvania, on which portions of a great army had bivouacked, the day broke on the morning of July 2 clear and beautiful, with abundant promise of heat after the sun had had a fair chance to climb up the sky. Jack, with his company, had been sleeping only three or four hours when they were aroused by orders to take position in the line of battle. After a hasty breakfast the boys had opportunity to look about them and in the course of the morning to study the situation. The division found itself posted, with the other troops of the Third Corps, on a ridge running north and south, with a peaceful intervale between them and a peach orchard nearly a mile away in their front, to the west, while beyond the orchard, which was on another ridge along which ran a public highway, were glimpses of forests, and still beyond, ten miles off, lay the blue and beautiful South Mountain range. Everybody expected that a battle would open at daybreak, but dawn and sunrise came, and indeed the whole morning passed away, without any attack on either side. Now and then a shot would be heard in the woods out beyond the peach orchard, but with that exception no fighting occurred until the day was three quarters gone. The most of July 2 was occupied with silence—the stillness, not of inactivity, helplessness, or repose, but the awful silence of reconnoitering and preparing for battle, the hush that goes before the storm.

While the troops lay in line early in the morning, ready to spring to their feet at a moment's warning when the signal might be given, Jack saw a friend riding along the Taneytown road—Captain Halstead, of General Doubleday's staff. Greeting his old friend, the boy asked for an insight into the "military situation." "We had a dreadful day of it," said the captain, summing up the experiences of the first day's battle. "The two corps that were engaged—the First and the Eleventh—were cut to pieces. We were in the battle from about nine o'clock till four in the afternoon—for the first three or four hours yonder along that ridge to the northwest of the town, which lies to our north two miles away; there Reynolds fell early in the fight, one of the ablest and most gallant officers in the Union army. If he had lived he would have been at the very top before long. About noon we had to look out for our flank and rear, which were threatened by Confederates who came in from the north and east, from Carlisle and York, so that we were liable to be caught between two fires. After struggling there to the north of the town for a while we were beaten at every point by an overwhelming force, and had to retreat to Cemetery Hill. The Confederates followed us through the town, which they occupied, capturing many prisoners, including many of our wounded who were left on the field. That, in brief, is the story of yesterday."

"Are our troops all here?" was the anxious question of the boy.

"Here come the Second Corps," said the major, "while we speak of them, up the Taneytown road, ready for battle. Hancock came yesterday afternoon and helped in the final arrangements for the battle that is to be fought here. His corps in part arrived last night, and this is the rest of it." And, while the two conversed, the eager, gallant men of the Second Corps, with their trefoil badge, with music and with banners, marched gayly by, ready for battle.

"The Twelfth Corps, under Slocum, came last night, and we are all anxiously looking for General Sedgwick and his glorious old Sixth Corps, who are on the march. If we are attacked before they arrive it may be a bad thing for us. They can hardly get here till noon, but they will do their best to reach us as early as possible, I'll warrant you."

"Where is our line of battle?" pursued the boy, anxious to locate himself in view of the topography of the region.

"This hill off to our left," said Major Halstead, pointing southward, " is Round Top, and as I understand it that is to be the extreme left. Our line of battle runs from that point northward to the other hill you see this side of Gettysburg, called Cemetery Hill, and thence off to the east, terminating at Culp's Hill, two miles or more from us off in that northeast direction. It is a splendid line of battle. The Army of the Potomac could not ask for a better position to defend."

"Do you think Lee will attack us?" said Jack.

"He cannot help it; he durst not waste any time; he cannot back out now; he had a lucky day yesterday, and his men are in high feather over their victory. They think they can do anything after their triumph. Certainly he will attack us sometime to-day. I wonder why he has not begun the battle before this; but perhaps he has not all his troops in hand either. He may be waiting for his concentrating columns to reinforce those already here before making his attack. But be very sure he is going to attack us, and we will have a dreadful battle This is the turning point. If Lee whips us here the Union is lost. If we win, Lee's army ought to be demolished before it reaches Virginia again."

The picture presented to the eye of Jack as the major uttered his closing sentence and rode away the boy can never forget. The morning was passing, noon was approaching; and still the troops waited on the ground seemingly idle, but really alert, watchful, intent. Suddenly a woman and a couple of children appeared on the scene, frightened, pallid, crossing the fields between the lines and making their way through the Union troops. She asked for one of the Pennsylvania reserve regiments, and was directed toward it not far away. Jack watched the scene, and saw a touching greeting exchanged between one

SHE ASKED FOR ONE OF THE PENNSYLVANIA RESERVE REGIMENTS.

of the soldiers and the group of visitors, who proved to be the veteran's wife and children, whom he had not seen for a year, and who had come from a farm near by, on the battlefield itself. They were escaping from the scene of conflict, had a lunch for the soldier, and with tears and sobs, which stirred the hearts of all the comrades, passed over the hill and out of sight down the Taneytown road.

Soon the division surgeon, Doctor Calhoun, rode up, arrayed with his green sash, to indicate the location of the hospital. "The wounded are to be brought over yonder to the tent erected near Rock Creek, in the valley beyond this hill, across the Taneytown road." And, having given his orders, and located his ambulance corps, away he went to see that his knives and saws were in order, and that the supply of chloroform and ether and liquor were ample for any possible demands that might arise during the battle.

Turning again toward the rear, Jack saw scores of cannon, battery after battery, parked on the hill a mile away to the east, with the ammunition train, packed full of various explosives ready for use, close beside. That was the park of the reserve artillery under General Hunt. Meanwhile, up and down the Taneytown road, aids were rapidly riding with messages from the different officers in command, and in the distance clouds of dust arose, indicating that troops were still marching to their place in the line. By nine o'clock nearly all the army was present for action except the Sixth Corps, which was hurrying with desperate speed to the field.

Jack, as the day wore away and the excitement of the first hours of preparation subsided, began to experience a distressing measure of reaction and nervous exhaustion. He lay on the grass in a very sober mood, now running his eye along the gathering lines of men, now peering anxiously across the landscape to the westward, noting the woods behind which the Confederates were concentrating their forces, and wondering why the battle did not open. It was fortunate, indeed, for the Union army that an early attack was not made. If Stonewall Jackson had been alive, and had opened his guns on the left of the Union army in the vicinity of Round Top at sunrise, as he would have been likely to do, he would have found our lines half formed and our army not all present and the soldiers exhausted with their fatiguing night marches. Instead of any such attack, however, the day wore away until nearly four in the afternoon before any real fighting occurred.

That last hour of waiting, how dreadful it was! Every man knew that a death struggle between two great armies was imminent; the next hour would summon all of them to face the storm of battle, and would doom thousands of them to wounds, maiming, death, or imprisonment. Quiet reigned all along that bristling line of battle, where the boys lay waiting for the orders to move forward or for the appearance of the attacking forces out beyond the peach orchard.

Jack, during this period of repose, had some very serious thoughts. Above all other meditations—thoughts of home, of loved ones far away, of the course of the battle—sounded in his soul the question, " What about the future ? Suppose you are killed, what will become of you ? In a few moments the tempest will break over this field and you will have to face it. You cannot now escape in any way from this emergency. In the face of the opening battle how about the future ? Are you ready to meet God and to face the issues of another world ? "

The boy sat on the grass troubled and aghast at the outlook. He had been trained in a religious home, had been taught to be a Christian from childhood, but amid the roughness, the exposures, the grossness, and the dissipation of army life for nearly two years many of these lessons and early impressions had grown dim, many of these admonitory voices which he had been taught to heed at home had ceased to influence him. Now, in a desperate emergency, with the possibilities of death before him, his sins rose up in alarming array, and his neglected soul was smitten with a sense of its needy and suppliant condition. " O Lord, have mercy on me!" was the single cry of his broken heart as he sought to keep back the tears, maintain his composure, and hide the tumult which disturbed his breast. Then he bethought himself of the Bible he carried, his mother's parting gift, the book that he had neglected and slighted of late. Turning to it and catching at it as a drowning man at a straw, he opened it at random. The leaves parted at the 121st Psalm, and the boy's eyes fell, as he glanced at the page, on these words: "The Lord shall preserve thee from all evil: he shall preserve thy soul."

The utterance seemed like a direct revelation from the skies. The boy felt as though there was some One who had taken knowledge of his destitute estate, his fears, his remorse, his sorrow, his anxiety, his cry for help. The words got hold of him, and he got hold of the words with a grip that has never ceased from that day to this. The vows made in that hour of danger and trouble were never forgotten, and while brooding on the passage so strangely applicable to his time of peril and want the boy's heart was lightened and at least a part of the burden was rolled away. He had scarcely put up the book and buckled on his sword in anticipation of orders to move, indicated by activity on the part of some of the troops near by, when an aid from General Sickles rode up at full speed and said to General Humphreys, "Berdan's sharpshooters are out yonder beyond the peach orchard and in the woods to our left. They send in word that Longstreet is massing a heavy force in that direction and is planning an attack against Round Top. General Sickles is going to move his corps out to the peach orchard. He directs your division to march out and form line along the Emmitsburg road at once."

Immediately the drums and bugle sounded the "assembly;" the orders were repeated all along the command, "Fall in, men!" The line was formed, and ten thousand men with turbulent hearts and knit brows and flashing eye, knowing that the hour had come on whose issues the destiny of the republic depended, heard the word " Forward," and marched forth to meet the advancing enemy. They had scarcely taken their advanced position before the battle of the second day opened with overwhelming violence. Inside of two hours half that gallant host, and as many of the foe, lay in blood and dust and death on the crimsoned soil of Pennsylvania. The struggle in the neighborhood of Round Top, where this portion of the battle of Gettysburg was fought, will require another chapter for its recital.

CHAPTER XVIII.

THE STRUGGLE FOR ROUND TOP.

IT was a brilliant sight— the march of the Third Army Corps, under Sickles, from its place in the line of battle near Little Round Top, half a mile toward the west and the southwest, to occupy a new position on the ridge in their front. Battleflags waved above the heads of the gallant soldiers; the bright gleam of their muskets flashed along their extended line; aids were to be seen galloping in every direction to execute the orders for the advance; bugles sounded out their stirring blasts, indicating the will of the corps commander, Major General Sickles, who, with his gayly decorated staff, some of them in showy Zouave costume, superintended the movement. While no engagement had yet taken place, yet the rapid " crack," " crack," of muskets beyond the hills, all along the skirmish line, afforded signs of fast-approaching battle.

'The division of Humphreys formed in line along the Emmitsburg road, beyond which, in the woods, across the fields, could be seen now and then glimpses of men in gray and brown uniforms, the marshaling hosts of the Confederates, massing for their attack upon the Union left flank. "It's plain to be seen that Gineral Sickles," was the remark of Sergeant McBride, as the boys marched out to the front to take their place on the advance line of battle, " does not belave in siege work. He is spilin' for a fight; he has the chip on his shoulder now; you can see it in his ivery motion as he rides along the ranks. He is intimatin' to Gineral Longstreet over yonder in the woods, wid ivery wink of his eye, and every motion of his head, ' Knock off this chip if you dare.' An' from the wicked way in which the skirmishers out there are exchangin' shots, and the hurryin' that's goin' on in the woods, I am of the opinion that the rebel gineral will not be slow in acceptin' the challenge."

Jack marched along by the sergeant's side, keeping his men aligned and noting the whole movement, wondering and anxious what the result of this advance would be. In a moment he replied to the Irishman: " We shall have no ' ditching ' here, that is clear, unless some of us get into ' the last ditch,' which is very probable from present appearances. If we have to fight let us have it out, and be done with it; that seems to be Sickles's motto to-day, and his men are with him in that sentiment." And the cheers that went up as the general galloped across the field showed that the Third Corps believed in the intrepidity and skill of its impetuous leader.

The men found the fences all down as they marched forward, the skirmishers having destroyed them in their advance, thus clearing the fields of barriers that might have impeded the movement. The line was soon formed, and a brief breathing spell was afforded before the death grapple of the two armies came.

Off to the left, on a hillock, Jack saw the batteries forming and the men of Birney's division going into position in the peach orchard of Sherfey. Looking to the rear of them, he saw Round Top looming up over the field, with rugged sides and big bowlders on its flank and front. The question to be settled within the next two or three hours was, " Who shall hold that hill ? " On the decision of that question hung the fate of the nation. Let the rebels capture Round Top, and the Union is lost ; if the Army of the Potomac can keep it the country is safe.

It is half past three o'clock in the afternoon, and suddenly a cannon shot is heard, followed by another, a sign that something is going to happen. General Sickles has been at Meade's headquarters, half a mile away to the rear on the Taneytown road, and the noise of the artillery brings him galloping to his corps, with General Meade following close behind, the two making a striking contrast, Sickles being a dashing and brilliant rider, while Meade, with his spare, spectacled figure and his ungainly look, was lacking in some of the qualities that usually arouse enthusiasm on the field of battle. It seems that Sickles had gone out far beyond the point that Meade had intended as the line of battle, several motives prompting the movement, one being the fear that the rebels might occupy the Emmitsburg road and thence advance against the Union line and break it in pieces. He judged that the line he now occupied was better than the other which Meade had chosen. As the two generals sat on their horses for a moment, not far away from where Jack was stationed, it could be clearly seen that both were in deep concern. Finally, after some discussion, Sickles said, " Well, general, I will withdraw and resume my former position back yonder if you give the command."

General Meade, rightly divining the movement then in progress on the part of the enemy, said, " The Confederates will not let you withdraw now;" and the words were hardly out of his lips when an exploding shell in the air almost over their heads showed that the battle was begun. In five minutes the batteries on both sides, which had been wheeling into position, were belching forth round shot and shell against each other, and the attack of the rebels against the Union left flank was begun in earnest. Although the battle did not begin until nearly four in the afternoon, yet it made up in intensity and in deadliness for its short duration. The next four hours were full of untold horrors, and when that waning July evening was done the gathering gloom that settled down on the field, illumined by struggling moonbeams, covered nearly fifteen thousand men who had been killed, wounded, or captured.

"Lieutenant Sanderson," said Captain Russell, of the division staff, as the fight opened, "General Humphreys says, deploy the company in the rear of the division, keep the ranks closed up, allow no straggling, and let no one pass to the rear except the wounded."

"All right, captain," said Jack, "I will obey orders," as he turned to execute the command. "Sergeant McBride, see that the men off to the left are aligned and properly deployed."

The sergeant turned to carry out instructions, his Irish wit coming to his aid even in the crash of the opening battle. With a merry twinkle in his eye he said, "Sure, liftenant, the gineral wants us to make a very thin line wid the company. I wish it could be made as thin as the air itsilf, so that no harrum could come to us from the murtherin' bullets. The thinner the better, says I."

Soon the seventy men were scattered over a space of about half a mile in the order of skirmishers (close up to the second line of battle, which had been massed and held in reserve), each man eight or ten paces from his next-door neighbor.

The battle, for a time, was off to the left in the peach orchard and in front of Round Top, and the division of Humphreys was not at first directly assaulted, but they had to take the stray bullets and shells that came in rapid succession from over the hill in their front.

The sound of tremendous cheering, along with dreadful musketry reports, attracted attention to Round Top in the early stage of the fight, and through the smoke once in a while the blue-coated men of the Fifth Corps could be seen hurrying over the rocks and forming into line, while cannon were drawn up by hand, just in time to prevent the hill falling into the possession of the enemy. The Texan Rangers, under Hood, ardent as the tropics themselves, full of impetuous and contagious valor, hardy sons of the wild Southwest, were pushing with frightful yells for the summit. The fight there lasted for two mortal hours, until the granite bowlders dripped with blood and the steep, rough slopes of the hill were covered with bleeding bodies of men of the South and of the North, intermingled here and there where the wrestling lines of battle came together.

Off to the left, in the peach orchard, hardly anything could be seen but shifting lines of infantry, coming to view once in a while through the smoke, which when it lifted for a moment revealed also the lines of cannon and the artillery men firing their pieces as fast as their lithe and muscular limbs could handle the ammunition and work the guns. Caissons with new supplies of grape and canister were flying, hauled by four horses, across the field; and just above the lines of batteries, which were massed—thirty or forty cannon in all in the orchard—shell after shell could be seen exploding, each piece of shattered missile fraught with death or wounds for man and horse. After an hour of fighting in the orchard, and beyond in the woods— where a pandemonium was raging, fierce and frantic shouts and yells, dreadful musketry firing, and appalling artillery explosions from that direction telling that a desperate conflict was raging there—after an hour of this sort of thing an aid from General Sickles's headquarters galloped across the field to General Humphreys and said, " General, we need help over on our left. Birney's line will be driven in hopelessly unless you can reinforce it. General Sickles says send a part of your division on the double-quick to his relief."

General Humphreys knew his own line was sure to be attacked, and that he would need more men than he had at hand to repel the assault imminent already, but he could not refuse, and in accord with the message sent Major Burns with the "Fourth Excelsior" regiment on the run to the relief of Birney's endangered troops. Off they marched with cheers, to be cut to pieces in front of Round Top as soon as they had fairly got into the swirling edge of the battle caldron.

By this time the round shot and minie balls began to fly thick and fast among the troops of Humphreys's division. Jack, as he looked along his own line, saw now and then a man throw up his arms and fall, or spin around like a top, with a fatal hurt that had suddenly come to him, while among the troops in the front lines more and more havoc was being wrought. It was evident that a direct attack would soon come against this part of the line, for in the fields directly in their front could be seen glimpses of troops in butternut apparel getting ready for some sort of an onset, and meanwhile Lieutenant Seely's battery opening fire upon them.

Suddenly there was disorder and confusion apparent in the peach orchard, as troops, some of them wounded and some in panic and dismay, in little squads appeared through the smoke, falling back out from among the peach trees. At the same time a heavy musketry fire came upon the front line of Humphreys's men, and at this moment an officer from corps headquarters rode up, his horse bleeding from a wound in the neck and his own arm in a sling, and cried in excitement, "General Sickles is wounded, and has been carried from the field. General Birney is in command of the corps, and directs that you change the front of your division so as to face toward the southwest. The lines are broken at the peach orchard, and you will be taken in flank in ten minutes unless you change front. General Graham is wounded and in the hands of the enemy, and his brigade is torn to pieces!"

While the words were being spoken the batteries on the right of the division were retreating slowly, and those in the peach orchard were drawing back a few paces after each discharge, while it was clearly seen that they could not much longer stand the terrific pressure that was brought against them. Before the change of front could be executed musketry in front, musketry on the right, and cannonade on the left told General Humphreys that he was attacked on three sides at once, and in the midst of this assault, made with indescribable fury, he must wheel his division, what remained of it, so as to make a half-face to the left. As though the regiments were on dress parade or executing a movement in review, without confusion or trepidation, they massed their columns, marched backward a few rods in the face of the enemy, wheeled to the left, formed line of battle again in the new direction, and began firing—one of the most difficult and skillful maneuvers ever done upon a battlefield.

Just then Jack looked off to his left toward Round Top, and in the intervale there was to be seen a touching spectacle. The Irish Brigade, with their emerald flag and the insignia of Erin in golden characters upon it waving above them, was advancing to go into battle in the region of the Devil's Den. Before they ventured into the actual battle they halted; the priest who was their chaplain stood on a rock high above the field, where he could be seen by the whole command, and, with the bullets flying about him and with the awful battle raging in his front, he pronounced absolution in behalf of his kneeling constituents. For a moment they bowed there while the priest commended their souls to the mercy of God, and then, with a united and terrible shout, they dashed forward into the bloody field, out of which hardly two thirds emerged unhurt.

The space occupied by the division of Humphreys by this time was the vortex of a caldron of fire, the crater of a volcano of destruction. Out of the seventy men under Jack's command, deployed as they were and not in the front line, and none of them having any chance to fire because of other duties in checking stragglers and caring for the wounded, one third were killed or wounded. It was seven o'clock, and the day was nearly over, but the fight grew hotter and hotter. It seemed as though it would be impossible for anybody to get out of that bubbling vortex of death unhurt. Jack, looking to the peach orchard, saw the lines there overwhelmed, flanked, and pressed irresistibly back. The batteries were surrounded, and one gun after another was captured by the enemy and turned against the Union forces, every horse having been killed and every man in the battery having fallen at his post. Against the weakened, struggling lines of Humphreys in the advancing twilight regiments of heroic Confederates were pressing with eager yells, trampling the wounded Union men under their feet as they pressed on, determined to capture Round Top before the night should fall. An enfilading rebel fire from the Emmitsburg road now tore its way through rank after rank, and from that direction also were to be seen fresh rebel troops flanking the division on that side. The pressure was too great to be borne, and, without facing about, Humphreys's men, obeying orders to retreat toward the hill, slowly and sullenly yielded, step by step, to the invincible attack that pressed them from their advanced position at the Emmitsburg road gradually back toward the Round Top ridge.

In some way Jack had failed to note any order to retreat. His blood was in a ferment, his brain distracted with the excitement and anxiety of the hour. He had for the time lost all thought of personal safety; this time there was no fear or thought of flight in his mind. One awful fact stared him in the face, the Army of the Potomac was being defeated on Pennsylvania soil! To retreat even half a mile seemed to him an irretrievable disaster. Perhaps it meant flight, panic for miles, with the rebels in full pursuit! He thought of his orders to keep the ranks closed up, and looked along his thin line of men, not fifty of them left, and not a dozen near enough to hear any command he might give. In his distraction he burst into tears and then shouted, "Don't let a man through your line!" The words were scarcely spoken when he found himself in the midst of the struggling division, which was being pushed back with irresistible force toward the ridge. His men were entangled in the confused throng; it was impossible to maintain regimental lines; yet the soldiers, without losing their heads or facing to the rear, were firing as fast as they could while falling back. In the midst of the mass Jack saw General Humphreys and Major Hamlin, cool but anxious, overwhelmed with anxiety and all but convinced that the only thing to be done was to die on the field, for it seemed as though the day was hopelessly lost. The general had to bring his little body of troops back over the field for half a mile from their advanced position so that they would fill in the vacancy in the original line in his rear. He had to do this while flanked and raked with a galling attack on both the right and the left and facing an overwhelming force in his front. The general afterward said that he thought at this juncture that all was lost, but if he did think so he never allowed any one else at the time to know the fears he suffered.

As Jack fell back with the division he was in an agony of sorrow and despair. It seemed to him that the Union was being destroyed forever; all hope of victory was taken away. A vision of slaughter off to the left added the climax to his overwrought emotions. Looking thither for a moment through the smoke and tumult, he saw a shell explode in the midst of a battery on the very top of the ghastly rock called "Devil's Den." The caisson was set on fire, and in a moment, with all its stock of ammunition, it exploded. Before the amazed and distracted eyes of the boy there flashed for a single instant against the sky the sight of wheels, limbs of horses and of men, pieces of timber, and scores of exploding shells, all inextricably interwoven into a spectacle of horror that almost drove his brain into madness. Then the smoke covered the scene, and backward the pressure still continued to drive the struggling men of the division.

Two things aided in restoring the frantic boy to something like the limitations of sanity. In the midst of the confusion he saw an officer who had lost an arm show himself possessed of the coolest sort of courage. His arm had been cut off above the elbow by a round shot; the stump was as smooth as though the work had been done by a knife. A comrade had made a temporary tourniquet to stop the bleeding, and the determined man, with a lighted cigar in his mouth and without a sign of trepidation, was deliberately walking to the rear to find a surgeon. This sight aided to reinforce Jack's self-possession. Further, nearing the hill in the rear, he heard a hearty cheer that seemed a token for good. Looking about him, he saw the familiar corps flag of the Sixth Army Corps, who were here at last, in time to help in the final struggle. The day was not lost, then.

after all! It was like passing from hell up to heaven to realize that there was really hope for the Union and that the rebels were not going to win. Still, the battle was not over yet. Off to the left, at Round Top, the glorious Pennsylvania Reserves could be heard cheering and shouting at the victory they had won in their magnificent charge down from the ridge, through the rocky valley, and out to the edge of that dreadful wheatfield, where Death, the reaper, had garnered a bloody harvest all the afternoon. Hancock the Magnificent, one of the most inspiring figures that ever roused and led men on any battlefield, was to be seen riding up and down the field, planting batteries, marshaling the reinforcements as they arrived, filling in the broken line, and aiding in the repulse of the advancing Confederates, who, in their eagerness to make a break in the Union line of battle, followed Humphreys close on his heels. Their line, it is true, was thin by this time, and was not well reinforced, but it made up in courage and spirit what it lacked in weight, and actually penetrated through the Union ranks at one point. Hancock drove them back, and the batteries now lining the hill swept the space in their front with grape and canister. Out of the confusion, the smoke, the battle shouts, the awful din of the conflict, there came something like order and quiet as the rebels realized that they had failed to capture Round Top, and the boys in blue woke to the fact that that commanding point was still in their possession.

Off to the right, at Cemetery Hill, and afterward at Culp's Hill, from six o'clock till nine the battle raged, keeping up the tumult and suspense until long after nightfall.

Jack in the tumult and retreat was separated from his command, and in the darkness and confusion knew not where to find any of his men. Heartsick, exhausted, wondering what the issue of the battle would be on the morrow, he sought here and

HANCOCK THE MAGNIFICENT.

there in the gloom for his scattered company. Stumbling over the stumps and through the underbrush at the base of the northern flank of Round Top, he heard a familiar voice, that of Colonel Burling, commander of the New Jersey Brigade, which had been detached from Humphreys and lent to Birney during the fight.

"How are you, colonel?" was the salutation of the boy as he halted for a moment at the spot where the officer was arranging a blanket in the darkness and getting ready for sleep.

"O," was the sad reply, "we have had a dreadful day. My command is cut to pieces! We left two thirds of them out in the wheatfield and in the peach orchard. Some of my choicest officers are dead, and my brave boys are killed and wounded, until there is but a handful of us left. I hardly know whether I am alive or dead. I appreciate the feelings of General Birney, who said a while ago, in view of the disasters that have almost demolished his brave division, 'I wish I were dead! I wish I were dead! My poor boys, I wish I were dead.'"

Out through the woods squads of men belonging to the ambulance corps could be seen going here and there over the field gathering up the wounded, and all night long their moans and cries of pain, from the hospital in the rear and from the field in front, smote upon the heart of the boy as he tossed on the ground and sought almost in vain for sleep.

Jack, before he slept, ran across Sergeant McBride, and the two rejoiced to find each other alive. "Where have you been?" said Jack.

"Sure, liftenant, I do not know where I haven't been, all over this infernal field, trying to help some of the poor fellows to the hospital. Sure it's a dreadful place! Dead horses iverywhere, dying ones kicking and groaning, dead men by the thousand lying on the ground, and wounded rebels and Union men lying together moaning and crying for water in ivery direction."

"What did you see off to the left during the fight?" said Jack, for the sergeant had gone with a message over to the region occupied by the first division late in the afternoon.

"One thing I saw, liftenant, that I'll niver forget. I saw Gineral Sickles after he was wounded. He was yonder by the Trostle farmhouse on a stretcher, wid his leg covered up wid a blanket, so that nobody could see how bad he was hurted. When they was about to carry him to the rear he asked for a cigar, and he lit it and began to puff the smoke out of his mouth as handsome as you plaze. But, liftenant, I could see the great drops of sweat, from the hurt of his wound, stand out on his brow; and yit for all that he spoke cheerfully to his staff, and niver let on that anything serious was wrong wid him. An' a cousin of mine, in the ambulance corps, Tim Maloney, saw him when the doctors tould him they would have to give him aither or chloroform and then cut off his leg. The gineral said he would not take it. The doctors did not know what to do wid him, until at last they said, 'It's yer one chance of life, gineral, to have your leg amputated.' And then the hero spoke up and said, 'Cut away, but give me a cigar first!' And, as sure as you are still alive and out of the fight of to-day, Gineral Sickles lay there without a whimper and smoked his cigar while the surgeons cut off his leg, he was that anxious that the boys of his corps should not find out how bad he was hurted when he was taken from the field. Didn't I tell you to-day Gineral Sickles was a dashing gineral? It takes the 'Excelsior boys' to know a good thing when they see it, and it's the 'Excelsior boys' that belave in Gineral Daniel E. Sickles!"

Jack now sank into a collapse, which for the time served as a sleep. With groans of wounded men sounding in his ears.

with his heart heavy and anxious about the morrow, sorrowful for the losses in his own company, and praying for God's blessing on the Union and the flag in the conflict that must come with the rising sun, the almost heart-broken boy subsided into a sort of slumber, from which he started in frightful visions again and again throughout that awful night which followed the struggle of the second day, in front of Round Top, at Gettysburg.

CHAPTER XIX.

GETTYSBURG—THE CHARGE ON CEMETERY HILL.

"WHAT will this day bring forth?" was the question which agitated the opposing hosts as they watched the gray dawn appear in the early morning of Friday, July 3. Two days of terrific struggle had passed without any decisive result; thirty thousand men had either been killed, wounded, or captured already, and both armies were suffering from the exhaustion and demoralization incident to such a desperate battle; and yet no victory had been won on either side. Would Lee attack again? Was he ready to retreat without further effort to capture the positions held by the Union army? Or was General Meade getting ready to assume the offensive? Had he made up his mind that it was now time for him to attack his great adversary?

These were among the questions that racked the brains of

those who were able, on account of their high commands, to overlook the whole situation. Wounded men, lying uncared for on the field, moaned and gasped for breath and for water, and in the intervals of their fever wondered what the issues of the day would be; and the whole of that great host, numbering now over fifty thousand men in line on either side, after only a brief respite from the battle, which had come to an end between nine and ten o'clock on the preceding night, after lying on the ground with arms at hand and meagerly satisfying their hunger with the now rapidly diminishing contents of their depleted haversacks, rose from the earth at four next morning to face each other again in the bloody fray.

Jack jumped from his bed of leaves and bushes at the dawn of day, roused by heavy musketry, into the midst of which the cannon soon sent their awful booming concussions. The boy had to rub his eyes for a moment to determine his whereabouts and locate the battle. Peeping over the hill to the west, toward the peach orchard, he saw that the lines of the Confederates were not advancing. Both sides in that vicinity were quiet; even the skirmishers had no apparent spite at one another, and were content with warily watching each other over the muzzles of their muskets, held so that they could shoot with fatal effect at the least sign of an advance on the part of their opponents. There was no fighting, then, the boy saw, in his immediate front. Round Top was in the hands of the Union army, and was filled with blue-coated soldiers, who had surrounded it with a line of breastworks. On its top were several batteries, and the artillerists stood by their guns, ready to fire at a moment's warning. The line of battle first indicated by General Meade was held, after the struggles of the preceding day, intact, just as it had been originally laid out. But where was the firing? It grew more fierce each moment, and came from the northeast.

Perhaps he might find out if he should go off in that direction after a bit. He could not get rid of this notion, and after skirmishing about for a bite of breakfast, and luckily happening upon a comrade who had successfully foraged for chickens in the neighborhood and who shared his spoils with him, and finding that no change of position was intended at once, he secured permission to take a view of the line of battle and do a little exploration in the direction of the battle that was then going on two or three miles away, off at the right of the Union line.

The boy started up the Taneytown road, and had not walked more than half a mile when he found himself at General Meade's headquarters, a little cabin by the roadside, with a garden round it, the locality being almost in the center of the whole line. In front, toward the west, were Hancock's men, massed several lines deep, and in all directions were to be seen officers of high rank, commanding divisions or corps, stationed close by or occupying staff positions at army headquarters. Dead horses, with distorted and swollen forms, lay here and there, and hospital attendants were still bringing in the wounded men and taking them to the hospitals in the rear.

As the boy walked on up the Taneytown road he found his way barred by batteries and lines of battle, and he had to leave the public road and climb the hill to his right, which was surmounted, he found, by a cemetery, now crested with cannon and occupied with troops in all its extent. From this point he could look upon the town, the first opportunity he had yet had of seeing the village, with its quaint steeples and its shade trees. On the west he traced the Confederate line of battle on a low ridge topped with woods and orchards; opposite the town their line left the ridge, ran through the village, and then on around toward the east and southeast, embracing the Union line in the shape of a fishhook. Everything in the town and along the

GETTYSBURG—THE CHARGE ON CEMETERY HILL. 819

rebel line, in the direction of the west and north, was quiet; but there was a terrific musketry fire going on in the woods off to the right, which Jack now found were located on a rough, rocky height called Culp's Hill. Thick volumes of smoke rose from the trees, and troops were hurrying across the depression that intervened between Cemetery Hill and that portion of the line now engaged in battle. Batteries were taking position, and further preparations were going on to make the hill still stronger.

The village cemetery was a frightful spot. The batteries on this eminence had been exposed to a devastating artillery fire and had suffered severely, as was shown by the numbers of dead horses lying about, the dismounted cannon and broken caissons which cumbered the ground, the defaced monuments and fractured tombstones which showed the effects of the shelling the place had received. Here and there were wounded men who had not yet been taken to the hospital, and hundreds of infantry lying on the graves or stretched on the paths, while the ground everywhere was covered with the litter and refuse and *débris* of the battlefield—broken rammers from the cannon, cast-off wheels, abandoned knapsacks, torn blankets, ruined muskets, discarded bayonets, saddles, harness, ammunition cases, caps, hats, coats, and an indescribable lot of other rubbish accumulated amid the confusion and havoc of the battle and lying on every side.

The arched gateway of the cemetery, Jack noted as he emerged from it and cautiously peered about him, had been battered by shot and shell; it was destined to suffer still more severely before the night should come again. In front of it ran the Baltimore pike, the road by which many of the Union troops had arrived on the field the day before. As the boy passed across the pike he saw that it was occupied by a battery of artillery; half a dozen field pieces were pointed down toward the town, so as to sweep the whole width of the road in case any attempt might be made to storm it. On the other side of the road he stepped over the broken-down fence into an open field, and walked a hundred yards farther, when he came to the top of the hill, which, on its northern flank, was steep and grassy and surmounted by redoubts, in the shelter of which were massed three or four batteries, their guns pointing in the various directions from which an assault was possible. As he sauntered along, noting that the sounds of battle were getting more violent off to the right, and wondering what the issues of it might be, he heard himself called by name, and looking around he saw, to his delight, an old school friend, somewhat older than himself, from a neighboring town near his home.

"Why, Jack Sanderson, is that you? Old fellow, how are you? Have you escaped the rebel bullets thus far? How did you find your way to this part of the line?"

It was the cheery voice of Lieutenant Brockway, of Captain Ricketts's Pennsylvania battery, stationed at that point in the battle. He was putting the redoubts in order, strengthening the fortifications, and cleaning up his guns, getting ready for whatever trouble might develop later on in the fight. The rifled guns had seen service, that was evident—wood work all battered and broken, wheels smashed, a field piece dismounted, one cannon spiked, half a dozen dead horses lying in the vicinity, and the earthworks bearing the marks of a terrific cannonade.

"Charley, old friend, I'm glad to find you alive. Is this your post of duty? I am just trying to get an idea of the extent and direction of our line. Our division is about a mile away on the Taneytown road, and while the boys are lying there in reserve for a while I got permission to do a little exploring. It looks here as if you had had something of a fight in this locality."

GETTYSBURG—THE CHARGE ON CEMETERY HILL.

"Fight?" said the lieutenant "fight? I wish you had been here last night about seven o'clock, and you would have said it was a fight!"

"Well, now, Charley, last night at seven o'clock I was where we had just about as much of a fight as I ever want to see. We were driven from near the peach orchard back to the line of the Taneytown road, step by step, in a whirlwind of battle. I was almost crazy for a while with fear lest we were being whipped out of our boots and with the terrible excitement of the hour. If you had any worse experiences over here than we had near Round Top I am glad I was not here to see it. But tell me something about your skirmish here last night. What was it all about? What did the rebels do? How far did they come up this hill?" This was the eager inquiry of Jack, on the alert to get an account of the fight from one who had been in it.

Lieutenant Brockway puckered up his mouth for a brief whistle of wonder and interest for a moment as he glanced across the landscape toward Culp's Hill and noted that the noise was becoming more tumultuous and the smoke more voluminous and dense as it rose from the woods, where great masses of infantry were struggling in deadly conflict, and replied: "How far did the rebels come up this hill? They actually took the hill, and right here where we stand, in the rear of our own guns, we had a terrible tug with them, hand to hand and face to face, for half an hour. It seemed as though everything was lost when we saw this center taken by the enemy."

Jack looked at his watch and noted that his time was nearly exhausted, and that in a little while he must return to his command, and said: "Tell me about it, Charley, if you can, in brief. I must return pretty soon, and I want to have your account of the fight here at the center before I go."

Lieutenant Brockway, stopping now and then to keep track of the squad of men who were strengthening the earthworks, getting the guns ready for action, and repairing damages wrought the evening before, began his story:

"We heard the sound of the opening battle out in the neighborhood of Round Top yesterday afternoon, but were not directly engaged until the worst of your fight was over. All the afternoon, during the fight at Round Top, the troops about us here—the infantry, I mean—were sent off to the left to help Sickles, Sykes, and Hancock, and when evening came on we had but a thin line of troops at the base of the hill yonder to support these batteries around us. About half past six o'clock the rebel batteries over yonder, a mile away, opened against us with a furious cannonade, and we replied in the same fashion. We got the range of their guns, and I sent one shell right into the midst of their gunners that I know must have made sad work with them. At sunset we found out what the bombardment meant. I saw a line of men march by the flank out from one of the streets of the village yonder and form in the fields to the east of the town. When they wheeled into line fronting toward us I knew what was coming. They were getting ready to charge these heights, with the 'Louisiana Tigers,' as I learned after they reached us from some of the prisoners we captured, in the lead. It was a grand sight to look on, that marching host of three brigades, with their flashing guns and their waving flags, and their line firm and well dressed as though out on parade."

"But," interrupted Jack, in his interest, as he almost saw the picture for himself, so vividly did his friend paint it before his eyes on the very spot, which was still wet and red from the blood of the contestants, "but, Charley, they did not maintain that line clear up this hill? You do not tell me that they actually charged half a mile across these fields and made their way into these redoubts and took these guns out of your hands?"

"Hold on, Jack," said the lieutenant, "I'm telling this story, if you please; you are in too great a hurry. We will come to that part of it soon enough. Of course they could not keep up a correctly dressed line half a mile in a bayonet charge, with our batteries blazing into them at every step, but it was a splendid sight, nevertheless, to behold them as they marched through the smoke across the fields, yelling, waving their banners, and at first firing volley after volley of musketry. Yonder, on their left, our batteries from Culp's Hill played on them so terribly that their line was broken—smashed to pieces, in fact. But here, right in front of our redoubts, they kept on in spite of all we could do. There was only a thin line of infantry at the foot of the hill yonder, in the breastworks, to support our guns. I hardly believed they could withstand long the assault which the rebels made when I saw how the gray-backs marched. We found out before long that the famous Louisiana Tigers led the charge, and they did themselves credit, I tell you.

"Their guns on yonder hill, a mile away, had been, as I said, concentrating their fire on us for half an hour before the infantry began to show themselves, and we had been replying to them, giving them as good as we got from them. Now, however, we found it necessary to heed the men with the muskets. They had to march half a mile, almost all the way uphill, before they struck us, and then they made the splinters fly! A hundred yards in our front the weak and scattered regiments that supported us fired off two or three volleys, and then had to run to keep from being captured, for the 'Johnnies' pressed right on in the face of their fire. We had twenty cannon here pointed down the hill, but we could not depress the guns to sweep the hill as we would like to have done; but we rammed down the shrapnel and grape and canister, and made those twenty cannon hissing hot before we were through. Those fellows never stopped for anything, but pressed right on up the slope, determined to take the hill. We could hardly see what was going on because of the smoke, but you may fancy how we felt when we found the infantry in our front retreating and close on their heels the Louisiana Tigers bursting through the smoke and running right into our teeth, coming in full ranks over the redoubts and falling with their bayonets on our gunners! My men would not give up their pieces, and hand to hand with the Confederates they struggled for the hill. Some of my boys were bayoneted at the mouth of their guns, and the two lines were so mixed up in the dusk of the evening that it was hard to tell 't'other from which.' I had been over to the right of the battery, but when I saw the rebels pouring in over the redoubt on the left I hurried over there, and found myself in the midst of a tussling, struggling, swearing, yelling mass of soldiers, bluecoats and butternuts all mixed up together! The rascals had spiked one of our guns, but my boys were whirling their handspikes, swinging their rammers, and using their fists all along the hill in the rear of the cannon. It had grown dark, but as the muskets blazed in our faces we could see that the rebels had gained their point—they had really taken Cemetery Hill, the very center of our whole line. I thought all was lost, but I was so desperate that I did not care what came to me personally in the battle, and so I pitched in with all my might. Right in front of me, as I came into the throng, was a Confederate who had captured our battery guidon and one of our horses, and the fellow was trying in the darkness to make off with both. I felt for my revolver, but I found it gone just when I needed it most. I determined I would not let that fellow steal our flag nor capture that horse, so I picked up a stone and knocked him

"I PICKED UP A STONE AND KNOCKED HIM TO THE EARTH."

to the earth with that, and down I pounced on him and grabbed the flag out of his hands, and as I lifted it into the air the staff was shot in two while I waved it aloft. I did not care for the stick, but I was mighty glad to save that guidon."

"Well, Charley, what next? I'll have to go back to the division pretty soon. How did the thing close? Who licked?"

"Why, we licked, of course. How could I tell you the story and show you the hill if we had not licked? In the midst of the fight we heard a voice like a bulldog's shouting out, 'Give 'em cold steel, boys!' and across Baltimore pike, from the cemetery, came a brigade with General Carroll—"

"Carroll!" said Jack; "I know him. He led our brigade at Fredericksburg. I shall never forget that voice, and I do not know anybody who is more reckless and daring than he is. He was a splendid commander to lead a forlorn hope. To hear his voice ordering a charge is worth a whole regiment in itself as a reinforcement."

"General Carroll," continued Lieutenant Brockway, "arrived just in time to relieve the pressure upon us and enable us to keep our post. We were overwhelmed, hemmed in, almost surrounded, and yet the boys of Ricketts's Battery and those associated with us clung to their guns and fought like demons to rescue them from the hands of the rebels even when it seemed a hopeless struggle. When Carroll's men came to our help we were almost ready to die in our tracks, and thus give up the ground to the Confederates; but we would not have surrendered our guns nor ourselves. We would have died first!" And the gallant lieutenant wiped the perspiration from his brow and drew a deep breath as he realized once more what a trying ordeal he and his brave boys had gone through the night before.

Meanwhile the firing on the ridge called Culp's Hill became more and more furious, and wild, fierce yells came from the opposing ranks, but it was impossible to tell which side was gaining any advantage. Jack bade good-bye to his friend and started back to the division, noting as he went that troops were being hurried across to the place where the fighting was going on, and also finding out, as he passed General Meade's headquarters, that the ranks in that vicinity were being rapidly and thoroughly strengthened by troops, which were massed in several lines of battle along the ridge facing the plain, on the other side of which, to the west, the rebels were arranged beyond the Emmitsburg road.

About ten years after the battle Jack lived for a while in the town of Gettysburg, and here one day he picked up an incident in relation to the charge of the rebels up the slopes of Cemetery Hill on the evening of July 2 which may be interesting in connection with the description of that affair which we have just given. A lady in the town, Mrs. Robert Sheads, a devout and patriotic woman, lived on one of the streets of the town traversed by the Confederates as they marched out to the field that evening. They were massed for half an hour or more in front of her house while the artillery was shelling the hill and trying to break the Union line of battle, and thus open the way for the infantry to charge. The boys were talking together of what they were going to attempt. One of them said, " Boys, we are going to take that hill where the graveyard is. It will be a steep climb, but we will do it or die."

"Yes," said another one of the command—the Louisiana Tigers—" we are going to take that hill and capture the guns that have been shelling our lines all day."

In a little while they marched out to the field and were lost to her sight; but her heart was almost broken with anxiety and dread lest their threat should be carried out. At last, in an agony of fear, she turned to her husband and with tears cried out, "Robert, let us go to God in prayer. Let us ask him to help our boys keep their battery." And while that battle of two hours was in progress, while the Confederates were pressing their way up the death-swept, fire-scathed slope, that woman was upon her knees in prayer, pleading that they might be helped and the battery might be saved. Who can tell how much the prayer of that wrestling soul accomplished toward deciding the battle and saving the day?

Off to the right about eleven o'clock the musketry firing grew less severe and finally ceased. There was a wild yell, a roar of thousands of voices, and then silence. The ground in that wooded height, at the close of the fight, was cut and torn to pieces with musketry. Trees as large as a man's body were sawed in two by musket balls, no artillery being used here at all. For seven deathful hours charge and countercharge were made, until the earth was finally covered with the mangled bodies of men in blue and men in gray, whose blood intermingled as it reddened the soil. At last Ruger and Geary, with their divisions of the Twelfth Corps, under Williams, drove the Confederates out of the intrenchments which they had occupied all night, and thus regained our former line of battle.

For two hours, from eleven till one, that day there was quiet. All the sounds of battle were lulled. What did it mean? What further movement was planned? Lee had first attacked the left flank of the Union line at Round Top, and had failed to make an impression there; next he had charged with the Louisiana Tigers on the center, and that attack had been repulsed; later, at nine o'clock at night on Thursday, July 2, he had driven in the lines of Meade on Culp's Hill; but this advantage had been neutralized by the charge of Geary, who had just now, at a little before eleven in the morning of Friday, retaken the intrenchments lost the night before, so that the original line of battle established by Meade on Thursday morning was now held as at first laid out, without an indentation or a break anywhere in its extent. Thus in turn Lee had attacked the left, the center, and the right of the Union position without obtaining a lodgment or breaking through the line. What would he do next?

The silence continued for two hours, oppressive and awful on account of the suspense and uncertainty that overhung the field, and because of the contrast between the awful hush and the tumult that had immediately preceded it. Jack fairly held his breath as the stillness grew dense and the silence appalling.

The broken division of Humphreys was placed in the rear of Hancock's men on the left center of the Union line. Here the soldiers were closed *en masse*, line after line, in solid blocks, in support of the divisions in the front, which were deployed in actual line of battle. Cannon stood along the ridge as thickly as they could be planted, while reserve stores of ammunition were close at hand. Jack felt a strange sense of awe; an oppressive and ominous dread of he knew not what came over him in that interval of silence. The nerves of all that army were held in the very tensest strain, and with a solemnity and dread that smote to the very depths of the soul the host waited for the next move to be made. When and where would that next blow fall?

CHAPTER XX.

GETTYSBURG—THE GREAT VICTORY.

AT five minutes before one o'clock on Friday, July 3, silence reigned supreme all along the embattled lines of the two great armies which stood face to face, taking their breath in anticipation of a final struggle, this time "even unto death." Three minutes elapsed and the hush, which had lasted almost two mortal hours, still continued. Then came a cannon shot, and at the interval of sixty seconds another, and then pandemonium! The heavens were on fire, the earth shook with an awful trembling, the air was torn and distracted with terrific concussions, furious and incessant explosions from booming cannon and bursting shells and whizzing round shot and screaming projectiles of various sorts, shapes, and sizes coming from about one hundred and fifty guns that had been ranged in batteries on the hills occupied by the Confederate line of battle.

Throughout the whole of the morning the rebel artillerists had been concentrating the aim of their cannon upon the left center of the Union line with the aim of breaking up and thoroughly demoralizing that portion of that army. They had massed their guns, skillfully arranged them so as to cover the threatened section of the Union troops, and at the given signal of two cannon shots had opened their fire halfway around the horizon. On the instant about twenty-five batteries of rifled or smoothbore cannon, six guns in each battery, of various caliber, and carrying all sorts of missiles, vomited forth each one a volume of flame, a cloud of sulphurous smoke, and a steel or iron projectile, perhaps filled with explosives and packed with other missiles, all ready at the proper moment to burst in the midst or over the heads of the Union troops. It was as though hell had broken loose when those dreadful engines of destruction began all at once their havoc, after two hours of breathless suspense and absolute silence. The noise, the confusion, the violence of a thousand earthquakes and thunderstorms all packed into one seemed to burst forth in a moment as the cannoneers obeyed the signal to fire and launched forth their implements of death into the air at one o'clock that afternoon.

On the other hand, General Meade had not been idle. His generalship in the battle was nowhere so clearly shown as in his foresight in connection with the final movement of the foe. He divined in advance the intention of General Lee; massed his reserved artillery on the hills, where he could best reply to the guns of his antagonist; packed his troops several lines deep along the threatened portion of his front; and when the desperate blow of the Army of Northern Virginia was at last launched in all its fury the Union commander was ready to meet it. He had hardly need to move a man, to change the position of a gun, to add a regiment to the forces already in rear of the part of his line which was the special object of the concentrated artillery and infantry attack of the enemy. He could hardly have made his plans better in this regard if he had been informed by Lee in advance concerning the objective point in the last move of the game.

After a few moments of delay on the Union side more than a hundred cannon replied to those which had opened the battle along the Confederate lines. The artillerists had stood on either side, lanyard in hand, guns in position, ammunition in large quantities within reach, cannon loaded and ready to go off with a single pull at the twine connected with the friction tube in the touch-hole. On the given signal the rebel cannoneers twitched the twine and tortured the atmosphere with the infernal tumult of their cannonade. In a little while the Union gunners, who had been standing, for half an hour at least, in readiness for whatever movement might develop, took their cue, made sure their aim at the opposing batteries, and responded with six-score fieldpieces. More than three hundred cannon altogether conspired to produce a furious series of explosions, a horrible, sky-rending, earth-shaking, soul-stunning tempest of fire, of smoke, and of thunderous detonations, never before or since witnessed on the American continent. No such cannonade as that which preceded Pickett's charge ever took place on any other battle-field of America. General Hancock spoke of it in his report as the "heaviest artillery fire" he had ever known.

The artillery, of course, was most exposed to this terrific storm of iron hail, this tempest of bullets and exploding shells. The infantry lay down flat on the earth, hid behind stone fences, if any were near, found some shelter in the rear of bowlders at certain points of the field, dug slight trenches in the ground, and in all possible ways shielded themselves from the pelting blasts of deadly projectiles that filled the spaces over their heads.

Jack, with his men close packed together, lay with the division, with columns closed *en masse* in reserve, in the second line of battle, in the very focus of the concentrated artillery fire of the enemy. It seemed to them that it was the unluckiest place in the line, for the front ranks were on the top of a slight ridge, or on the slope of the hill toward the enemy, and the guns of the rebels were so aimed as just to miss this hilltop and fall over it on the slope occupied by the troops held in reserve, supporting the Second Corps, to which detachment Jack and his men now belonged. The howls, the infernal screams, the unearthly shrieks, and the fiend-like wailings of these various projectiles no man can now describe or fancy. He must have listened to them to be able to picture them to his imagination. And yet there were revelations of pathos and merriment even in the very midst of the eruptions of that volcanic and fiery cannonade.

Sergeant McBride, for one, could not be repressed, although almost every moment the wild screeching of a bomb, or the explosion of shrapnel shells, or the whizzing of a round shot, or the rattle of fragments of exploding missiles of various sorts upon the rocks and earth imposed silence on every tongue but his and pallor on almost every face. The merry Irishman joked to keep his courage up; and "Mishter Lee," he muttered to himself as a screaming projectile passed just over his head and struck in the road a few yards behind him, making the gravel fly and the dust ascend in a whirlwind and scattering pieces in all directions, "Mishter Lee, be careful now wid your hardware. Betther save some of it for another occasion. Remimber that iron is scarce in the South an' it's hard to run the blockade, and foundries are not plinty in the Confideracy. By the sowls of all my ancestors in ould Ireland," he continued, as a wild, piercing, wailing scream like that of a demon in torment came from another missile, issued from an English Whitworth rifled gun, and falling close by the witty sergeant, "they've exhausted purgatory and opened the door into the lowermost regions, for that noise came from some crayture in deadly pain. Sure it sounds as if they had the spirits of the dead in their guns and were firing them at us this day. The Lord and all the saints presarve us, for that sounds as though the ould divil himself, which St. Paul says is the prince of the power of the air, had sure enough got after us this day. D'ye hear him scraych and yell and howl and whine and groan all through this sulphureous atmosphere. It smells like him, too. Phew, wid all this gunpowder in my throat I've had a taste of the very ould Satan himself this day!"

Just as Sergeant McBride finished this sentence an explosive with an uncommonly dreadful noise accompanying it passed over him, barely grazing the place which his head had occupied a moment before. The sergeant, alert and wary, had dodged just in time to escape death by sprawling on the ground with an instantaneous movement downward, which left him collapsed and wriggling on the earth. To Jack and his comrades it seemed, so quick was the whole performance, that McBride must surely be killed, but in a moment they were relieved to see him half rise from the ground and put his thumb to his nose and look toward the rear, where the projectile had just burst, and cry out, "I chated ye that time, ye ould Confiderate divil, ye. I heard ye comin' and squatted quick. Sure, if a man is born to be hung you cannot kill him wid an ould rebel murdherin' shell!"

Jack broke in on the Irishman now with a command: "Sergeant McBride, keep your place in the line, and do not rise until you are ordered to. You have no right to get up and expose yourself needlessly. Keep your head down now, and maybe you will cheat the devil and get through the battle without harm."

Some of the boys had lighted their pipes and were trying to calm their excitement and keep themselves in equipoise by the soporific power of tobacco; but with all the power of discipline and tobacco combined it was a trying thing to lie still and take that awful cannonade and quietly wait for whatever desperate assault might follow up the roar and destruction wrought by the thunderous guns.

The batteries of artillery suffered the most, after all, from this dreadful duel, some of them being actually torn to pieces, guns dismounted, caissons blown up, men shot down, earthworks destroyed, horses killed. Prodigies of valor were performed by these heroic men in the midst of the havoc and violence and smoke and slaughter that raged about them with more than volcanic force. Not very far away from where Jack was stationed in the line was a battery belonging to the regular artillery, in the very focus of the storm that beat from the Confederate guns upon the Union line. A sergeant of this command fell a victim to the explosion of a shell which burst in the very midst of the guns whose fire he was directing. In a moment others rose from the earth unhurt, but he lay gasping for breath; one of his comrades came to speak to him and find out if he was injured. He saw at once that the sergeant was fatally wounded, the blood from a shocking hurt in his breast rapidly ebbing away. The comrade stooped to give the dying man his hand and a helpful word, when the latter said, "Have you water? Give me a drink." And with the request the eyes of the dying man began to fail and his breath came in gasps and sobs, and it was clear that he had not long to live. The comrade replied, as he shook his canteen and found it empty, and saw that the fight was getting more fierce and terrible, every man's energies being occupied with the work of manning the guns, and additional explosives falling every second in their ranks and among their

GETTYSBURG—THE GREAT VICTORY.   337

rifled guns, " O, my boy, I have not a drop of water, and the battle is too hot for me to get any now."

The dying artillerist caught the words, and for a moment roused himself from the stupor which was overwhelming his faculties. Then he exerted his dying energies to lift up his body and raise his voice so that he might be heard by his comrades

"BOYS, NEVER GIVE UP YOUR BATTERY!"

around him. It was his last message, and even amid the confusion and noise and tumult that raged on the hill many of his comrades heard the stirring words, worthy to stand in history alongside of Lawrence's immortal utterance, " Don't give up the ship!" The dying man expended his waning strength in one supreme effort, and shouted with heroic fervor, "Boys, never give up your battery!" and fell over dead.
22

After an hour and a half of artillery work the Union guns suddenly ceased firing. General Meade, and General Hunt, his chief of artillery, at the same moment, one at one end of the line and the other at another point, gave the command to cease firing in order to save ammunition and bring on the final attack, which they clearly foresaw would be made. General Lee took it for granted, in view of the sudden silence of the guns of the Army of the Potomac, that its batteries must be destroyed and its forces disorganized. He proceeded at once to carry out, therefore, a movement which he had been getting ready for all day. In McMillan's orchard and in the woods that crest Seminary Ridge he had been massing his choicest brigades of infantry with the purpose of making a final, desperate charge against the left center of the Union line after the cannonade had demoralized and broken it to pieces. Longstreet had command of the general movement, but the charge itself was committed to the care of General Pickett, with his brigade of Virginia troops as his main support to lead the van. Fourteen thousand men in all were picked out early in the day, and massed behind Seminary Ridge they patiently awaited the summons to charge. The hour of destiny for them, and for the world as well, had come, and, without waiting for the orders which Longstreet in his foreboding that the movement could not succeed was hardly able to frame, Pickett assumed leadership and sounded forth the command to march forward across the plain.

Standing on the hill where the Union troops are posted let us try to picture that almost matchless movement. A stone fence is immediately in our front, with batteries of artillery lining the slope. Look about you: here are bronzed and worn veterans in blue, with a set and dogged expression on their lips and in their eyes, line after line of them, massed on both slopes and on the crest of the ridge in support of the batteries. In

GETTYSBURG—THE GREAT VICTORY.

front, toward the west, is the advanced line of Union troops, and beyond them are pleasant fields rolling in beauty; the fences are mostly broken down; the road to Emmitsburg crosses the landscape toward the southwest, and a mile away toward the region of the setting sun Seminary Ridge, crested with woods and orchards, limits the view. Over this plain and against these batteries and upon this stone wall more than ten thousand men are about to be led with a furious and indomitable courage not to be paralleled by any other martial achievement hitherto wrought by the Army of Northern Virginia. As we look with bated breath and quivering nerves on the landscape we behold the shimmer of steel along the distant ridge, and then the flutter of banners and then an advancing line of men emerging out from the cover of the orchard and the woods. They reach in length almost a mile as they come into view, with battle flags waving and muskets glittering in the July sun, which with pitiless heat beats down on the field. Another line appears behind the first, and then another still, Pickett's select body of Virginians leading the advance, and all of the warriors clad in uniforms of butternut or gray.

They are at the start fully a mile off, and they are not yet ready to charge; but with steady, determined tread, with the bearing of men who know on what a desperate mission they have been sent, and who have resolved to carry the Union line or perish, indeed, in "the last ditch," they come across that rolling plain. No man who looked on the scene can ever forget it. There was at the outset no impetuous, hot-headed Southern valor, but a cool, disciplined steadiness that won the admiration of all who beheld the attack.

Almost from the start the Union cannon were trained upon them, and in the distance solid shot plowed their way through the Confederate ranks; as these came nearer shells were sent skillfully among them, exploding in their faces; sixty or seventy pieces of artillery got the range of the advancing line and began a terrific fire as soon as the infantry came out from cover. From Round Top the charging host were assailed by shot and shell from forty cannon, which took them in flank at the distance of over a mile. No sign, however, of demoralization was noted as the fruit of this artillery fire, for as fast as men fell dead or wounded others crowded up to take the vacated places. Clouds of smoke soon covered the field, but now and then a puff of air cleared away the mists of the battle, ever and anon revealing that embattled host, with solid front of glistening steel and with invincible heroism, making its way over the fields and pushing with wild, shrill yells for the position before them, the summit of the hill.

> "O now let every heart be stanch and every aim be true!
> For look! from yonder wood that skirts the valley's farther marge
> The flower of all the Southern host move to the final charge.
> By heaven! it is fearful sight to see their double rank
> Come with a hundred battle flags—a mile from flank to flank!
> Trampling the grain to earth they come, ten thousand men abreast;
> Their standards wave—their hearts are brave—they hasten not nor rest,
> But close the gaps our cannon make, and onward press, and nigher,
> And yelling at our very front again pour in their fire!"

Pickett's men have now reached the Emmitsburg road in the Union front, and here he halts to re-form his line, which is rent and torn with canister and grape-shot from the Union batteries. After only a brief stay he issues the command, "Forward!" and with exultant and eager tread, moving soon into the double-quick, his magnificent men speed on their way. Will anything check them? Are they indeed to carry the hill and pierce the Union line of battle?

The Union infantry have been reserving their fire until the rebels should come within close range. Now they are but a hundred paces off, and their firm, well-aligned ranks of men in brown and gray can be clearly seen at intervals in spite of the smoke from the batteries. The men along the Union lines can be restrained no longer. A sheet of flame and smoke bursts from their guns. When the smoke lifts for a moment the first line of the Confederate division is melted as the frosts are dissolved before the beams of the morning; but the second presses on with the fierce Southern battle yell which can never die out in the memory of those who have listened to it. Fifty battle flags are waving in the fight, ten thousand men are charging our works; with wild yells and bayonets at a charge they rush against our barricade. The two lines at last have come together, and they mingle in a tumultuous, infernal, bloody struggle which can never be forgotten by anyone who was there to get even a glimpse of it.

The outermost line of the Union troops were overwhelmed by the savage and desperate pressure of the charging lines, and was pressed back toward the top of the ridge. Commotion and tumult ensued, which threatened to spread disaster in all directions. An appalling tremor thrilled like a pulse of terror through all the ranks of excited men. Could any force withstand this mad onset, this living catapult, which had been hurled for a mile across the plain, and which solid shot, shells, grape, and canister had failed to swerve from its deadly course?

Armistead, the leader of one of Pickett's brigades, headed the advance with an ardor, an impetuosity, and a magnetic bearing that were worthy of a better cause. Foremost in the line, leading the charge, he leaped upon a barricade that had been thrown up as a sort of intrenchment for the Union troops and urged his men forward. With his hat off, and waving his sword high in air, and followed by scores of his bravest men, he dashes down into the forest of bayonets and strives to make a pathway for his followers through the bloody ranks of men in blue, who vibrate to and fro in the terrible crisis that is upon them. The batteries can no longer fire, lest they may hurt their own men; but before they cease firing Lieutenant Alonzo H. Cushing, a young West Point graduate, only twenty-two years of age, barely two years out of school, a model of youthful gallantry and grace, crowned his heroic career with a final act of patriotic devotion. All of his cannon but one, in the battery he commanded, had been disabled, and he had been bleeding and suffering from dreadful wounds for two hours, but had not left his place in the line. Now, in this critical hour of the fight, he was smitten with musket balls while his last gun was being loaded. Staggering with his death-wounds, he still did not yield up his life at once. He pulled the lanyard, crying to his superior, General Webb, "I'll give them one more shot," and dropped dying to the ground, as the projectile sped forth on its mission of destruction right into the faces of the advancing Confederates, who were then almost at the mouth of the gun, at the very moment when General Armistead, the foremost figure in the Confederate ranks, not far away from Cushing, had reached his utmost point of assault and fell down to the earth pierced with Union bullets.

Just then a desperate act of gallantry was done by a Union staff officer, Lieutenant Haskell, of General Gibbon's staff, who saw the Union ranks wavering and about to give way at the point of contact between them and the Confederate troops. The lieutenant happened to be the only officer just at that moment on horseback, all the other horses having been sent to the rear or hurt by the enemy's fire. Without hesitation, prompted by the emergency of the hour and fearing that the division was about to retreat or be driven back in confusion, he bravely rode forward, galloping between the two lines, waving his sword, urging the Union lines forward again into the breastworks. His

"I'LL GIVE THEM ONE MORE SHOT."

horse received many wounds and he was also hurt, but out of the storm of bullets he emerged at last with his life, having aided with singular skill and valor to steady the quivering Union line of battle. Meanwhile caissons are exploding; wounded, riderless horses are galloping aimlessly to and fro; rebel and Union troops are mixed up together, so that in the smoke and tumult one can hardly be distinguished from the other; the generals —Hancock, Gibbon, Hays, Humphreys, and others—dismounted, and their aids also, are in the midst of the struggling masses; bayonets, sabers, clubbed muskets, handspikes, are used in the dreadful fight, where twenty thousand men, bleeding, cursing, yelling, trodden under foot, climbing over the stone fence, using perchance their clinched fists when all other weapons are gone, are heaving, tossing, groaning, crying, under the stress and strain and upheaval of the fiery whirlpool which is devouring them.

In front of the point where Jack was stationed was a gallant little Vermont brigade under Stannard. These Green Mountain boys were in their first battle, having but just joined the Army of the Potomac. Hitherto, for months, they had been drowsing away their time behind the safe, quiet fortifications of Washington. As the rebels came upon Gibbon an unusual opportunity was afforded for a Union flank movement. Suddenly the New England men heard the command shouted above the turmoil of the strife, " Second Vermont Brigade, change front, forward! Double quick, march!" As though they were on dress parade the brigade hastened to execute the orders, and with the coolness and precision of regimental drill they swung around against the rebel right, pouring forth at short range a destructive fire. Hundreds were shot down, yet on the desperate rebels pressed to the very mouth of the cannon. The grimy cannoneers, their canister and grape now exhausted, sprang to the mouth of their guns and beat back the daring and desperate foe with rammer and sponge staff. Surely braver soldiers never breathed than those who charged across that plain and those who, with equal courage, beat back the men in gray.

Confusion now appears to reign supreme in that seething mass of wrestling, screaming, bleeding, desperate men; but amid it all the Union line finally emerges unbroken. Its defenders crowd together in ranks from four to ten deep; regimental organizations are dissolved, and officers of all grades are intermingled with privates, and no one can tell where one battalion ends and another begins, but they all stand firm throughout the whole line. The Confederates dash up against the Union men again and again, but all in vain;—they reel back into the plain, stunned, crestfallen, and defeated. They have done all that it is possible for martial courage and desperate valor to accomplish, but they cannot penetrate that line. The supreme effort of the Confederacy has been made, but it ends in rout, ruin, overwhelming and irretrievable disaster. Hancock's men are blazing in their faces; part of the First Corps is pouring a deadly fire into their flank; three fourths of their number are lying in blood upon the ground; their blow has recoiled with crushing force upon themselves. Hemmed in on every side—bayonets and batteries in front, musketry pouring a murderous fire into either flank—hundreds throw themselves upon the earth to escape the tempest of fire that sweeps the field. The unhappy remnant, wounded, bleeding at every pore, their cause lost, their hopes blighted, their generals dead or dying, their flags captured, their magnificent corps literally cut to pieces, go back again across the plain over which they had so eagerly and jubilantly marched an hour before, but now broken, discomfited, crushed, defeated. The battle is over, the issue of the war is decided, the victory has been won by the patient, long-tried, and at last triumphant Army of the Potomac; victory, after the reverses on

GETTYSBURG—THE GREAT VICTORY.

the peninsula, with its ditches and retreats and ineffectual valor; after the shame of Bull Run and the disgrace of Chancellorsville, and the half-won battle of Antietam, and the dismay and havoc of Fredericksburg; victory, that would send a tidal wave of dismay and terror throbbing to the utmost corner of the doomed Confederacy, that would gladden the hearts of our prisoners in Libby and in Andersonville, that would assure other nations that the republic was no bubble glittering for an hour, but a star of hope and promise kindled in the western sky with splendors that would last through time; victory that would crown the names of Meade and of Gettysburg with undying renown!

With one glad impulse that victorious Army of the Potomac rose from their breastworks and sent out their glad rejoicings. The enemy had made his final attack and had failed. His culminating assault had resulted in his humiliation and defeat. Cheer after cheer arose from the triumphant boys in blue, echoing from Round Top, reechoing from Cemetery Hill, resounding in the vale below, and making the very heavens throb with the exultant cries, the jubilant and stormy shouts, of the victorious Army of the Potomac!

CHAPTER XXI.

AFTER THE BATTLE.

THE battle was now over, but nobody knew it! The repulse of Pickett's charge was really the defeat of the Army of Northern Virginia, but it required two days to make known that decision. Until Monday morning, from Friday afternoon the two armies stood at bay, glaring like two wild beasts which had fought one another almost to death, watching for a stroke or a motion, and listening for a growl that might indicate a further continuance of the struggle. General Meade hardly durst venture out against the Confederates after the defeat of Pickett, and General Lee was too weak to undertake any further movement except in retreat, unless he should be attacked. So the two armies waited for developments.

The higher a bird flies into the air the lower must be its descent back to the earth again. So the reaction and collapse occur after the wild excitement and tumult of the battle. In the engagement men are stirred up into madness, to the utmost fury; they are beside themselves in their frenzy. The awful noise of musketry and cannon, the swiftly moving cavalry, the charging hosts, the varying, shifting phases of the fight, with defeat or victory all the while trembling in the balances, wounds, blood, hurrahs, deaths, all together rouse the soul into a tempest, the like of which is unknown anywhere else. When the bloody work is done the descent of the soul into weakness, gloom, and despair is swift and sudden.

There have been few such sights and circumstances as those amid which the two armies found themselves at Gettysburg when the fight was over on Friday afternoon, July 3, 1863.

As Pickett's men reeled back across the plain some of the Union generals who saw the sight were in favor of pressing after the fleeing fugitives and crowding them into retreat and panic, if possible. Others said, "Not so; we are not able to make such a venture. Let well enough alone. If we charge after them we are liable to be driven back again. We may endanger our flank and lose what we have already gained. Wait and watch to see what the enemy intends to do." And this was the policy that Meade actually followed.

Some cannon on either side kept up a scattered fire, and some of the Union troops pressed their line out toward that of the Confederates, in front of Round Top; and after a bit of a skirmish the Confederates withdrew, retreating back to the Peach Orchard.

By this time it was night, and thousands of men were lying unattended, scattered over the field, mingled with broken gun carriages, exploded caissons, hundreds of dead and dying horses, and other ghastly *débris* of the battlefield. At once the poor victims of shot and shell nearest our lines were brought in; others farther out were in due time reached; and the surgeons and nurses, all night long, and for days and nights after that night of horror, kept up their work of ministering to and caring for the wounded, of whom there were more than twenty thousand in our hands.

It was possible, as night came on, to make a bit of a fire, here and there in the rear, and boil water for a cup of coffee, which was a boon to be grateful for. While the boys sat or lay on the ground, eating a bite of hard-tack and eagerly, in their hunger, devouring the succulent salt pork, which was about the only nourishment to be secured, relays of men with stretchers, and hundreds of others helping the wounded to walk to the rear, passed back and forth with their bloody freight; now and then a groan or a suppressed shriek telling the story of suffering and heroic fortitude.

"Listen, boys!" was the shout of one of Jack's men, as they lay on the ground near division headquarters that night. "The fight must be over—listen! There is a band in the rear beginning to tune up. Surely that is a sign that the battle is done. If there was any sign of danger those musicians would not venture back here." And while the boys kept up their humorous and sarcastic comments *versus* the trumpeters, the band had begun to play. It was a sight and a situation long to be remembered. The field was covered with the slain; the full moon looked down with serene, unclouded, and softened luster on the field of Gettysburg, trodden down for miles by the two great armies; surgeons were cutting off limbs, administering whisky, chloroform, and morphine to deaden pain; hundreds of men were going back and forth from the fields, where the actual fighting had occurred, to the rear, with the mangled bodies of the wounded; and about a hundred thousand men—the survivors who were left out of one hundred and sixty thousand in the two armies—were waiting to see what would come on the morrow, when suddenly a band of music began to play in the rear of the Union line of battle, down somewhere on the Taneytown road. One of the tenderest and most beautiful airs ever set to music was breathed from their instruments. Down the valley, and up the hill, and over the field, into the ears of wounded and dying men, and beyond our line into the bivouac of the beaten enemy the soft, gentle, and melting tune was borne on the evening breezes, already laden with the premonitory mists of the approaching storm which, as usual, had been incited by the cannonade, disturbing the mysterious forces of the atmosphere and setting free the rain, now soon to drench the waiting troops.

"Home, Sweet, Sweet Home," was the tender air that was breathed from the brazen instruments that evening. It brought visions of palmetto trees and orange groves and cotton fields and sunny southern skies to thousands of Confederates, dying in the hands of their foes; it induced pictures of fertile prairies and pioneer cabins and glimpses of great lakes and a breath from the northern forest before the fast-glazing eye of hundreds of brawny men from Michigan and Wisconsin as it brought them under its magic spell; before the eyes of New Englanders, bleeding, exhausted, losing consciousness, drifting out into another world, it unfolded panoramic views of a rock-bound coast indented with picturesque harbors; or a factory village with a busy stream babbling by its doors and in the distance the great old mountains; and as it touched the memory of the wounded Bucktails from the northern boundary of the Keystone State they fancied themselves once more on the tops of the Alleghenies, hunting deer and bear, felling the trees, and clearing out new ground, in the intervals of their delirium.

The next morning was the Fourth of July, but it seemed at the time to those who were at Gettysburg a somber and terrible national anniversary, with the indescribable horrors of the field, as yet hardly mitigated by the work of mercy, before the eye in every direction. The army did not know the extent of the victory; the nation did not realize as yet what had been done. The armies were still watching each other, although the Confederates had withdrawn from the town of Gettysburg and concentrated their troops on Seminary Ridge. The people in the village came out of their cellars and other places of refuge, and as the day broke upon them opened their doors. They had been under a reign of terror for over a week, ever since the alarm caused by the raid ten days before, indeed, when Early had passed through on his way to York. During the night they had suspected a movement of Lee's troops, for they had noted in their places of concealment occasional hurried sounds as of men, wagons, and cannon passing through the streets; but whether these betokened withdrawal or preparations for another attack on the Union lines it was impossible for them to tell. Now, as they came out of doors, they cherished new hopes, for they could see no rebel soldiers. All had seemingly disappeared, except, now and then, indeed, a straggler hurrying away after his fellow-rebels toward the west, or hiding in an alley or outhouse to escape further service in the "lost cause." It is almost daybreak, and some of the citizens venture to stand out on the pavements to watch for the development of events and note what is going to take place. They see a squad of men coming toward them down the main street from the south, bearing a banner. It is too dark at first to tell whether they wear the blue or the gray, whether the Confederates have returned to capture the place, or whether the boys in blue are advancing from Cemetery Hill. The watchers hold their breath in suspense, until in a moment the dawning light reveals to their longing eyes the glorious flag which the advancing troops are carrying, the Stars and Stripes, torn with the marks of battle, stained with blood, but wreathed and crowned with victory.

On that very morning, the nation's birthday, the Fourth of July, 1863, while the troops of Meade planted their triumphant banner on the recaptured heights of Gettysburg a similar scene of victory was displayed a thousand miles away to the southwest.

THE GLORIOUS FLAG.

There, in front of beleaguered Vicksburg, a great chieftain had been encamped for months before the doomed city, grim, silent, relentless. Baffled in one direction, he had sought to find another avenue of approach, and now at last, after heroic assaults and months of besiegement, he was waiting to receive the surrender of the army of Pemberton, which, starved into submission, beaten, long ago hemmed in and surrounded, assailed by gunboats from the river and siege guns and lines of circumvallation ever encroaching nearer and nearer upon them by land, was now about to march out of its captured fortress on the natal day of the Union, the glad Fourth of July. Grant, at Vicksburg, that glorious day, beheld twenty thousand prisoners, with vast stores of guns and appliances of war, become the property of the Union, while at the same hour, in the southern verge of the Keystone State, Meade rejoiced in the dawn of the glorious truth, which we receive now in all its fullness, that the victory of Gettysburg was the decisive battle of the war, determining that during the rest of the rebellion there would be no further invasion of the North, there would be no recognition of the Confederacy, there would be only a defensive warfare on the part of the South, until on every side the troops of the Union advanced to the center and crushed the Confederacy to pieces. Gettysburg and Vicksburg, the twin victories won by Meade and Grant, the one repelling invasion and deciding that final victory would surely come for the Union, and the other, in the graphic language of Lincoln, "allowing the Father of Waters to pass unvexed to the sea"—surely these were two great events for one day. The nation did not know of them, indeed, for several days afterward. It was not until Monday's dailies came out—Monday, July 6—that the flaming headlines announced the news from Gettysburg: "The Great Victory—The Rebel Army Totally Defeated—Its Remains Driven into the Mountains—It is There Surrounded and Hemmed In—Its Retreat Across the Potomac River Cut Off—Twenty Thousand Prisoners Captured—A Great and Glorious Victory for the Potomac Army!" Thus the *New York Tribune* gave the news to the world. On the following Wednesday, the 8th of July (the news had to be brought up to Cairo, Ill., by boat, and sent thence by telegraph, which took several days), the same paper gave the following lines at the head of its news columns: "The Fall of Vicksburg!—More

AFTER THE BATTLE.

Glorious News!—Pemberton Surrenders—Bag, Baggage, Cannon, and Cattle—The Stronghold in Our Possession!"

Then what a frenzy of joy swept through the land, and inspired our other armies in the field with new hope and fervor and zeal, which did not die out until peace finally came and settled down upon a reunited Union!

But, nevertheless, among the troops themselves that Fourth of July, 1863, at Gettysburg, was a wretched, dismal, and foreboding day, a day of uncertainty and suspense for both armies, which still faced each other. Each had thrown up fortifications and strengthened its line of defense, and was watching to find out what the other would do. Neither Meade nor Lee, just at that time, was anxious to bring about a renewal of the fight, and the time was occupied in caring for the wounded and burying the dead. A heavy rain storm set in about noon, which made the roads and fields in the course of a few hours a sea of mud. Without tents, with hardly shelter even for the wounded, of whom there were still thousands on the reeking earth to be cared for, and amid the beating tempest that swept the whole region round about, the situation of the two armies was forlorn enough.

At a pile of fence rails along the Taneytown road, by a flickering, sputtering camp fire, which was fighting in the face of the storm in order to maintain its right to burn, with a rubber blanket about him and in the midst of a dozen shivering, comfortless, dilapidated, and rain-drenched men, stands Jack, trying bravely to keep up his spirits and cheer his men. Word has just come in from the skirmish line that some sort of a movement is going on among the rebels. One of Berdan's sharp-shooters, with his familiar green uniform and his unerring rifle, worn out with four days of continuous service, night and day, along the left flank of our army, has just come in to get some rations for his comrades out on the front line beyond Round Top, where they are watching the operations of the Confederates.

"Hello, what is the news out on the left?" is the rallying question of one of the boys in blue by the bivouac.

"We are watching the Johnnies with a sharp eye, and are tired to death with our task," was the answer of the sharpshooter, as he stopped to warm his hands by the fire and ask for a bit of hard-tack and some "salt horse." While he eagerly munched his rations and rubbed his hands to start the circulation he was plied with a multitude of eager inquiries.

"What is Lee going to do? Will Meade move out to attack him? Is the rebel army retreating? Do you think the 'Johnnies' will get away from us now, and escape back to Virginia again? Are they trying to flank us? Have you any word from General Couch? Is it true that he is getting in on the rear of the rebels? What are the orders for to-day?"

These questions, with scores of others equally pertinent, and some perhaps impertinent, were fired at the exhausted skirmisher in the intervals of his hungry bites at a meager luncheon until he was almost distracted.

"Look here, boys," finally he exclaimed, "I am not a bureau of information, nor a committee on the conduct of the war, nor an authority on tactics and strategy, nor the commander in chief. I do not know what in blazes General Lee does intend to do. I hardly think he will attack us again after the repulse of yesterday. He cannot flank us, for our cavalry has command of the roads off to our left, down toward Taneytown and Emmitsburg. But do not ask me any more questions; I am so tired I do not want to think. I have been on the skirmish line near and in front of Round Top ever since Wednesday night, with hardly a wink of sleep, and I am just ready to drop; but I must get some bread and meat and take it back to the boys out there or they will starve. Where is our commissary?"

"Down yonder in the valley to our rear," was the reply, and, in obedience to the direction, the weary skirmisher plodded his way through the mud and across the soaking meadows to the park of wagons where the commissary of subsistence had stored his rations for distribution.

Then the boys began to wonder and talk and exercise their wits in the effort to solve the questions their quick and anxious brains had been springing on each other until orders came for further details to go out over the field and bring in the wounded and bury the dead. The day passed without any alarm or movement. All sorts of rumors, however, were flying here and there from mouth to mouth throughout the army. Everybody knew that the Confederates had drawn in their lines and had fortified their front very strongly along the Seminary Ridge. What they would finally do was only guesswork.

When the day was over the soldiers, anxiously and in discomfort, lay once more on the soaking earth, trying almost in vain to keep up the smoldering fire at their bivouacs; and then, when the night had gone and Sunday morning arrived, July 5, there was news indeed. Before daylight the rumors spread far and wide, and they were verified by advance of the skirmish lines all along our front, "The rebels have retreated back toward the Cumberland Valley!"

It is only a candid statement of the truth to say frankly that everybody was relieved when that fact was finally known. The enemy had withdrawn, the battle of Gettysburg was over, there would be no further struggle in the vicinity of the town nor on Pennsylvania soil. But what would be the issue of the campaign? Would Lee get off without further harm? Would he be able to escape to Virginia? Would he be able to foil the

Union commander and take his army back to the old stamping ground without molestation?

Everybody asked these questions, but nobody could answer them. The Third Corps, to which Jack belonged, was the last to leave Gettysburg. Early on the morning of Sunday, July 5, the whole command was alert. A staff officer from corps headquarters rode rapidly past where Jack was stationed, on his way to General Meade, with news that Birney's skirmishers had found the works in their front, on Seminary Ridge, vacated, and that, upon feeling their way westward they had discovered the enemy in force two or three miles out on the Fairfield road. This news might indicate that an attack was to be made, and the boys were in line at once. No further advance, however, was made that day by the Third Corps, although on all the roads leaving Gettysburg the other corps were seen marching with eager haste, it having been demonstrated that the rebels were retreating full tilt and anxious to get away as far as possible from their antagonist.

Jack, with a comrade or two, secured permission to go into the town for a little while, and set off on a tour of exploration. The road leading into Gettysburg was covered with cast-off uniforms, broken artillery caissons, ruined muskets, and here and there a dead soldier, and with scores of dead horses, which indicated places where the batteries had made their gallant fight. The boys wondered whether much harm had been done to the houses and the people of the town during the battle.

On their way down from the cemetery into the village they found a curious crowd assembled at a little house along the road, and on inquiry they discovered that a woman had been killed here. One of her friends stood at the door and told the story. Her name was Jennie Wade, and she was baking bread for our men on the first day. During their retreat a musket ball came flying through the house, struck her, and she died without knowing what had happened. "She was a good, kind soul," was the tearful comment of the survivors.

At the foot of the hill, where the houses of the town actually begin, the two skirmish lines had almost touched each other. Passing this point, the boys entered the village, which was a scene of confusion and wretchedness, nearly all large buildings, schoolhouses, churches, warehouses, barns, and other structures, besides the college halls, being occupied as hospitals. Near the entrance of the village the boys stopped to note the damage that had been done to a house by a solid shot which had come from a rebel cannon, lodged in the wall near the roof, and then fallen down to the earth. An old gentleman was near, shaking his head in doubt at the condition of the building. "This is the Methodist parsonage, and the old parson got a hard fright when this shot struck his house, but nobody was hurt. I heard he had come down in the evening and secured the ball, and was going to have it plastered into the wall."

Immediately opposite was a little girl pumping hard at an old pump to get a pitcher of water. The boys stopped to talk to her, and she prattled for a while until an old lady called to her to come in. "It was just awful when the rebels were in town. They fought right in front of our door, and we all had to go down cellar, but we could hear them, and we thought we should all be killed. Some of the bullets struck our house; see there," she said, pointing to the impressions made on window shutter and wall by the flying minie balls, "and we were almost scared to death. Those great cannon almost deafened me. Three wounded men hid in our back yard, and one of 'em got into an old oven, and another got away up garret and stayed there till the fight was over. I heard the rebels shout, 'Kill the Yankees;'

'Surrender, lay down your arms!' and then the muskets went off like everything, and I thought we should all die."

Just then a voice came from a neighboring house, "Tillie, hurry up with that water!" and the little girl vanished with her burden.

In the Presbyterian church near the center of the town scores of Confederate and Union soldiers were found lying side by side. One of the nurses, a lady of the town, who had been caring for the wounded since the opening of the fight, in the intervals of her work found time to say a word to the boy and his comrades, this being among the incidents she told: "Dear me, how we have come through these days of danger and trouble I cannot tell now. Why, on Wednesday I thought we had our hands more than full when they brought in about fifty men and filled the church with cots and blankets. There were our own boys and rebels all mixed together, and they were all saying that there would be a worse fight next day. I just broke down, and I said, Why, boys, what will we do with them? We cannot take care of them!' Then a Southern soldier said, 'O, you Lincoln women will have to tear up your dresses and make bandages for the wounded before this thing is ended!' And I turned to him, noted his gray uniform, put a spoonful of panada to his lips and said, 'Yes, we will do that very thing! We will tear up every dress we have to make bandages for dying men, whether they come from Massachusetts or South Carolina.' Another of his comrades then said, 'We whipped your men to-day, and to-morrow we will drive them a-kiting toward Baltimore!' Well, I was not going to be beaten by a rebel, and so I said to him, just as bravely as I could, 'You do not know anything about it. You do not know what a strong position our army has, nor how many men we have, either!' And that man also hushed up—but, la me, I did not know anything about it, either; still I did not give one inch to the Confederates; but we cared for them just as kindly as we could."

While Jack was exploring the town artillery fire was suddenly heard toward the West, indicating that the troops of Meade had caught up with the fleeing foe and that another battle might be on hand. The boy reluctantly turned back from his investigations in the town, which he had no opportunity to revisit for several years after the battle. Eight years afterward, however, in the turning of the wheels of destiny it happened to be his lot to be sent to Gettysburg as a Methodist itinerant, and his home was in the very house that had been damaged by the solid shot near our skirmish line; and the road he took to his country appointments lay directly across the varying lines of battle in different directions, so that, for three years, Round Top, and Cemetery Hill, and Culp's Hill, and Seminary Ridge, and all the other points on the field became to him familiar as household words.

CHAPTER XXII.

BACK TO OLD VIRGINIA.

THE Third Corps stayed at Gettysburg until July 7, and then marched to Emmitsburg, and thence by Frederick City across the old Antietam battle ground, noting the traces of the awful engagement that had taken place there less than a year before, in September, 1862, yet fresh and ghastly on every side; and in the course of three or four days they found themselves in front of the rebels again near Williamsport, Md. The other corps had marched by different routes to the same point, and now the two armies were concentrated again, face to face. What would be the issue?

"Hurrah, boys!" shouted Sergeant McBride, after arriving at the meeting place of the two armies, "I've heard news for you. Our division commander, Gineral Humphreys, is goin' to lave us. Gineral Meade wants him to be his chief of staff, an' that is the ind of his lading this division as he did at Gettysburg."

At this there was a hubbub in the camp, for although General Humphreys had not been with the division very long, yet he had led it with such skill and gallantry as to win entirely the esteem and confidence of both officers and men. A graduate of West Point, an officer of engineers of the very highest ability—afterward occupying, at the end of the war, for years the post of chief of engineers in the United States army—the soul of honor, a trained soldier, wise, scholarly, he proved himself one of the very best men in the field that the Union produced, and it was no wonder that General Meade wanted such a man in the important and confidential place of chief of staff. "Who is going to lead our division?" was the inquiry at once, and the words were hardly uttered before the new commander appeared, a gentleman in middle life, with a full iron-gray beard, stocky and well built, reserved, quiet, a West Pointer, a major and paymaster in the regular army; this was the new division leader, Brigadier General Henry Prince. "And there's more news yet," said Jack to the group that had hardly yet stopped their hurrahing for the outgoing and the incoming commander. "General Sickles is gone, of course, to the hospital. Whether he will recover from that amputation of his leg or not no one can tell. But he has led his glorious Third Army Corps for the last time. He cannot serve again in the field with one leg, I reckon. General Birney is ranked by the commander of the new division that has just joined us, General W. H. French. By the way, there he goes now with his staff. He is going to be the corps commander of our corps. How do you think you will like to go into battle under him, boys?" It was a question to be pondered. General French had a big, burly, pursy body, and a fat, red, weather-beaten face, and a habit of stuttering and winking very rapidly as he spoke, and altogether he did not exactly present to the boys that beau ideal of soldierly appearance that one might expect in a corps commander. Nobody knew how much liquor he drank, nor how much he could hold, but the red face that he carried was a suspicious-looking sign. Still he proved to be a gallant commander, and did effective service, although his habit was to "swear like a trooper." And, now that some new commanders have taken charge of their troops, and the two armies are facing one another, what of the issue?

Four or five days were occupied at Williamsport, Md., on the brink of the Potomac, by the two armies, now and then a skirmish taking place, each side strengthening its position, and, in turn, each one anxious, for a part of that time at least, that the other should attack.

From July 9, until the morning of the 14th, the Army of the Potomac and the Army of Northern Virginia stood at bay, while the nation, on both sides of the bloody chasm, looked on with bated breath, wondering whether Lee would finally make good his escape into Virginia again, or whether he would be driven to the wall and forced to surrender.

"Boys," said Jack at the bivouac, one night before "taps" had sounded, "did you hear the rebels cheer yesterday? It sounded like their old battle yell, and made the woods and the hills ring again. It echoed all along their line, and resounded from the sky. Who can guess what was the occasion of the cheering?"

"Maybe," said Sergeant McBride, "they have found a stray cow that has wandered off into their lines and have made soup for their fifty thousand gray-backs out of her carcass; or perhaps they have heard the news from Vicksburg, and are glad to hear that the Mississippi River is free once more; or maybe they are joost littin' on, and tryin' to git us to run our heads butt up against their breastworks. Who can tell what they were cheerin' about?"

Just then one of the division staff, happening to pass along, was able to give the information desired: "A deserter came in from the other side a while ago and told us that Lee had issued a proclamation cheering up his men, and urging them to do their best in the present crisis. His army cheered wildly when the order was read in their camps, and that was the noise of the shouting that we heard."

"Let 'em holler as loud as they please," said one of the boys as the staff officer rode away. "All that we ask is to be let loose on the army of Lee; we'll clean 'em out this time. We want to close up this trouble here on the banks of the Potomac, near Harper's Ferry, where the affair began with old John Brown's raid four or five years ago. For one, I do not want to go 'traipsing' back across this Potomac River again down into old Virginia. Boys, let us bring this matter to an end right here and now—that is my sentiment."

Eagerly all about the bivouac fire there came instant responses, "So say we all of us;" "No more Virginia in mine;" "Count me in too;" "I'm with you, boys;" and so on all round the circle of bronzed veterans in the intervals of smoking their corncob pipes and other like evening pastimes.

The newspapers often represented the army as "spoiling for a fight." This writer never saw that description actually realized except at Williamsport, Md., on this occasion, when, the battle of Gettysburg over, the rebel army in retreat, the swollen Potomac in their rear, their pontoons swept away, their ammunition short, and with no reinforcements at hand, a final victory seemed to be within the reach of the Union forces.

For five or six miles, in semicircular form, the lines of battle extended over a pleasant landscape, with nooks of woods and rolling pasture land and little bluffs now and then intervening. It was easily to be seen from the Union lines that with every hour of delay in making an attack the rebel lines were being strengthened, until, after three or four days of waiting, their position was a series of intrenchments—one little fortress after another crowning the hilltops, and each elevation occupied by artillery. If these positions were to be stormed it would be at great cost of life, but there surely would be no time afforded now for anything else. No siege work would do here. At the very first chance Lee would retreat, and what must be done needed to be done at once. The soldiers were eager, enthusiastic, wild in their anxiety to be led against the Confederate intrenchments and end the war on the banks of the Potomac.

Everybody was kept on the *qui vive* of excitement, knowing that the battle might break out at any moment of the day or night, and knowing, furthermore, that when it did come it would be a desperate one, fairly rivaling the engagement at Gettysburg for bloodiness and intensity of purpose and heroic work. Now and then a bit of skirmish, a sharp sound of rattling musketry, a booming note, and a deep reverberation indicating that a cannon had been fired off would send a fresh thrill of expectation and excitement through the waiting armies.

A rumor of a council of war pervaded official quarters one night. It was said that Meade had called his generals together to determine whether he should attack or not, and no one could tell what the results of the consultation might be. As the boys sat about the fire or paced to and fro along the picket line there was hardly a doubter or a faint-hearted one among them. All were this time "in fighting trim," eager to advance. The voice of every man was for war, and each soldier, in view of what might be done by an immediate, urgent, heroic attack, said in his heart or in his talk with his comrades, "O for some one to order us forward—to lead us on ! This is the hour to strike; this is the time to defeat the enemy for good and all; this is the very place to make him surrender. He is hemmed in, he is out of ammunition, the river has swept away his bridges, he cannot evade an attack, he must surrender. O for some one to say, 'Forward, boys!'" At last it was noised along our line, "Boys, we are to attack in the morning! Be ready, with plenty of ammunition, bright and early. Sleep on your arms to-night, and be ready to advance at seven."

Now, at last, it really seemed as though the final hour of decision, of attack, of victory, was near. With its approach, however, came rain that dampened everything, even the ardor of the eager soldiers, who tried to keep their cartridges dry and get a little sleep in view of the advance and battle to begin in the early morning.

In the morning the men began to press forward, expecting —what? Nobody knows now exactly what they expected, but they found all along the intrenchments only deserted rifle pits and empty lines of fortification. "Look out for an ambush," said some of the cautious commanders. "They are drawing us on!" And so, slowly and cautiously, the troops moved ahead, until the news was announced, "The rebels have escaped. They have crossed the Potomac again. Kilpatrick has captured some of their rear guard and taken a few of their guns, but they have repaired their bridges, crossed in the night, and are safe back in old Virginia again!"

What a disappointment that was! The men who were eager to end the war at Williamsport, to bring the rebellion to a close on the banks of the Potomac, well knew what this news meant —long and weary marches through the dusty roads and barren, smitten fields of Virginia; siege and charge and camp fire and campaigns, and long months, perhaps years, of fighting, before the war should be brought to an end.

It seemed as though a great opportunity had been thrown

away; but, looking at the case from this end of the vista of time, we may conjecture that the hand of God was in the series of events that sent the two armies back into Virginia again. If the war had been ended just after Gettysburg by the surrender of Lee's army, the Confederacy would have fallen, possibly, without the destruction of slavery. There would have been compromise on that, and on other questions perhaps, that were settled finally at Appomattox. It was well that the war continued until it had wrought its perfect mission.

In a day or two the Third Corps advanced across the river, with the rest of the Army of the Potomac, after Lee, on pontoons at Harper's Ferry. They saw the old armory where John Brown had been besieged, where the war began, and where that old crazy hero who loved the souls of men and was an enemy of human slavery sought to bring the system of bondage in America to an end. The boys saw the place where the old man, wounded, at bay, a strange mixture of tenderness and heroic firmness in his nature, with his little band set at defiance the State of Virginia, and with a handful of followers undertook to set all the slaves of the South free. Now the soldiers from the great, united, loyal North, singing,

"John Brown's body lies a-moldering in the grave,
His soul is marching on,"

were crossing the same river and marching through the same town against the upholders, adherents, and defenders of the Confederacy which he foresaw and tried to obviate—the friends of the system of bondage, which he tried to destroy, now in retreat, and the boys in blue in full pursuit of them.

One day, soon after crossing back into Virginia, the army, going through one of the beautiful valleys of the Blue Ridge, came upon a great vale overgrown with blackberry bushes, which were covered with luxuriant fruit, ready to drop at a touch. The inhabitants had been long ago driven out of this region, and the rebel army had not used this road of late. Such a sight was too tempting to be withstood. What mattered it if other troops were pressing on behind—what if the rebels were to be headed off yonder in the valley of the Shenandoah, and the hosts of Lee were to be intercepted? Here were hungry soldiers, and here, also, were great acres of rich, tempting, luscious blackberries! At once the boys spread out as skirmishers all over that valley, far and wide. All thought or care for discipline, commander in chief, batteries in the front or rear, wagon trains impeded, and all other vicissitudes were scattered to the winds (only there were no winds on that hot July day); and the soldiers began feasting on blackberries.

"Can you tell me," said Sergeant McBride, "why this is like an African funeral?"

"No," said Corporal Jones, "I give it up;" and he crowded down his throat a handful of berries, and reached out to gather more.

"Why, do ye not see, it is a black-berrying expedition, d'ye mind now?" replied the merry sergeant while plucking and eating as fast as he could.

Meanwhile, in the rear, other troops were crowding on. The road in front was clear, and this halt on the part of Prince's division had impeded things all along the line. There came a hurrah from the rear, "Those greedy Third Corps men are stealing all the blackberries and leaving none for us." And there was a fierce yell from thousands of hungry throats. The general ordered the bugles to sound "Forward," but the men kept on eating. Nobody stirred. Even the officers had dismounted and were eating their fill of berries. Men with faces smeared with berry-juice, gorging themselves with ripe, delicious fruit, were to be seen to the number of three or four thousand. At last it became a question how to start them. "Lieutenant Sanderson, you have command of the rear guard, have you not?" Jack replied by lifting his hat to General Prince, the division commander, who had asked the question. "Where are they?" "Here, picking berries." "Get them into line at once!" Jack succeeded in doing so with some difficulty. "Now," said the general, "deploy them in the rear, order them to fix bayonets, and close up ranks with speed." Jack spurred his horse forward, gave the order, and soon had his men in position. Then came the tug of war. "Forward, men!" was the cry. "We are not through eating yet." "That makes no difference, 'Forward!' is the order! Other men are waiting behind us to crowd through this valley. You must go on." Still nobody moved. "Provost guard, fix bayonets—charge!" was the command. And in among that scattered division of blackberry pickers the provost guard walked, bayonets at a charge, and slowly, sadly, and at last successfully, the blackberry patch was cleared.

One of the most picturesque and vivid scenes recalled by the boy is connected with the pursuit of Lee by the Army of the Potomac, after Gettysburg. A race took place between the two armies in their efforts to reach and command the mountain passes. Meade was trying to cut his antagonist's forces in two, and Lee was striving to get back to his old position, if possible, without a battle. In this race the Third Army Corps, under French, was in the advance, and as it entered the pass in the mountains called Chester Gap, it found before it, splendidly arrayed, on a high hill commanding the neighborhood, a portion of the Confederate army. The battle of Wapping Heights ensued, if the struggle, brief and brilliant while it lasted, can be called a battle, rather than a skirmish. A deep valley separated the two forces, and in this valley the struggle took place. On that sunshiny afternoon of July 23, Jack looked on a glorious picture. Far away in the distance was the Shenandoah Valley, opening out in its beauty, with wagon trains and glimpses of troops belonging to the enemy, to be seen by means of the glass. To the rear, looking back toward Washington, one might see Union troops by the thousand, artillery, cavalry, and infantry intermingled, pressing forward into the Gap. French, finding that the enemy was in his front, ordered a line of skirmishers forward, and, as they deployed, the Second Division, to which Jack belonged, formed line of battle. From where Jack was posted he saw every movement down the valley, once in a while carrying an order and cooperating in the work. On the farther slope of the hill he could see the marching columns of the Confederates forming into line and getting ready for the battle. Finally all was ready, and the rattling fire of the skirmishers opened out in the front. Then the batteries began to play, and then the infantry marched into the battle with shouts and hurrahs and stunning volleys of musketry. The whole scene, in which twenty thousand men, perhaps, were engaged, was laid out before the eyes with panoramic distinctness and beauty. Perhaps there was not an occasion during the war where the paraphernalia and machinery of battle on both sides were so clearly outlined and magnificently defined as in this little battle of Wapping Heights, which amounted to nothing in its results, however, for when the next morning came Lee had taken his army and vanished. But that little battle of two or three hours, on the hills of Wapping Heights, in which the foe was dislodged and driven from his works, was one of the most striking, thrilling minor scenes of the war. After that incident the army settled down for a rest on the Rappahannock, no special event exciting it for weeks, both sides rejoicing, perhaps, at the opportunity for rest and recuperation.

One day an officer of the staff said to Jack, " Lieutenant, let us ride over to the Fifth Corps and see the execution that is to take place. Five deserters are to be shot, and about twenty-five thousand men are to witness the sight, for the sake of the effect it may produce on the army at large."

In accordance with the invitation the two set off on horseback across the country to the camping ground of the Fifth Corps. They soon found that officers from all the army corps were in large numbers riding also in that direction, and by the time they reached the ground the region was covered with a brilliant array. From all directions the various divisions of the Fifth Army Corps were assembling. It was a queer mixture of a holiday and an execution; bands were playing, soldiers were gayly marching, riders were galloping in all directions, the focus of all eyes being a single spot, carefully guarded by a line of sentries, where all could discern an open grave, five ghastly-looking coffins, and the same number of forlorn-looking, depressed, despairing men who were to be executed for the crime of desertion.

"Who are these poor fellows?" was the inquiry of Jack, as he saw the parade organized, the sad procession begin its dismal march, the prisoners with their coffins borne in advance of them, the bands playing a dirge, and three ministers accompanying the men who were to die.

"They are all foreigners," was the reply of some one who stood near. "Three are Prussians and two are from Italy. They are hard cases, all of them, and it seems that they have been singled out as victims, to convey a needed lesson to the army that desertion must be stopped. They are vicarious sufferers, if we may use that expression, who are dying as a sort of object lesson, to warn the Army of the Potomac that this crime must come to an end."

"Probably they are not the worst of deserters; men worse than they are have got safely away and have pocketed bounty after bounty in their offense against the army and the country, deserting again and again. They are victims of circumstances. It is a pity to have to shoot them for the sake of making an example and a spectacle out of them."

By this time the parade was ended. The procession had passed in front of the whole corps, had been seen by every soldier, and now the priests, the doomed men, and their guards with the coffins had arrived at the spot where the execution was to take place.

"What is delaying them now?" said Jack, as he saw some disturbance or sign of friction in the little crowd of people at the grave-side. "Let us go and see." And they pressed near to find out what was going on. They found there a Protestant minister, Chaplain O'Neil, of one of the Pennsylvania regiments, and a Catholic priest in full canonicals, and a Hebrew rabbi, attending the unfortunate men. A dispute had arisen between the rabbi and the priest as to which should lead off in the service. The priest claimed that his was the rightful privilege to precede, as his was the true Church, and the rabbi made the same claim because his was the oldest and primitive religion. The rabbi finally was allowed precedence, and then brief services were held, the consolations of religion being administered. A detachment of fifty soldiers, with muskets, was drawn up in line before the poor victims as they sat on their coffins, and ten men were assigned to each one of the prisoners. One gun in each set of ten was loaded only with a blank cartridge, so that no man would know whether his own particular gun contained a bullet or not. The rabbi recited passages from the Psalms in Hebrew, and his disciples repeated them after him; the Catholics kneeled before the priest to receive absolution, and then sat down on their coffins; the Protestant chaplain prayed with his friend and whispered a word of cheer into his ear. Then the captain in charge of the shooting squad spoke in a low, agitated voice to his men, "Ready—aim—fire!" Like the shot of a single gun the fifty muskets sent forth their explosion, the five deserters fell dead, and the tragedy was over.

During that season of August–October, 1863, Meade and Lee made a number of marches and countermarches, each one seeking to outgeneral the other. An incident took place that claims record, during the retreat of Meade from the Rappahannock. A day or two after the troops had reached the outer circle of the fortifications of Washington, Jack was in his tent one sultry afternoon quietly resting, and glancing at the late daily papers which had just come in. Hearing a rap on the tent-pole, he looked up and saw one of his men who had been, since morning, out on the picket line, not far away, standing in front of the tent with a seedy-looking individual in farmer costume in custody. In answer to Jack's look of inquiry the guard replied:

"Lieutenant Sanderson, we found this man trying to get through the picket line, and the colonel in command out there sent him in as a suspicious character under arrest."

"Have you searched him?" said Jack.

"We went through his pockets and clothing, but did not find anything except a very small bit of tobacco," was the answer of the picket.

"Did he make any resistance?"

"None at all. He has been very quiet, and came right along without any trouble."

"Was he armed?"

"No," was the reply; "he had no weapons and made no resistance. He said he lived just outside of the lines, and that he had been at a neighbor's whose family had been sick and was away from home when our forces fell back inside the fortifications and was only on his way home."

"All right; here is a receipt for the prisoner. You can go back to the picket line, and I will send the man on to corps headquarters," said Jack, as he summoned another of the provost guard and wrote a line to the assistant provost marshal general of the corps. When the note was written Jack took a good look at the prisoner. He was a lithe, angular specimen, with tawny beard, dark eyes, and weather-beaten complexion; a very

JACK TOOK A GOOD LOOK AT THE PRISONER.

innocent-looking farmer, sure enough, he appeared to be. Jack cross-questioned him keenly, but found out nothing suspicious. The man had been caring for a sick neighbor, had been away from home for a week, did not know of the army's presence till he found himself inside the lines, and in his anxiety to get home he was simply trying to pass through at a point where the line was very thin, and was taken prisoner. That seemed all there was of it, and Jack finally sent the prisoner with a guard to corps headquarters, half a mile away, and settled back to read the papers again. He had not gone very far in his reading when he heard a musket shot followed by another, and then some excited shouts, and then he saw a number of soldiers run down the road which had been taken by the guard and his prisoner a few minutes before. Jack saw that there was trouble of some kind threatening, and, picking up his revolver and starting out, he soon met the guard returning without the prisoner.

"Where's your prisoner?" said Jack.

"Why, lieutenant," said the soldier, gasping and breathless, "as soon as we reached that piece of woods the man leaped like a deer into the thicket and vanished from sight. I fired after him and hit him, I thought, but he did not stop. I followed, loading as I ran, and fired again, but the man was gone!"

"Send out word in all directions; detail a hundred men to beat the bushes and go through the woods and find him; he must not be allowed to get away!" was the instant order of the boy. The commands were at once obeyed, and the region was scoured in all directions; word was sent to the pickets for miles around warning them of the matter, and every house in the neighborhood was searched—all in vain. No man was found, and the disappearance of this prisoner so suddenly and inexplicably seemed forever relegated to the long list of "mysterious disappearances."

There was a sequel to the story, however. A few weeks later the Third Corps was in camp on the estate of the Hon. John Minor Botts in Culpeper County, Va.—a camping place occupied successively by both armies as they swept back and forth across the wasted plains of that region. Mr. Botts was a Southern Union man who had been, in Congress and in political life in his State, and indeed in the nation, a conspicuous figure in other years. Through the desperate struggle he remained at home on his farm, which was trodden down by each army in turn, and here he met and was familiar with the leading generals in the Union and Confederate forces. Soon after the Union army had advanced again to the neighborhood of the Rappahannock, and the division of General Prince, at whose headquarters Jack was now serving, had encamped on Mr. Botts's place, one day the general and several members of his staff and some of the Virginian's family were enjoying themselves in the grassy yard, under the shade of the big trees, when Mr. Botts said:

"General Prince, one of your old friends in the rebel ranks, General Ewell, was with us in familiar intercourse last week. He had his headquarters just where your tents are erected, and was in good spirits over the fright which he said the Army of Northern Virginia had given Meade when your forces retreated under the cover of the fortifications of Washington."

"Perhaps General Ewell may not be able to see the funny side of this campaign when we get through with it," said General Prince in reply. "I do not wonder, however, that he did enjoy our retreat. I do not know anybody in the army who does understand the philosophy of that movement, except, perhaps, General Meade. It is one of those strategical movements whose significance is not apparent to the ordinary mind!"

"General Ewell," continued Mr. Botts, "was not all laughter, however, while he was here. He said that he had experienced a loss equal to that of a whole regiment in the death of a single man during the campaign, one of his secret service men, a scout of remarkable daring and skill, who was shot in your lines and who soon afterward died."

"What were the circumstances? Tell us the story," said several voices at once, as every ear was attent.

"In brief," said the Virginian, "General Ewell said that he had in his employ one of the most skillful spies and scouts in the whole Southern army, a man who spent a good part of his time inside the Union lines, and who seemed to be able to deceive the very elect, going back and forth almost at will without detection. He had access, by some means, occasionally to the War Department, got on the track of pending legislation in Congress, secured the earliest information concerning the movement of troops, gave the Confederates the names and membership of the new regiments, and, in a word, kept them supplied with the very latest news from the inside of the Union lines. 'During the early movements of our late campaign,' General Ewell said, 'this scout, Harry Anderson, was in Washington City getting information for us. He had made a circuit of inspection of the whole line of Union fortifications, had noted the best points for an attack, had found out the positions of the troops, and was loaded down with information that would have been invaluable to us. In his eagerness to get back to me and give me the news he ventured to pass through the Union lines in daytime dressed as a farmer, under pretense that he wished to go to his home just outside the Federal picket station. He told the story that he had been caring for a sick neighbor, had been absent from home when the Union army suddenly had appeared in the vicinity, and he had found himself shut out by the picket guards from his own house. He was arrested at the picket line, and while being taken from one camp to another for safe-keeping he broke away from the guard who had him in charge and ran into the woods in the hope of escaping. The guard fired at him and wounded him severely, but he kept on running until he reached a cave which he had used a good many times before in the woods. At night he managed to creep out of his place of refuge and crawled to the home of a Southern man close by, where his wounds were dressed and where he died in a few hours. As soon as the army moved away from that region the friend at whose house Harry died ventured by a roundabout course into our lines, and came to my headquarters to give me Harry's dying message. The poor fellow only regretted that he had not been able to reach me with the news he had in mind before we fell back to the Rappahannock.' General Ewell," said Mr. Botts, "could hardly keep back the tears as he finished his story, and said, 'I could better have afforded to lose the best regiment in my corps than to have lost Harry Anderson, the best scout in the Southern army.'"

Jack had listened closely to the story, and now could hardly contain himself as he broke out, "That was the very man we captured inside the lines at Centerville the day after we reached there. We had that very scout in our hands and under guard, and while he was being taken to corps headquarters he 'broke and ran,' and although a hundred men were ordered out in search of him, yet not a trace of him could be found except an occasional clot of blood, showing that he had been wounded. It seemed as if the very ground had opened to swallow him up, and that, it appears now, was really the case, for he hid, like David in Bible times, in a cave. That man, then, was Harry Anderson, the scout of General Ewell. What a prize we had, and did not know it!"

CHAPTER XXIII.

STAFF DUTY IN WASHINGTON.

THE Army of the Potomac was back again in its familiar tramping ground along the Rappahannock, and the winter was near. The roads were beginning to become difficult for teams, and the outlook seemed to be that no movement would take place again, in force, until spring. Jack was thinking what sort of a shelter he would erect for winter quarters when he was one day summoned into the presence of General Prince, where he found that officer and Major Charles Hamlin, the assistant adjutant general of the division, in conversation. After the usual salutations had been exchanged Major Hamlin said, "Lieutenant Sanderson, here is a document that concerns you; it comes from the War Department, and is a serious matter." As the officer spoke he assumed a grave expression and held the official paper in his hand, as though he feared to unfold its contents to the anxious boy, who began to wonder what he had been doing, and to rummage through his memories of the past, seeking for some possible ground for interference with his affairs on the part of the War Office at Washington. He did not recall any delinquency that would justify dismissal from the service or court martial inquiry, or any other matter that would in reason account for a document from army headquarters in which he might be personally interested. At last Major Hamlin handed Jack the paper, laughing as he did so, and exclaiming, "It is not so serious a matter, after all; you need not be afraid to read it."

The boy now took the paper and with eager eyes perused it, holding his breath meanwhile, and wondering whether he was dreaming or awake. The paper was covered with indorsements, in military fashion, having been referred from one commander to another, from the War Department at Washington, through General Meade's headquarters, down to the commanding officer of the Eighty-fourth Pennsylvania Volunteers, Jack's regiment. The document, in brief, was an application from Major General Casey, at Washington, for the assignment of Lieutenant Jack Sanderson to serve as the recorder for the board of examiners, of which the general was president, and which was engaged in examining applicants for commissions among the colored troops, which the government had then but lately begun to muster into its service. Secretary Stanton had referred the application to General Meade, and that officer had referred it to General French, commanding the Third Corps, and thence it had been referred down to Colonel Opp, then in command of the regiment. Colonel Opp had replied, speaking in cordial words of the boy's standing as an officer, saying that there were already two officers with the company to which he belonged—a number which in the depleted condition of the regiment was sufficient—and that he would not interpose any objection to this proposed assignment. Now the paper had come back to General Prince for his action in the case. He said, "Lieutenant, would you like to spend the winter in Washington?"

Jack's eyes brightened as he replied, "Of course I would if I thought it was the right thing to do. I do not like to go away from the front, however, if there is going to be anything to do here."

The general laughed at this, and said, "My boy, you need not hesitate on that account. There is not an officer that I know of who would not be glad of such an opportunity just now. There may be nothing but picket duty to attend to here for months to come; and while I shall regret to spare you from your post at my headquarters, yet, if I were at your age and had the chance to enter upon staff duty with an officer as illustrious as General Casey, and in such a post as he offers you, I would accept it without question and at once. It is a great opportunity, and if you are desirous of accepting the place I will recommend it and say that you will ' fill the bill.' "

Major Hamlin joined in at this point, and said, " I would be glad, if I could get away for a few months, to spend the winter in Washington, and my counsel also would be, Accept the post *instanter.*"

With this counsel Jack needed no further urging, and General Prince forwarded the document back to army headquarters with the recommendation that the detail be made. In a few days the assignment came. The boy hardly knew whether to laugh or cry. It seemed like breaking up his home to leave his comrades in the field and betake himself to Washington for duty there—almost like "playing soldier." But he packed up his baggage—a work which at that time did not require much time—paid his respects to the officers at division headquarters, where he had been on duty for six months, said good-bye to his friends in the Eighty-fourth, took the train at Brandy Station.

and in a few hours was in the city of Washington. Here, after making himself presentable, he reported for duty to Major General Casey. He found half a dozen noble-looking officers—all of them veterans, men of courage and experience—engaged in the work of examining candidates. The boy saw that his youthful appearance placed him in strong contrast with everybody else on the board of examiners, for he was not yet out of his teens, and almost literally a beardless youth. But he soon ascertained that his work of keeping the records of the board required only promptness, accuracy, courtesy, and application, and he settled down to his task with assiduous devotion. General Casey was the author of the *System of Infantry Tactics* then in use in the army, had been from his youth a skillful soldier, having served more than forty years in the army, and seen service in Mexico, in California, and in all sections of the land, besides displaying great courage and skill in command of his division at Fair Oaks, in 1862, on the peninsula. He was now in command of the camps of organization for recruits in the vicinity of Washington and at the head of the examining board already referred to. The work of this board had become so large that it was now necessary to divide it into two sections, and Jack, at the suggestion of a friend on the board, had been asked for as one of the recorders, Major E. P. Halstead, who had seen two years in active service at the front, being the other one.

Soon after assignment to duty here General Casey promoted Jack to the additional office of aid-de-camp; and as this assignment gave him a horse and afforded him ingress and egress within the fortifications of the capital on both sides of the Potomac, by night and day, and brought him in contact with many leading officers, the added honors and emoluments were heartily welcomed. As it happened, Jack was kept on duty with General

Casey almost till the close of the war, now taking troops to the front, now conducting them to New York to be shipped to the South by sea, and meanwhile conducting correspondence, keeping the records of the board, and performing the usual service of a staff officer. Some of the pictures indelibly fixed in his memory during this closing period of the conflict may be recorded here.

One of them is the advent of General Grant into Washington City early in March, 1864. One day it was announced that the newly appointed general in chief of the armies would arrive in the Capitol that afternoon, and would be at President Lincoln's reception, at the White House, in the evening. Jack and a friend agreed to attend, but when they arrived at the Executive Mansion they found thousands of people exactly of their state of mind surging about the entrance, barricading the sidewalks, and striving to gain access to the place. With some difficulty the two made their way through the crowd, found ingress by favor of a friend at court through a side door, and had a chance to look about them for a little while. Here were senators and members of the House and scores of officers in uniform. The most elegantly dressed officer present that evening was not a general, it was noticed, but a second lieutenant of the newly organized Invalid Corps, whose light blue uniform and gorgeous sash and gold epaulets and dashing, self-conscious air made him a center of observation, if not of attraction. President and Mrs. Lincoln, in the midst of a crowd of friends and various celebrities, were engaged for an hour in receiving the multitude before the particular guest of the evening appeared. The President had a kindly greeting for everybody, but appeared tired and preoccupied; there were lines of suffering on his furrowed face, and his eyes at times seemed to be fixed on objects outside the crowd, as though he were noting far away lines of battle, watching troops marshaling for an advance or lying wounded and dying on the field. It was a notable privilege for the boy as he passed on with the crowd to take the hand of Mr. Lincoln and to look for a moment into his kindly eyes. A little before ten o'clock there was a thrill of excitement which vibrated through the densely crowded rooms, where many hundreds were jammed together. There was a shout from the corridor, "Hurrah for General Grant!" and a rush toward him which almost took him off his feet. President Lincoln pressed toward him in the throng and greeted him with great cordiality, finding him accompanied by several military officers and escorted by Secretary Seward. The multitude cheered, waved their handkerchiefs, strove all at once to get a sight of the general, tried to reach him in order to greet him, and for a little space there was danger of suffocation to everybody. At last Secretary Stanton, President Lincoln, and Secretary Seward pushed, hauled, pressed, and struggled with the terrific crowd, which was almost a mob, until they transferred General Grant to one side of the great East Room, where the general mounted a sofa and reached out both hands helplessly to the people. His face was pale, his cheeks were blanched, his speech was gone; he had not a word to say. During the war, up to this date, he had been at the front with his army, and no popular ovation had been rendered to him. He was not prepared for any such reception. He trembled with timidity, and seemed literally scared out of his senses. For half an hour he stood on the sofa the helpless victim of popular favor, while Secretary Seward sat on the back of the sofa, his eyes twinkling with suppressed merriment, the bushy eyebrows underneath his splendid forehead fairly shaking with his sense of the ludicrousness of the scene. The people called out, "Speech! Speech! Grant! Grant!" But all in vain; not a word could be extorted from the silent man. His reticence stood the strain and came off conqueror. All who could touch his hand with a tip of a finger went away that night rejoicing that they had shaken hands with the new general in chief of the armies of the United States.

A few weeks after this reception Grant began his Wilderness campaign, and the whole land waited in untold agony for tidings from the front. After days of suspense and conflicting news—nothing being certain but that the most terrific struggle yet known was going on in the dense thickets beyond the Rappahannock—came the word of cheer which gave hope and assurance of victory to the world, the dispatch from Grant, " I propose to fight it out on this line if it takes all summer." From that utterance the nation knew that the end was assured, if not nigh; and that there could be but one way for the war to close—with the Union restored and slavery dead.

Among the items that came from the front was one that filled the boy's heart with deepest sorrow, the news that Lieutenant Colonel Milton Opp, in command of the Eighty-fourth Pennsylvania, had been fatally wounded and had died from the effects of the injury. He was one of the noblest soldiers in the army, a man of scholarship, devotion, sympathy, with a singular mixture of chivalrous courage and womanly tenderness in his make-up. Jack went down and searched the embalming establishments of the city to see if he might be able to find the body of his beloved commander. That sight he can never forget. Scores, nay, hundreds, of dead officers and men from the front had been forwarded to be cared for and sent on to their homes in the North. Jack failed to find Colonel Opp's body, but he was thrilled with horror at coming suddenly upon the stalwart form of Captain Eayre, the assistant adjutant general of the brigade to which the regiment belonged. When Jack had seen him a few months before this officer was the personification of health.

manly strength, and military valor. Now, half naked, cold, and stiff, his splendid form lay stretched out before the eyes of a former comrade, a little bullet hole right over the heart showing where the messenger of death had sped upon its fatal errand.

Once in a while, in the intervals of shipping troops to the front and attending to the duties of recorder at the board of examination, Jack found time to take a run through the hospitals, filled with thousands of sick and wounded, in the city. Here he sometimes saw President Lincoln, Walt Whitman, the poet, and other celebrities of that day, caring for the wounded, or at least going from couch to couch with a kind word and a cordial grasp of the hand. Here, also, one hot day in May, he was summoned to see his captain, who had been severely wounded in the arm, almost losing it, in the Wilderness. Captain Bryan was as cheery and patient, however, as though he were on a picnic instead of in a hospital.

So the weeks and months of 1864 went rapidly by, bringing Jack toward the close of the year a captain's commission, so that he was now "almost" Captain Sanderson; almost, I say, for the regiment was so depleted that none of the promoted officers could be mustered into service with their advanced rank for the present, so that Jack, with a captain's commission, was only "almost a captain." At the opening of 1865 his term of service expired, his three years were up, and with his company he had no alternative but to be mustered out of service, although some of the companies of the regiment, now consolidated with the Fifty-seventh Pennsylvania, prolonged their time of enlistment by taking service as veterans; but Jack's company in the consolidation was wiped out, so that now for him soldiering was over. He was not satisfied to quit the service, however, and while waiting for an opening General Casey said to him, " Why do you not come before the examining board and accept service as an officer of colored troops?" Jack finally concluded to do this, went before the board, stood his examination, and was recommended to the War Department for appointment as lieutenant colonel. This recommendation stirred anew his military ambition, and he cherished now the hope of being at least a field officer.

CHAPTER XXIV.

THE PAGEANT FADES.

MEANWHILE, as the boy waited for his appointment, coveting eagerly the opportunity of going again to the front and aiding in the closing campaign of the war, he had the privilege of seeing, among other notable spectacles, some of the ceremonies and parades associated with President Lincoln's second inauguration.

The 4th of March proved to be a dismal, sloppy, and wretched day, the stormy weather spoiling the military and civic display, and almost preventing anything like a parade. There was, however, in spite of the rain and tempest, a procession, and through the wet streets the carriages went, headed by soldiers, and welcomed by crowds lining the pavements. Precisely at the hour—a little after noon—when Mr. Lincoln stepped forward to take his place on the platform on the east front of the Capitol, to deliver his inaugural and assume anew his oath of office, the storm broke away, the sun peered through the clouds, the transfiguring light falling upon the rugged, furrowed, homely face of the President. Those who saw it were stricken with awe, and some said to themselves, "Is this a sign of divine interposition?"

On the next day, Sunday, March 5, Bishop Simpson preached in the hall of the House of Representatives. The scene which the boy then and there beheld can never fade from his memory, as the multitude assembled in that historic spot, the President, his cabinet, the ladies and their households, distinguished generals, foreign embassies, almost the entire membership of both houses of Congress, governors of various States, with other dignitaries from various parts of the country—a congregation representing the very flower of American civilization. The future of our land was not yet quite settled; although enough had been done even then by Grant and Sherman to indicate to hopeful and believing hearts the ultimate triumph of the Union armies, yet many were saying, "What will the spring campaigns bring forth? What policy will President Lincoln pursue? What will be the final fate of our now distracted nation? Will the war ever end?" In the midst of his sermon, which had for its text the words, "And I, if I be lifted up from the earth, will draw all men unto me," the bishop related the incident of the day before with brevity, dignity, and touching simplicity; and then with his utmost power of eloquence he dwelt upon the event as an omen of coming prosperity. He pictured the sunshine of peace breaking through the clouds of war, illuminating not only the radiant features of Mr. Lincoln, but bathing distracted homes and bereaved hearts and crowded hospitals and the entire war-smitten land, with its battlefields, its ghastly sights of sorrow, its myriads of sufferers, in benignant and enduring light. The marvelous words of the bishop, whose services to the nation thus far during the years of war everybody had recognized, melted, penetrated, overwhelmed that whole audience ; and with shouts, applause, sobs, and tears every heart was lifted up to the mountain-top of prophecy where the orator stood, like one of the old Hebrew seers, his face aflame, his form transfigured, his soul entranced by the vision of assured peace and union for the divided nation near at hand. Without question the voice of Bishop Simpson that day was like a voice from the skies for the bruised and bleeding heart of Abraham Lincoln, the vicarious sufferer for the nation, soon to be the typical martyr of the ages, and for those who, with him, were striving to "bind up the nation's wounds" and "keep the jewels of liberty in the family of freedom."

One bright morning early in April, 1865, just at the time when General Casey was ready to offer Jack a regiment of troops, and the boy was pluming himself with the ambition to be at least a field officer, he was walking along Pennsylvania Avenue, near the War Department, when he saw a great throng pour out of the building, and soon from the offices in the neighborhood excited swarms of clerks and soldiers filled the streets. Jack looked up along the windows of the War Department, and saw there the familiar face of an intimate friend, Mr. D. H. Bates, then the confidential telegrapher of Lincoln and Stanton. Mr. Lincoln's customary salutation to young Bates when he visited the department in search of news was, " Well, Homer, has anything 'drapped' this morning?" Jack, adapting Mr. Lincoln's question to suit his needs, cried out, " Halloo, Homer, what has 'drapped' this morning?" Bates waved his handkerchief in reply and shouted, "News has just come that Richmond has surrendered and Lee is in full retreat!" No one can reproduce the thrill, the happiness, the enthusiasm, the overwhelming joy of that hour. The streets of Washington were filled with a tumultuous throng of soldiers, citizens, women, and children overflowing with rapturous gladness, waving flags, frenzied with excitement, shouting till the sky resounded with their songs and cheers, halting at the office of Mr. Stanton and listening to his words, hearing speeches from him and from Vice President Andrew Johnson full of patriotism and joy, and meanwhile, at inter-

"RICHMOND HAS SURRENDERED!"

vals, joining in the songs of that day, "Rally 'round the flag, boys," "The Battle Hymn of the Republic," and others. Everybody was decorated with the national tricolors, and flags floated from almost every window. When night came the whole city was lighted up with splendid illuminations, as the streets were crowded still with excited and rejoicing people, exultant at the dawn of peace, and beside themselves with gladness that the

Union was about to be restored. Then came that tragedy which can hardly be brought vividly to mind to-day without pangs of immedicable sorrow, the assassination of Mr. Lincoln. To the boy it seemed, as he threw himself on his bed that awful day and turned his face to the wall and wept with breaking heart for the loss which the army, the nation, and the world had sustained in the death of the martyr President—to the boy it seemed as though the sun would never shine again.

The boy's plans for reëntering service were disappointed, however, and he resumed his studies again at school, taking up his books at the point where he had left them off four years before, and eager to make up for what might be called " lost time." That expression, however, would be a misnomer for the period spent in the army. These years gave the boy a knowledge of military and national affairs, a series of glimpses of the resources and possibilities of the nation, a love for freedom, and an appreciation of the blessings and advantages of a republican form of government that could have been secured in no other way. Experience in the army was an education of itself of the most valuable sort. It taught those who were subjected to its discipline the worth of military training, and especially of West Point education, the virtues of promptness, courage, patience, fortitude, and the value of the nation, as no other drill or experience could have afforded. The best institution the boy ever attended was Uncle Sam's "School of a Soldier."

A single other picture remains to be added, and these sketches are ended. The boy stands in the midst of a vast multitude on the steps of the Treasury Department, in Washington, looking toward the Capitol, whose magnificent dome looms aloft into the sky. He is waiting, with countless thousands, for the triumphal appearance of the men who placed that massive structure on new foundations from which it shall never be removed. Far and wide over the city floats the banner of the republic. It means something now, far more than it ever did before; it is the actual symbol of freedom, it is the flag of the free, its stars are the luminaries of liberty, its stripes are interblendings of our institutions into bonds never to be broken. Sidewalks are crowded with spectators; a great sea of surging faces lines the avenue, waiting for the armies that have saved the republic to appear. Listen! Far off is the sound of music; the bands are playing in the distance; the soldiers are beginning their march of triumph—their toils over, their victories won, their work achieved, their crowns of glory assured. A signal gun sounds on the air, and far away, coming into range of vision, a mile distant, appears the head of the column at the Capitol. Tumultuous cheers fill the air and resound from the throats of more than a hundred thousand spectators. Division after division wheels into the avenue, while the masses wait with breathless interest, the excitement making every nerve to tingle and burn. Now the head of the column draws near, with Meade leading the way, the conqueror at Gettysburg, the leader of the Army of the Potomac to final victory, surrounded by his staff and greeted with shouts and hurrahs on every side. His horse is decorated with garlands, and he is kept busy bowing right and left to the cheering crowd. This is the first day of the review, and the Army of the Potomac has the right of way; this is their day. Custer, with his dashing cavalry, accoutered magnificently, follows Meade, and heads the advance of the cavalry corps, preluding the advent of the other corps of the glorious Army of the Potomac, while the sidewalks, houses, and windows are lined with fluttering handkerchiefs, waving banners, and garlands lifted high in air.

On the second day Sherman's army was reviewed—at the head Sherman himself, then Howard, his one arm laden with flowers, and Logan, tawny and dashing, and the " bummers," car-

PEN AND INK SKETCH OF GENERAL PHIL. SHERIDAN, 1863.

rying their spoils, now and then making merriment in the parade —bronzed with southern suns, weather-beaten, not as well dressed as the Army of the Potomac, but a splendid body of men. The boy, on the second day, opposite the reviewing stand at the White House, saw Grant, the conqueror, Stanton, the organizer, Seward, still weak and pallid, and President Johnson, greeted with rousing cheers. Sheridan, unluckily absent from the parade, was in the Southwest, watching our Mexican frontier.

The boy watches the marching columns, thrilled with the magnificent spectacle and with the memories of bivouac and battle which throng to his mind, admires the swing of victory which all the troops have acquired, and comments to himself, as one after another commander or regiment familiar in other days passes swiftly along, after this fashion : " I was with you on the Tennessee River—I saw you last at Fort Donelson—I remember your splendid charge at Pittsburgh Landing—I waded with you through muddy trenches in the siege of Corinth—I helped you on recruiting service—I was with you at Fredericksburg—I spent the winter with you at Falmouth—I was in the thorny thickets and scrub oaks of Chancellorsville with you in May, 1863—I marched with you to Gettysburg—I trod the journey with you back into old Virginia again." And so, all along the line, for two days, old scenes and memories came thrilling to the front, until the boy's heart was overfull.

When, toward the end of the first day of review, in Mott's division of the Army of the Potomac, the boy's old regiment marched along he broke down. The colors, torn to rags, stained with blood, and blackened with battle-smoke, floated over the thinned ranks, which the boy saw dimly through tears, his beloved captain, now Major Bryan, and the bronzed comrades of former days, covered with dust and with glory, proudly mingling with the splendid pageant.

Here and there in this marching army the boy noted an old friend, a comrade, who had shared his shelter tent, ridden beside him in battle, lain with him in the trenches, been a companion on picket duty, or had "drunk from the same canteen."

The boy, as he gazed, saw other forms, misty and shadowy at first, but then assuming substance and form and life—the figures of those who had fallen in the four years of war. Tears washed from their dust-stained faces, wounds all healed, health recruited, toils over, they took their place in the procession, and marched by the side of their comrades of the olden time, they, too, rejoicing that slavery was dead, the Union restored, and the nation saved. At the head of this shadowy army in review stood Lincoln, the typical martyr, the greatest man of his age, exultant and triumphant that, after the cares and sorrows, the anxieties and battles, of the past the nation had had a new birth unto freedom.

Then the vision faded, and with it came to an end "What a Boy Saw in the Army."

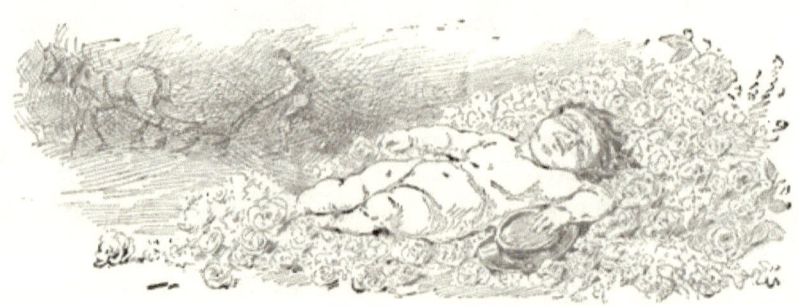

PEACE AND LIBERTY BORN FROM THE MOUTH OF THE CANNON.

www.ingramcontent.com/pod-product-compliance
Lightning Source LLC
Chambersburg PA
CBHW030408230426
43664CB00007BB/791